COACH FELLAS

HERITAGE, TOURISM, AND COMMUNITY
Series Editor: Helaine Silverman
University of Illinois at Urbana-Champaign

Heritage, Tourism, and Community is an innovative new book series that seeks to address these interconnected issues from multidisciplinary and interdisciplinary perspectives. Manuscripts are sought that address heritage and tourism and their relationships to local community, economic development, regional ecology, heritage conservation and preservation, and related indigenous, regional, and national political and cultural issues. Manuscripts, proposals, and letters of inquiry should be submitted to *helaine@uiuc.edu.*

The Tourists Gaze, the Cretans Glance: Archaeology and Tourism on a Greek Island, *Philip Duke*

Coach Fellas: Heritage and Tourism in Ireland, *Kelli Ann Costa*

COACH FELLAS

Heritage and Tourism in Ireland

Kelli Ann Costa

Left Coast Press Inc.

Walnut Creek, California

LEFT COAST PRESS, INC.
1630 North Main Street, #400
Walnut Creek, CA 94596
http://www.LCoastPress.com

ISBN 978-1-59874-406-4 hardcover
ISBN 978-1-59874-407-1 paperback

Library of Congress Cataloguing-in-Publication data:

Costa, Kelli Ann.
Coach fellas : heritage and tourism in Ireland / Kelli Ann Costa.
    p. cm.—(Heritage, tourism and community)
    Includes bibliographical references and index.
    ISBN 978-1-59874-406-4 (hardcover : alk. paper)—ISBN 978-1-59874-407-1
    (pbk. : alk. paper)
1. Ireland—Description and travel. 2. Tourism—Ireland. I. Title.
    DA969.C67 2009
    338.4'791417—dc22
    2009002323

Printed in the United States of America

♾™ The paper used in this publication meets the minimum requirements of American National Standard for Information Sciences—Permanence of Paper for Printed
Library Materials, ANSI/NISO Z39.48–1992.

Printed on partially recycled paper

09 10 11 12 13   5 4 3 2 1

Cover illustration by permission of CIÉ, *córas lompair Éireann*, Dublin, Ireland.

To

Lesley Alan Daunt

Contents

Preface

For many years, I have been an active observer of and participant in the tourism industry in Europe; initially in Austria (Costa 2001) and for the past several years in Ireland (for example, Costa 2004, 2006). I have been particularly interested in vernacular material culture and its increasing commodification on the tourist market (see discussion in Costa 2001). Over the past several years, I have concentrated on the commodification of the built environment, especially that of the ancient past, and the "modified natural landscape" of Ireland. As an archaeologist, I have a natural curiosity about and concern for ancient and historic landscapes and the ever-increasing pressures of modernization and development on them. Nowhere is this pressure more acute than in Ireland. The heritage of Ireland is tied to its landscape and the more than 9,000 years of human intervention upon it.

The landscape and the many ancient and historic remains found on it (and in many cases within it) are integral to the "branding" of Ireland: the country's three pillars of cultural heritage marketing are "people, place, and pace" (Tourism Policy Review Group [TPRG] 2003: xi). Without clear and intensive marketing of the three pillars and effective visual stimulation (Brett 1996), Ireland as destination would be more real than imagined. This imagined Ireland, the anachronistic, backward, rural, ancient Ireland, is the Ireland desired by the visitor. This desire is encouraged through effective—and affective—marketing. For many American visitors, in particular, to Ireland, the land represents an ancestral heritage brought about by the massive Irish diaspora that began in the 19th century and continues—though at a much reduced rate—today. Other visitors from Canada, New Zealand, and Australia, especially, also understand the Irish landscape as ancestral ground. Even I was drawn there as a moth to a flame, because of the tremendously varied archaeological landscapes, the beauty of the environment, and the people themselves—the core concepts of people, place, and pace chosen to brand the island to visitors.

Tourism is predicated on visitor satisfaction, and of central importance to visitor satisfaction are the people within the tourism industry who serve as the "primary interfaces" (TPRG 2003) between destination (or product) and guest. As many tourists from outside Ireland participate in organized coach tours, including city tours and day trips, the coach driver is often the only "live" informant available.[1] Tour guides and coach drivers, who are often one and the same, are responsible for imparting background information and insights on the heritage sites and other places visited by their groups. Despite this, they are easily forgotten, ignored, and often challenged by the uninformed. Thus, this book is about mundane, white, working class men as much as it discusses heritage and tourism. In Ireland, almost without exception, it is men who drive the tour coaches and men who toil at the day-to-day tasks of shepherding tourists. Women can, and often do, act as guides, but they very rarely serve as drivers or driver-guides. During my study I never met a woman driver-guide, and, although it was rumored that a few existed, no one I spoke to had ever seen one.

Ireland's current booming economy, a direct result of its attractiveness as the "gateway" to Europe or America for industry and its early membership in the European Union, has brought about an intensification in infrastructural and domestic development that at times seem out of control. Real estate now stands as among the most expensive in Europe (Economic and Social Research Institute [ESRI] 2005), centered primarily in Dublin and its surrounding suburbs but increasingly in other areas throughout the island as well. A recent article in *The Corkman* newspaper reported that in the southwest region of Ireland alone, house prices have risen 267% since 1996, calling the growth "staggering" (16/02/06, accessed 20/02/06).[2] Ireland was also reported as the second wealthiest country in the world behind Japan in the summer of 2006, an astonishing reversal of fortune (Radio Teleféis Eirean [RTE] July 2006). As the population of Ireland has grown wealthier (and younger—30% of the population in 2005 was 30 years of age or under), a dramatic upsurge in automobile traffic has heightened demands on roads, bridges, slip roads, and car parks. Road construction and repair are a constant presence in Ireland, aiding in the alleviation of traffic woes but also altering, destroying, and damaging vast areas of historical significance throughout the country. As housing estates crop up across the landscape, enormous tracts of rural Ireland are also disappearing. One benefit to archaeologists is the availability of constant employment and the dramatic proliferation of cultural resource-management firms owing to this expansive growth.

To a great extent, the tourism industry has served to ramp up these modernization efforts as the number of tourists to Ireland has also swelled considerably over the course of the last 30 or so years. It is within the context of modernization, tourism, the heritage market, and the people who work within the tourism industry—in particular, the people who serve as driver-guides—that this book is written. Unlike many current views, my position on tourism and heritage interpretation is not negative. I see each as essentially necessary to aid in the preservation and rescue of archaeological landscapes in the modern world. While there are many conflicting issues regarding both tourism and heritage site management, the reality is that they exist, and effective methods of working within the provisions of the economic benefits and constraints of each must continue to be created by all stakeholders in the tourism-heritage-archaeology trilogy.

Acknowledgments

Many people have been instrumental in the development of this research, and it would be difficult to list them all here. I would like to thank Franklin Pierce College for its support of my research despite the hardships it caused in staffing my position and covering my classes when I would "disappear" to do research. I am grateful to the incredible patience and understanding of Susan Rosa, who served as Chair of Behavioral Science, as well as the support and advice of Robert Goodby, Lorettann Devlin-Gascard, Phyllis Zrzavy, Jefferson Allen, Emlee Kohler, Bill Costa, and Tom Taaffe, my colleagues and friends. The College also financially supported my research in Ireland through a series of Faculty Research Grants. The Whiting Foundation and the CIES/Fulbright Commission also have generously funded this project. Yorke Rowan and Uzi Baram read and commented on, and subsequently published (Costa 2004), an early version of my research on heritage tourism. Maíread nic Cráith and Ullrich Kockel also saw promise in my work (Costa 2006). Finally, I would mention the support E. Moore Quinn of the College of Charleston has always given this project throughout its development.

In Ireland, I would like to thank the tour directors, coach operators, heritage site managers, archaeologists, government representatives, and tour guides who have been so generous with their time as this research has evolved. In particular, I would like to recognize the staff of the Cruachan Aí Centre (in particular, Carolyn Candish), the Ulster Archaeology Society, Christopher Lynn, Niall Brady of the Discovery Programme, Nic Brannon, Audrey Horning, John Bennett, Ros O'Maolduin, Kate Leonard, Hannah Ulrich, Oscar Ryan, Mick Monk, the National Museum of Ireland, the Dublin Institute of Technology (especially Kevin Griffin, Bernadette Quinn, Pat Dargan, Sheila Flanagan, and Theresa Ryan), Fulbright Ireland (in particular Sonya McGuinness), Liz Morgan, Feargal Barton, The Tourism Research Centre, Owen Mohan, and Fáilte Ireland.

Finally, this project would not have been completed without the assistance, cooperation, and encouragement of the Coach Fellas. I am indebted to them one and all. I am especially grateful to Lesley Daunt, who drove me and 20 college students through Ireland for three weeks in 2005 and 2007, taught me to play snooker (badly), watched over my fiercely independent students, and never lost interest in this project. This book is for Lesley and the boys on the road. It is also for the students who took part in the Field Experience in Anthropology at Franklin Pierce College in 2003, 2005, and 2007. I would also like to thank my assistants in the field in 2005 and 2007, Jessica Norton, Caroline (Care) Haley, Jessica Guertin, and Tristan Downing, who assisted in teaching and who photographed and filmed the field school, and my research assistant Tyler Brown, who has read, edited, corrected, and constantly griped about my "unique" understanding of the English language as this project has progressed; they are great students all. I am also grateful to the anthropologists, who saw integrity and value in a work about the true backstages of tourism and heritage and the people who populate the places of interest there and make them accessible to the visiting public. Finally, I would thank Mitch Allen, Helaine Silverman, and Stacey C. Sawyer at Left Coast Press for taking on my project.

The opinions expressed in this book are mine. Any mistakes, omissions, ambiguities, or lack of clarity are my responsibility alone.

Figures and Tables

Abbreviations

CERT	Council for Education, Recruitment, and Training
CSO	Central Statistics Office
CTTC	Coach Travel and Tourism Council
DMC	Destination Management Companies
EC	European Community
EEA	European Economic Area
EEC	European Economic Community
ESB	Electricity Supply Board
ESRI	Economic and Social Research Institute
EU	European Union
GAA	Gaelic Athletic Association
ICOMOS	International Council on Monuments and Sites
IRA	Irish Republican Army
IRB	Irish Republican Brotherhood
ITA	Irish Tourism Association
ITIC	Irish Tourism Industry Confederation
ITOA	Irish Tour Operators Association
M50/M3/N4	Main motorways
NDP	National Development Plan
NSS	National Spatial Strategy/Survey
NTDA	National Tourism Development Authority
OECD	Organisation for Economic Cooperation and Development
OPW	Office of Public Works
PCO	Professional Conference Organisers
RTÉ	Radio Teleféis Éireann
RTO/A	Regional Tourism Organisation/Agency
SME	Small-Medium Enterprise
TAP	Tourism Action Plan

TPRG	Tourism Policy Review Group
UNESCO	United Nations Educational, Scientific and Cultural Organisation
WHS	World Heritage Site
WTTC	World Travel and Tourism Council

CHAPTER 1

Tourism: A Consideration of the Literature

THE TOURIST

Thorstein Veblen referred to them as the "leisure society" (1899). "They" were the people during the Victorian era who could afford to engage in forms of travel for leisure (often under the veil of education or health) and other such nonnecessary, non-utilitarian forms of pleasure. Since that time, the tourism demographic has changed, the nature of travel has changed, and the ways in which tourists and travel are understood have changed. Once the venue of the idle rich, travel and tourism are now widely available; whether in local or domestic destinations or in far-flung areas of the world, nearly everyone in the developed world will go on holiday, take a vacation, or see the sights at least once in a lifetime—if not several times a year.

As a social category, "the tourist" has often been vilified in a wide range of literature. Many people who travel do not wish to be identified as tourists and will not self-identify as a tourist when asked to describe their status. People who travel often differentiate between "travelers"—who are understood as socially sophisticated and who travel for the cultural value of it—"trippers"—who may travel for a variety of sentimental or emotional reasons or for adventure—and "tourists"—who are understood as somewhat vulgar, uncomfortable, and superficial (Gmelch 2004; Lury 1997). Tourists do not engage with local people; rather, they are served by them. Trippers seek out an "authentic" cultural experience;

travelers "know" the culture. These contrived categories of identification can serve as bounded entities through which the world of the touristic experience is understood.

But do these categories truly encompass the entirety of the culture known as *tourists*? Many tourists suggest that they evolved from one suggested category to another over the course of a holiday; some suggest that they devolved, falling from a cultural sophisticate to a kitschy, souvenir-collecting, poorly groomed outsider. However, the taxonomy of the tourist extends beyond these simple classifications. Along with *why* people travel, *where* people travel and the reasons they choose to travel to that particular place must also be understood—how they choose to see the places they travel to; when they choose to travel (high season, low season, shoulder seasons); the emotional, nostalgic reasons for the trip, if there are any; whom they travel with; how long they remain in a place; how, and in what contexts, they interact with others; and how they comprehend the culture and the landscape around them. Is the experience itself a reason to travel and observe?

THE SEARCH FOR THE AUTHENTIC: THE TOURIST—IN THEORY

As suggested by MacCannell (1999 [1976]) and others (for example, Bruner [1994]; Corkern [2004]; McManus [1997]), what tourists seek when traveling often is authenticity, the authentic, or an "authentic experience." For something to be authentic, it must conform to fact; be worthy of trust, reliance, or belief; have a verifiable origin or authorship; and not be copied or counterfeit (*American Heritage Dictionary* 2000). Authenticity infers the quality of being authentic, trustworthy, or genuine, but it also suggests something that is honestly felt or experienced, that is free from hypocrisy and dishonesty (ibid.). As such, an authentic experience is something that is felt and that has an emotional context. A tourist's authentic experience may simply be something a tourist would not normally experience in daily life, something he or she may not see at home, whether or not what the person is seeing or experiencing is genuinely "authentic" or not. In many cases, tourists are perfectly happy with simulated experiences of once-authentic occurrences (such as the simulated winter solstice sunbeam at Newgrange referred to in Chapter 3).

Davydd J. Greenwood, in his widely read "Culture by the Pound: An Anthropological Perspective on Tourism as Cultural Commoditization" (1977, 1989, 2004), suggested that tourists, in their quest for the authentic ("local color" in his words), and the tourist industry, by capitalizing on this quest, have made "peoples' cultures extensions of the modern mass media" (2004: 164). Over the course of 27 years and numerous republications and revisions of the article (only three of the many are listed here), Greenwood has persisted in his view that tourists and tourism are essentially at fault for the changing (sometimes destruction) of "culture," which exists only in places other than those the tourists come from. He uses the term *ethnic tourism* to differentiate between the observer and the observed, Valene Smith's "hosts and guests" (ibid.: 158). In Greenwood's study, a Basque ritual commemoration, the Alarde (a reenactment of "Hondarribia's victory over the French in the siege of A.D. 1638" (ibid.: 160) is described as a form of inaccessible sacred history to outsiders that was co-opted by the Ministry of Information and Tourism to draw tourism revenue to the area (ibid.: 161). Upon its cooptation, the once powerful and inclusive ritual was discarded by the locals. This "collapse of cultural meanings" is seen as a violation of sorts by Greenwood, both of the people and of the ritual. He suggests that the invitation of tourists to the ritual and the ritual's subsequent commodification destroyed the ritual's "authenticity and its power" for the Basques of the Hondarribia (ibid.: 164). Although in 2004, he does reflect on his transparent anger in the original script of 1977 and apologizes, after a fashion, to the discipline of anthropology for being "professionally self-serving" (ibid.: 167), Greenwood remains convinced that tourists seeking authenticity, promised by the tourism industry, are in effect exploiting defenseless people. The tourist as capitalist predator.

Nelson Graburn referred to the tourist experience as a "sacred journey" (1989: 24) and then as "secular ritual" (2004: 23) in opposition to the profane work-a-day world tourists leave behind. He even went so far as to compare souvenir collecting and other evidence of journeys (photos, postcards, rocks, and sea shells) to the "Holy Grail"—that mythic sought-after goal of the ultimate journey (1989: 33). Graburn suggests that the greater the authenticity of the item (he breaks down souvenir-collecting tourists into experiential categories such as environmental, hunter-gatherer, ethnic), the nearer to a religious experience tourists have; tourists return home with an item of nearly sacred proportions, evidence of their special status, their participation in a cultural pilgrimage (1989). Like many scholars, Graburn identifies a tourism performed by a (relatively) wealthy elite from the developed West that is visited on an unprepared underclass somewhere else. Dennison Nash, in the same volume as Graburn above, compares the tourist to a "conqueror" and tourism to a form of imperialism (1989: 38). These types of binary arguments are prevalent in most tourism literature—tourists are bad, the cultures they visit are good; tourism is inherently destructive, negative, and without conscience and is placed in opposition to the innocence and positive existence of the cultures it invades. Tourism is modernity without check; tourists (and the somewhat awkwardly labeled "post-tourists") are uncaring, egocentric, and culturally insensitive. The tourist experience is undertaken always at the expense of "the Other." The tourist as parasite.

Perhaps the most cited scholar in tourism literature is Dean MacCannell, author of the classic text *The Tourist: A New Theory of the Leisure Class* (1999 [1976]). MacCannell begins by suggesting that the word *tourist* has two meanings within the context of his book: the actual person(s)—"sightseers, mainly middle-class, who are at this moment deployed throughout the entire world in search of experience"—and the metasociological term that represents "modern-man-in-general" (ibid.: 1). Though MacCannell challenges the propensity to see tourism as somehow uncouth (calling it "the rhetoric of moral superiority" [ibid.: 9]), throughout *The Tourist* he uses tourists and tourism as whipping posts for the eroding away of cultural values—they are among those responsible for the "dumbing-down" of society. In MacCannell's estimation, the search for the authentic experience is paramount in the tourist world and the tourist's mind. MacCannell famously concludes, however, that tourists have little regard for the genuine in that they are, as a class, unsophisticated. What "the tourist" may understand as authentic or as an authentic experience is masked behind or within a series of "stages" such as those one might find in live theatre. The farther one peers backstage, the less magical and mystical the production becomes. Much the way Toto uncovered the man behind the curtain, evaporating the looming godlike presence in the Wizard of Oz, a tourist who is privy to the behind-the-scenes machinations of the tourist product may be ultimately disappointed, or, as MacCannell suggests, the backstage may also not "trick, shock, or anger them, and [tourists] do not express any feelings of having been made less pure by their discoveries" (ibid.: 105). MacCannell's writings on tourism have consistently suggested that "modern humanity has been condemned to look elsewhere, everywhere, for authenticity, to see if we can catch a glimpse of it reflected in the simplicity, poverty, chastity, or purity of others" (ibid.: 57). Therefore, the authentic experience is obtainable only "out there," somewhere other than "here." The tourist as pilgrim.

Edward M. Bruner has dissected the experience of authenticity by tourists in a number of offerings—of particular importance to this discussion in "Abraham Lincoln as Authentic Reproduction: A Critique of Postmodernism" (1994), "Tourism in the Balinese Borderzone" (2004), and "The Maasai and the Lion King: Authenticity, Nationalism, and Globalization in African Tourism" (2001). In his critique of postmodernism, Bruner explains his views on authenticity and tourists (or, more precisely, visitors to living museums such as Lincoln's New Salem) and asks that we see beyond the binary arguments of authentic/inauthentic or original/copy (1994: 397). Bruner introduces four cultural dimensions of authenticity based on "verisimilitude, genuineness, originality, and authority" (ibid.: 401). He argues that along with these multiple, shaded meanings, the reasons behind a museum or cultural excursion must also be weighed: Are visitors there primarily to be educated? Are they "consuming nostalgia" (ibid.: 411)? Are they "buying the idea of progress" (ibid.)? Are they somehow commemorating traditional society and social values, sorting out the origins of a national ideology or fetishising a mythic past?

Bruner takes these constructivist notions further when he serves as a tour director in Bali for a group of knowledgeable, educated adults. Here Bruner finds himself crossing over and back through many discrete identities of professor, tour guide, tourist, insider, and authority figure as he leads his group to witness Balinese and Javanese cultural performance: dance, gamelan music, costumes, cuisine (2004). He exposes the "romantic characterizations" that tourists have when they are among Indonesian cultures (and I would argue Irish and other cultures as well); these characterizations, often used in advertisements and brochures, and a variety of other media, not only suppress the "true conditions" of life among the visited but usually also "depict a culture that never existed" (ibid.: 220). Bruner also introduces the term *borderzones*, which in effect are the liminal spaces of the visited rather than those of the visitor, which have been widely discussed in recent tourism literature (ibid.). These liminal borderzones are areas of engagement where the visited leave their normal lives to interact with tourists—in the case of the Balinese, to dance, sell souvenirs, expose the public areas of their culture. These are the spaces in which culture is produced for consumption by an "other"; the consumption may not be in the form of market exchange, with which the West would be most familiar; it may simply be that area of life where outsiders are "allowed" to move freely through.

Among Bruner's most evocative discussions regarding his Balinese experiences is his comparison of First and Third World peoples: "in First World cities the Other is a social problem; in Third World places the Other is an object of desire" (ibid.: 222). Many Western visitors to Bali want to be close to this exotic Other in their liminal borderzone—they, too, occupy liminal space and are suspended in a place of new experiences, new faces, new feelings. Beyond the borderzone, the desire recedes, becomes a source of visual and cultural pollution or disgust, a symbol of backwardness rather than exoticism (ibid.). Bruner includes a familiar term—the *suspension of belief*—in his discussion but suggests that a tourist's willingness to suspend belief is what makes a cultural performance both gratifying and believable for the viewer. In the end, he reminds us that tourism has not only helped shape Balinese culture (and others), but it has also been absorbed by it. Cultures that occupy the tourist zone can live their lives as tourist objects; in Bali, this has been true since the 1930s, when Bali was popularized by Gregory Bateson and Margaret Mead's ethnographies.

Among the Maasai, Bruner investigated three different cultural exhibitions, all highly constructed for the tourist gaze (2001). One reflected the colonial relationships between the Maasai and the English; one was a modern dance performance directed toward urban, middle-class Maasai promoted by the national government; and one was based on the film *Out of Africa* and took place in a safari camp near a game reserve. Here he introduced the notion of the "questioning gaze" of the tourist, wherein the tourist may cast doubt on the authenticity of what is being presented. Even though tourists generally have a manufactured "Hollywood" version of a culture in mind, Bruner suggests that they are willing to question the presentation of a culture that does not meet with the preconceived notion that they carry with them. He found that tourists were generally more comfortable with cultural performances that did not attempt to disguise the Maasai as participants in a premodern world but rather as fully modern humans with strong traditional links to a tribal past. Bruner's willingness to accord tourists with this degree of interpretive agency, to imbue them with active roles in their own explorations of the Other, is rare in tourism research (and may not be true in all cases of the touristic experience). The tourist as intellectual.

No discussion of tourist theory would be complete without mention of the influence of John Urry's "tourist gaze" (1990).

The tourist gaze relates to the visual consumption of places and peoples that are not familiar. It is a highly anticipated sensory function, one that allows tourists to look at scenery and people with fresh eyes, to observe with great interest, and to satisfy their curiosity about the Other. Yet, Urry contends, this anticipation of new visual stimuli is "socially organized and systematized" by many (called "experts") in the tourism industry who "help to construct and develop our gaze as tourists" (2002: 1). We (tourists) measure the quality of our tourist gaze against what we keep in our everyday field of vision; it is the opposite of what we normally see—it is a new and unnecessary pleasure. The tourist gaze has evolved since the days of the Grand Tour and Thomas Cooke—the scenic is more than a pleasurable view; it is a signposted area that defines the place as worthy of the tourist gaze. The gaze may include the less pleasurable as well; red-light districts, Killing Fields, slums, and assassination points may be part of the postmodern tourist gaze. No matter what the subject, it is out of the ordinary, and it takes on a special significance to those who view it. Urry suggests that "different countries, or different places within a country, come to specialize in providing particular kinds of objects to be gazed upon" (ibid.: 45). In Ireland, each province, region, county, and city has become associated with a particular "brand" of gaze-ability, and many tourists are attracted to specific areas because of the unique branding that is their advertised foci (such as Dublin's cityscapes, pubs, and cosmopolitan atmosphere). The tourist as voyeur.

DISCUSSION

The tourist as capitalist predator, parasite, pilgrim, intellectual, and voyeur—there are inherent problems with each of these theoretical characterizations, and some have more than others. I begin where I ended, with Urry's tourist gaze. The main difficulty with the tourist gaze is that Urry reduces the participation of tourists to a single sensory involvement. Tourists experience the places and peoples they visit in much more complex and profound ways; at the very least, they taste the food, smell the air, hear the voices, they touch the fabric of the culture in ways that may defy description. They engage with one another and often with the visited culture in ways they may never have done before—they may become more or less inhibited, they may fall in love (or out of love), they may be frozen with fear by the mere thought of engaging with the Other. Their time in this out-of-the-ordinary place filled with strangers may be a life-changing experience—it may not, but it could and has happened. Urry's gaze is oversimplified and is closely aligned with the negative stereotype of tourists as passive participants hopelessly mired in their own cultural milieu. Tourists are more than voyeurs when they travel, and their memories of peoples and places are more than snapshots of a moment in time.

Bruner gives the greatest latitude to his tourists—they are individuals with the full range of human emotions, quirks, and capabilities. Bruner's tourists have agency and intelligence (and this may be why "his" tourists seem so alien; everyone else's tourists have a litany of repulsive traits that we have all come to despise!). As a constructivist, he understands culture as a product of its own micro-evolutions—that culture(s) moves, bends, adapts, and shifts by necessity and sometimes by compulsion. He awards tourist culture this same opportunity. In Bruner's tourist world, both tourists and hosts understand the difference between real life and performance, although for the performance to be enjoyed, it is the tourist's responsibility to "let go," to suspend belief, to absorb what is presented, and perhaps to believe. This is the authentic experience—that moment of intense engagement with the performance, whether the performance is a Balinese dance or a guided tour through a Neolithic passage tomb. Not all host-guest relationships are performance-based though, and not all tourists seek out an authentic experience—sometimes they just lie on a beach, have as little to do as possible with the locals, and return home with a sunburn and a new Speedo. Tourists also interpret their experiences differently. For example, on a fine spring day at Stonehenge in 2002, I witnessed a variety of tourists' reactions to the site. A few visitors were overcome with emotion and literally wept as they walked around the stones;

some were so busy snapping photos of the stones, their friends and families in front of the stones, and themselves with friends and family in front of the stones that the site simply became a colorful backdrop; others were unimpressed with the stones, bored and disinterested—for them, the site was simply part of the orthodoxy of musts; they had been, seen, gotten the T-shirt, fridge magnet, and the ticket stub. This multiplicity of reactions and interpretations of experience is the wild card in all tourism development.

Perhaps the most challenging to critique is MacCannell—if only because of his presence as the father of modern anthropological studies of tourism. The authentic experience, the pursuit of authenticity, is understood as the primary goal of the middle-class tourist. MacCannell's neo-Marxist view of tourism essentializes the activity as one of economic and power relationships, with the tourist object being reduced to what is available in a plethora of manufactured presentations and performances. His front- and backstages (the façade and the real world) have been analyzed by any number of scholars, and these analyses are not revisited here. Suffice it to say that the frontstages are sanitized spaces, created for the market, while the backstages are grubby, real-life storerooms full of personal and cultural secrets—these are authentic. According to MacCannell, it is the endless search for these areas of authenticity that drives the tourist class forward and sustains them while they are away from home. Convincing though MacCannell's arguments can be, again there is no room for the tourist who does not seek the authentic. In *The Tourist,* MacCannell challenges Daniel Boorstin's contention that "tourists want superficial, contrived experiences" (1999: 104), suggesting that in his studies, literally *none* of *his* tourists would accept this. In nearly the same breath, MacCannell concedes that even though tourists may eagerly and intentionally seek out backstages, they also understand that "what they see in the back is only another show" (ibid.: 105). This statement indicates that all backstages finally accessed by the tourist are equally created, that perhaps the authentic either does not exist or, like the Holy Grail, only encourages them to look harder and the object(ive) to be more cleverly hidden. Tourists on pilgrimage, though progressing in increments through and across stages of understanding, experiences only a "regression of stages" until they come to the place of "increasingly *apparent* authenticity proffered by tourist settings" (ibid.: 106). At some point, they accept defeat, have lunch, and go home. Ultimately, the creation of an authentic experience lies with the tourists themselves. The preservation of the memory is the sole responsibility of the tourist; therefore, it is only the felt need of the tourist that is the point of interaction between host and guest—the rest is really up to the tourist.

Graburn and Nash, as well as many others who have studied tourists and tourism, have presented the tourist as something that can exist only when attached parasitically to another living culture. This other culture is the touristic support mechanism of host communities that tourists are compelled to visit. Through this relationship, tourists can accomplish their personal goals, which may include anything from bedding cabaña boys, to climbing Mt. Everest, to seeing the Mona Lisa. The identity of "tourist" allows people not of the community, culture, or state to often move with much more freedom across a variety of landscapes than local people can. This freedom of movement, the inequalities in wealth between host and guest (the implication is that guests are always better off than hosts are), and the superficial contact between host and guest are all taken for granted as existing *a priori*. The relationship is understood as more real than apparent, although in the case of Ireland and many other tourist destinations of the 21st century, the opposite may be true.

Finally, Greenwood suggests that tourists and tourism are vile and ruinous and responsible for the utter destruction of traditional "real" cultures the world over. Much as the Irish and Ireland are not allowed to evolve in the tourist imagination, Greenwood understands many of the changes among these "real" cultures as being unwanted and forced on them through the very act of visitation. Rather than suffer the consequences of being swept aside by modernity, Greenwood's cultures in many cases may have seen the benefits of participation in it. Contact with cultures other than one's own has occurred over many millennia, and not all contacts have been to the detriment of the contactee. Although tourists and tourism may contribute to the ultimate shifts, modifications, and minirevolutions some cultures may experience, they are not solely responsible for them. Cultural evolution affects every culture everywhere and fairly constantly, whether it is welcomed or not, and whether tourists are there or not.

In this study, I situate myself as a reluctant advocate of tourism and heritage development. To clarify: I support the measured and sustainable development of heritage tourism and its use as an educational opportunity for visitors. I do not support the uncontrolled expansion and development of sites and sights that ultimately destroy significant cultural entities. I see the tourist experience somewhat differently than do most researchers, although I maintain a constructivist approach similar to Bruner's. In all my years of exploring the connections among tourism, liminality, and heritage, I have found that, by and large, the people who come to Ireland on holiday come for reasons other than rest, relaxation, and nightlife (although these are certainly important). They come to fulfill a need to connect with a memory they may not have created but have only inherited. In this sense, they are within a liminal space and time from the moment they begin planning their trip until long after they return home. In some cases, this liminality, specific to Ireland and Irish culture, exists on the fringes of personal life and ethnic or cultural bonds present within the visitor's family for years before they arrive in Ireland. In essence, the visitor to Ireland, especially of Irish descent, strives to reify the memory of generations past by touching the existing landscape of the Ireland of the present. In some ways, this action may release such a visitor from inherited memories, enabling him or her to then pass on new memories, genuine memories, memories of experience, which in turn may validate the previously unproved inherited memories.

CHAPTER 2

Heritage Tourism and Discourse
in Ireland

DEFINING THE COMPONENTS OF TOURISM

Tourism has been defined and redefined many times through a variety of theoretical and practical viewpoints. Tourism has often been understood as the leaving of one's familiar surroundings for the purposes of leisure, but tourism in the modern globalized world goes far beyond this. Tourism is also an industry developed from the elite class's "Grand Tour" of the Victorian era. The anthropology of tourism may be said to have begun with Thorstein Veblen's Victorian-era commentary on the leisure class (2001 [1899]). After World War II, travel became widely available to more than the elite classes. As long-distance travel became more affordable and common, beginning in the 1970s, travel to "exotic" places became a reality for the middle classes. The modern era of the field is usually traced to Dean MacCannell's path-breaking *The Tourist* (1976). MacCannell observed that tourism "is an alternate strategy for conserving and prolonging the modern and protecting it from its own tendencies toward self-destruction" (1976: xix). This backward look at the purpose and outcome of tourism implies that a form of seriousness of thought takes place over the course of the touristic experience, that tourism in and of itself is something other than a separation from the familiar. There is an assumption that the release from the familiar will somehow instill a quality of reflection in the tourist that was not present prior to the experience. We (the tourists) observe the places and people we visit, make thoughtful decisions on our own positions in the world, and take measured steps to preserve ourselves and our modernity *because* of these observations.

Valene Smith argued that a "tourist is a temporarily leisured person who voluntarily visits a place away from home for the purpose of experiencing change" (1989: 1). Sharon Gmelch, in a slight revision of Smith (1989), suggests that tourism is "temporary travel for the purpose of experiencing change" (2004: 5). It is true that tourists leave their familiar spaces and places of comfort to experience something different from the everyday. They are "away," they are seemingly unobserved by those who routinely judge them, and they are, by virtue of their position as "tourist," in a position of higher (or at least different) status than are those who work around them rather than with them. They are in new and unfamiliar surroundings and are paying for the experience. If they travel regularly, they develop places of preference and may return to those places repeatedly. The purchase of second homes in favorite holiday destinations may follow, creating a new class of temporary visitor.

Oriol Pi-Sunyer (1989) points out that tourism often acts to polarize relationships between and among visitors and the hosts who serve them. Jamaica Kincaid (1988) reminds us of the social and often racial inequality in *A Small Place* in her discussion of the host/guest relationship on Antigua. Erve Chambers (1997) examines tourism as a "mediated activity" that contin-ually shapes, influences, and reshapes the way in which hosts and guests interact in social worlds. The mediators are not necessarily the hosts and guests but the vast numbers of significant others who reside in the tourism industry, such as government and local authorities, tour companies, guides, travel bureaus, and theme parks.

Mediation can also take place through advertisements, films, and travel shows on television and in many other media-driven venues. John Urry (2002) has examined tourism as essentially a "visual activity," referring to it as the "tourist gaze." Urry suggests that we go away in order to gaze on the unfamiliar and out of the ordinary, but the gaze is "socially organized and systematized" by a variety of forces including the society, culture, class, and history (or historical era) of the tourist (ibid.: 1). He also includes the active role of tourism professionals who develop, market, and manage destinations. The output of their efforts results in "anticipation, especially through daydreaming and fantasy, of intense pleasures" that are beyond the tourists' normal reality (ibid.: 3).

Adrian Franklin (2003) places tourism within the postmodern, an integral part of the new world order, a plan of discovery, a way of "being modern." Others have seen tourism as inherently dangerous and damaging, a postmodern, postindustrial massive and temporary colonization of seasonally oppressed people (see, for example, De Kadt 1979; Greenwood 1977; MacManus 1997; Nash 1989).

Tourism is consumption. The development of theme parks, vacation oases, and targeted regions (for instance, foliage tours of the northeastern United States, the Kerry-Cork region in Ireland, the Disney phenomenon), with their accompanying glossy advertisements, television exposure, and organized tours or packaged holidays, have made vacation planning less stressful. The internet has further increased access and ease of planning.

Mass tourism also relieved the pressure of planning a holiday from the point of view of both tourists and tour operators. Smith refers to mass tourism as a "continuous influx of visitors who inundate" vast areas of the world developed for tourism (1989: 13). It is a quintessentially middle-class movement that includes a wide variety of participants from backpackers to package holiday takers, but, according to Smith, they share a need and expectation for "Western amenities" (ibid.). These amenities include same-language communication at the destination (for example, English-speaking staff), comfort, and cleanliness. Pi-Sunyer reminds us that mass tourism is a "manifestation of mass consumption" in developed countries and that, in many cases, the ability to consume has opened vast areas of underdeveloped regions to the working and lower classes of affluent nations (1989: 191). Mass tourism also gives the visitor the security of finding others who share language, culture, and similar social experiences despite the confines of tourist identity. Undoubtedly someone from "home" will be in the destination.

IRELAND

In Ireland, tourism has developed from a return to the homeland for émigrés in the early 20th century to a massive global industry. Much of the Irish economy is directly dependent on tourism, and it is of central importance to the country's economic stability and continued growth. By the new millennium, Ireland saw over 4 billion Euro in earnings from tourism (approximately 5 billion USD) (cso.ie/statistics 2005). The range of tourism experiences in Ireland is vast; from the focus on Dublin as a hub of international travel to the rural countryside of Connemara to the Ring of Kerry; from rail and drive opportunities to organized bus tours to religious pilgrimages; from pub tours to literary tours to tours of Irish cuisine; from castle stays to golf excursions to manor houses to hostelling, Ireland is able to provide niche holidays for everyone.

As a product to be consumed, Ireland and the Irish are a self-conscious expression of a desired ideal. Since the 1970s, Ireland has been able to position itself as a destination whose tourist traffic has continually increased yearly (the exception being 2001, with the combined post-911 season and the foot and mouth disease scare)—as the 1990s came to an end, an estimated 7 million people were staying in Ireland for at least one overnight stay (Hickey 2005). Ireland-as-destination has had to develop new sources of entertainment and attraction in order to keep up with the growing and changing tourist population. Hotels, guest houses, and other forms of accommodation; roads, parking, rental cars, airports; shopping areas and restaurants that have a wide appeal; sources of accessible information have all been the subjects of frenetic specialized sector development, especially since the late 1980s.

Ireland has exploited its reputation as a friendly, open, aesthetically pleasing country. It is the land of a "thousand welcomes," and *Ceád Mile Fáilte* hangs over the doorways of pubs, guest houses, and restaurants across the land. Its tourism organization, including Fáilte Ireland (the corporate arm of the

Ministry of Arts, Sports and Tourism), is tight, well-trained, and streamlined. Its banks are prepared for tourists—exchange counters, kiosks, and ATMs (called "holes-in-the-wall" by locals) are located everywhere; many mobile ATMs are even trucked into hot spots as temporary points of access for tourist exchange. It has courted internationally recognized chefs and restaurants to its cities to further attract the tourist and adjusted its pub cuisine to accommodate the international palate. It has become necessary to hire tourism sector workers (wait staff, bar tenders, bus drivers, tour guides) from across the European Union to fill jobs that Irish workers cannot or will not owing to Celtic Tiger attitudes and opportunities. As a created community, the land of Irish tourism differs greatly from the day-to-day realities of Ireland as lived. Ireland as lived is not the goal of the industry or that of the tourist; the dreamland of Ireland, the Ireland caught in a past, that still photograph of never-ending green fields and bucolic farms and thatched cottages is what tourism in Ireland is. The frantic urban landscape of Dublin with its tourist-oriented target zones of Temple Bar, O'Connell Street, and Grafton Street attracts visitors as well; pubs and shopping and historic city tours, as well as seasonal sporting events (Gaelic Athletic Association [GAA], soccer, Dublin Horse Show, among others) draw a wide array of Irish and international tourists to the city. Cultural events abound—theater, opera, traditional and other music events, lectures, museums add to the cosmopolitan attraction of the "most globalized nation in the world" (Foreign Policy 2003: 61). Tourism is a kaleidoscope of opportunities, tuned to any individual's wants, needs, and expectations.

The Irish government and development sectors are also creating further tourism opportunities in "Gateway" cities: Dublin, Cork, Waterford, Limerick, and Galway have been designated to represent the urban landscape of modern Ireland through the National Spatial Survey (NSS). The National Spatial Survey 2000–2020 is not infrastructural in nature, although its relationship to infrastructural development is clear. The NSS is "a planning framework . . . of investment" (2001) for the areas of development. In addition to the existing gateways, Dundalk and Sligo are slated to be new gateways, with Letterkenny/Derry in the north and Athlone/Tullamore/Mullingar in the country's midlands positioned as "linked" gateways. The NSS has also identified nine medium-sized hubs: Cavan, Ennis, Kilkenny, Mallow, Monaghan, Tuam, and Wexford, with "linked hubs" of Ballina/Castlebar and Tralee/Killarney. While the NSS is explicit in explaining its plans as a way, among others, to relieve transport pressures and to develop employment opportunities for the changing agricultural sector, it also includes tourism as a driving force behind the creation of gateway/hub cities and towns.

DEFINING HERITAGE

Heritage is that which is inherited. In the world of tourism, heritage has taken on the additional characteristics of destination, market, and area of development potential. It is a term much used in the tourism market and by archaeologists, human geographers, and others, but it remains an ill-defined and ambiguous word in all these instances. In 1999, ICOMOS (International Council on Monuments and Sites) defined heritage as including both tangible assets (cultural and natural environments, landscapes, historic places and sites, and the built environment) and intangible assets (customs and traditions, collections, knowledge, experiences). Inevitably, heritage is a contested zone—for instance, a political subject of national discourse, often utilized as defining characteristics of emergent or re-emergent nations.

Graeme Aplin explains that heritage depends on an individual's or a people's "background, life experiences, and personality . . . common socio-economic, cultural, or ethnic background," but he adds that the chosen heritage is often that of the "dominant group"; the issue of power and decision making must be examined as heritage sites are being filtered through the political and social fabrics of the cultures observed (2002: 14). Bob McKercher and Hilary du Cros point out that heritage *assets* "are identified and conserved for their intrinsic values or significance to a community rather than for their extrinsic values as tourism attractions" (2002: 7). Although heritage as a marketable product exists in many forms throughout Ireland, for the purposes of this book I am most concerned with the ancient heritage landscapes of the Republic—in particular, the archaeological landscapes that give Ireland an additional mystique and attractiveness to the visiting public. Within this focus is the discourse of interpretation and knowledge exchange that occurs between visitors and those who guide them—in particular, the coach [bus] drivers who serve as "primary interface," escort, and caretaker for organized tours.

"The heritage," as defined by Chambers, means inherited property, inherited characteristics, and anything transmitted by past ages and ancestors (1992 cited in O'Donovan 2000: 1). This definition was utilized in the 2000 publication *The Heritage of Ireland* as an umbrella term for archaeological sites, industrial and urban landscapes, natural resources, literary works, and other focal objects that are the subject of tourism and development within the rubric of Ireland's unique cultural legacy (Buttimer, Rynne, and Guerin 2000). This sizeable volume also examined the business of heritage in Ireland, as well as how heritage is interpreted. John Harrison discussed the evolving nature of heritage interpretation in Ireland, as well as the controversies involved in it in recent years, typically found within the context of museums and heritage site centers (ibid.: 385–392). He found that heritage interpretation has gone through a series of public and professional impressions ranging from a panacea for heritage site marketing through a "destroyer of landscapes and a sign that [the Irish] had lost touch with [their] past" (ibid.: 385). Harrison suggests that interpretation is

> an educational technique used to bring visitors closer to a specialized subject than they could normally get. The aim of interpretation is to reveal the inner world of a subject in a simple and meaningful way and then to inspire people to find out more on their own. (ibid.)

It is the link between heritage site, heritage marketing, and heritage interpretation that can both enlighten and confound the visiting public. Despite Harrison's desire that interpretation encourage self-discovery, it is clear from my own and others' (for example, Franklin 2003) empirical research that many members of the visiting public leave heritage sites uninspired, bored, and uninformed. This is one example of the problematic role of heritage placement within the "tourist gaze" (Urry 2002): there is no control over the amount of information that will be effectively disseminated to the public, and there is no effective way of determining the filtering of that information once it is given.

I experienced this disconnection at the megalithic tomb of Newgrange, where I observed a number of tours between 2002 and 2007. Visitors were reluctant to spend time in the exhibition area, where they could have learned background on the prehistoric development of the Brú na Bóinne valley. In many cases, this reluctance was due to the time constraints placed on groups who are on bus tours—the limited time and tight scheduling often interferes with opportunities to engage more deeply with available information at many sites. Many watched the 7-minute video, which overmystifies the sites of the valley (especially Newgrange and the solstice). Many also went to the "library" (actually a book-gift shop), where they bought postcards and other souvenirs. Few paid any attention (Figure 2.1) during the

Figure 2.1 Newgrange. The guide is in the grey sweatshirt in front of the standing stone in the center of the photograph. Very few people in this mostly American audience are listening (© Kelli Ann Costa 2002).

tours and lectures, and many were interested only in going inside the passage grave, seeing the simulated solstice, and getting back to the center to have something to eat.

As I followed a few of the visitors (mostly white, middle-class people from Europe and North America who were in Ireland on their holidays) around the outside of Newgrange, many had not understood that the tomb had been completely reconstructed and reinterpreted by the Office of Public Works (OPW) and the late archaeologist Michael O'Kelly in the 1970s, despite the guide's repeated reference to O'Kelly's excavations. Some doubted that the ancient Irish had made the monument. (Egyptians, Phoenicians, Greeks, Vikings, space aliens were mentioned as more likely to have made the mound.) There was also a pervasive feeling among many of the visitors traveling back to the center that they had "been there," taken their photos, and could now move onto the next site. A few remarked that they were glad to have another one "marked off the list."

Newgrange and the Brú na Bóinne have been fully absorbed into the "orthodoxy of musts" that so clearly drives much of the tourism market worldwide; these are prescribed places and routes, preferred and picturesque areas that have to be visited and recorded by guests (see Brett 1996 for an insightful discussion of the picturesque in heritage establishment). The area is heavily marketed by tour operators, the government, and travel agents and has become synonymous with visiting Ireland. The swirling inscribed designs on the stones have been reproduced on everything from T-shirts to paperweights to bed linen, all of which are available for purchase in tourist-oriented shops throughout the country. Visitors can even visit Newgrange without ever leaving the visitor center by virtue of a recreated "tomb" inside the center and well-mounted telescopes that allow people to gaze across the Boyne Valley toward the monument.

The orthodoxy of musts includes other governmentally ranked sites (based on importance, significance, locality, preservation, and so on) and tourism trails and routes that guide the visitor across the island. According to Claude Moulin and Priscilla

Boniface, routes are particularly effective mechanisms in tourism, especially when "a major attraction act[s] as the 'anchor' of a route, the others linked to it may be visited by tourists as an outcome of that association" (2001: 246). One prime example is the Boyne Valley Drive, where Newgrange/Brú na Bóinne serves to anchor the other sites of Tara, Drogheda, Monasterboice, Old Mellifont Abbey, the Hill of Slane, the Battle of the Boyne site, Trim Castle, and Kells Heritage Town.

In Ireland, a discernible tension exists regarding the choice of markers for the heritage landscape. Some represent the ancient and mythical past, the past that cannot be fully comprehended, such as Newgrange. Others are sites situated throughout the country that remind visitors of Ireland's monastic and religious histories: monasteries, white martyrdom sites such as Skellig Michael, holy wells, and churches. There are other sites that are linked with the rural landscapes of the 18th and 19th centuries, such as the preserved cottages of Glencolmcille and the deserted medieval village of Achill Island. Still others are stark reminders of Ireland's history as an occupied colony— the Strokestown Plantation and the Famine Museum among others. In every sector of its visible society, Ireland offers nearly everything to nearly anyone. All these sites are chosen as representations of the national heritage landscape of Ireland; inseparable from its turbulent past, they are symbols of the recovered nation of Ireland, the Ireland that has survived its own history. The symbols evoke both a backward gaze and a forward glance that leaves the visitor relieved that they live in the present and can look toward to the future. As such, they also symbolize Ireland's modern present and its future participation on the global frontier; having survived unimaginable strife, Ireland will prevail and thrive.

NATIONALISM AND THE SYMBOLS OF THE NEW IRELAND

The history of Ireland since Independence in the 1920s is well documented, but there has been limited discussion regarding the carefully chosen symbols of the Irish nation that are preserved on the landscape. As Ireland struggled to break away from England in the immediate post-Rising years, it needed to establish distinct symbols of nationhood that would resonate with the people of the newly formed nation-state of the 1920s and 1930s. The poverty of the nation and its people had left the landscape in disrepair and the country with few modern roadways or conveniences. Centuries of colonization by the English had embittered the Irish people, and the newly formed government strived to institute a national ethos that would establish an Irish nation separate from England.

The formation of a nation is founded on a simple combination of factors: shared culture, shared belief, shared language, shared boundaries. Marguerita Díaz-Andreu and Timothy Champion suggest that the "emergence of political nationalism at the end of the 18th century converted the production [of a propagated past] into a patriotic duty" (1996: 3). In the partitioned Republic of Ireland, shared culture was an agricultural, rural, newly independent, and economically emergent one; shared belief was a strident, militant Catholicism; the shared language was Irish, and, though few in the land spoke it routinely, the government moved fairly rapidly to institute the learning of Irish in schools as an educational requirement. The Irish government also looked to distinguish a landscape that would represent an essential Ireland: a highly recognizable, immediately identifiable landscape that was "thematically" unique. In stark contrast to the sophistication of England (urban, modern, organized), the landscape of Ireland was wild, ancient, mysterious, anachronistic. After centuries of imposed poverty, the Irish faced decades of recovery, and changing the landscape through infrastructural improvements was beyond the economic capabilities and scope of the nation. The ancient, musty, underdeveloped Ireland was recreated as heritage, and today that landscape remains the idealized vision of the country. The battered and backward but breathtaking landscape of Ireland was re-imagined as the traditional and well-preserved (Hobsbawm 1983).

This idea of the Irish landscape was and is inextricably tied to the idea of what it is to be Irish in Ireland. The politics of Irish identity today also has its roots in the country's separation from England and is founded on a revival of the heroic Celt, communitarian ideals (O'Kelly 2004) and a unique combination of highly stereotyped "gifts" that have blessed only those with the fortune to be Irish. These gifts include gab, good humor, toughness, a quick temper, brewing skills, wistfulness, addiction to sport, a lyrical genius for language, and generosity of spirit—among countless others. The agrarian history of Ireland ties the Irish to their land; the new breed of wealthy urban dwellers is not exempt from this; they, too, are connected with their tangible heritage, the symbols of which flow around them as they hurry through their complex post-industrial lives.

CELTIC TIGER

Economic recovery began with Ireland's inclusion in the European Community (EC), beginning in 1965. The EC evolved into the European Economic Community, or common market, which Ireland has held membership in since 1973. At the same time, the effort to capitalize on the building tourism market began. The Irish diasporic population, which began with the Famine of the 1840s and continued through the 1980s, was an obvious audience toward which to direct tourism marketing. Millions of people across the globe could claim Irish ancestry, and with travel becoming a common form of cultural exchange among more than the upper classes, the attraction of the homeland of Ireland was explicitly developed by the government and tourism organizations in the Republic. After another downturn in population, related ostensibly to economic reasons from 1965–1975, Ireland's economy slowly recovered. By the 1993 signing of the Maastricht Treaty and the establishment of the European Union (EU), Ireland was beginning to witness what has been referred to as the Celtic Tiger, a powerful upsurge in its economic power. The EU was brought about as a way to enhance political, economic, and social cooperation among the member states, with the ultimate goal of establishing this cooperation across Europe. It also provided funding for member states' development, among the most important aspects of which was explicitly recognized as tourism.

There is no question that tourism in Ireland is among the most important of the country's industries. According to the World Travel and Tourism Council (WTTC), Ireland is ranked 31st worldwide in its tourism driven economy (2005). Tourism accounts for over 8% of total employment, over 9% of total gross domestic product, over 5% of total exports, and 16% of total capital investment (ibid.). The Central Statistics Office (*An Phriomh-Oifig Staidrimh*) found in 2004 that there had been a 3% increase in the number of visits to Ireland over 2003, with 6,574,000 overseas visitors (26 April 2005). Earnings directly related to visitors to Ireland were over 4 billion Euro (CSO 26 April 2005). And, as mentioned above, the number of foreign visitors increased to 6.7 million by 2005 (Hickey 2005) and was in excess of 7.5 million in 2007. In Ireland, travel- and tourism-related employment is estimated to be over 160,000 jobs. The WTTC suggests this is 8.5% of total employment, or 1 in every 11.7 jobs, although jobs in the travel and tourism industry itself account for 2.9% of total employment, or slightly more than 67,000 jobs (2005). (The WTTC differentiates between "related employment" and "industry employment.") In order to capitalize on the projected increases in tourism-related earnings and activities, the Irish government and the tourism industry in Ireland have had to develop sites/sights and attractions with a wide and consistent appeal. Without resorting to a "Disneyization" of the landscape, the government and industry have made Ireland itself the attraction (although O'Hagan [2004] suggests "the marketing of Disneyfied images of Irishness is big business worldwide," and MacManus [1997] suggests that overproduction of the heritage landscape—a Disneyfication of the past—both distorts and oversimplifies the past; Ritzer and Liska [1997] also discuss it in terms of the "post-tourist"). The systematically chosen and labeled symbols of the nation and its heritage are the foci of visitors' experiences. To keep the Celtic Tiger going, these symbols must remain at the forefront of visitors' expectations and imaginations.

The Tourism Policy Review Group (TPRG) found that "the Irish tourism industry is, arguably, the most important Irish-owned sector of enterprise, national and regional wealth creation, and employment generation" (2003: 4). Despite this, they found that the competitiveness of the Irish tourism industry had experienced a downturn based primarily on the value for money factor owing to the high costs of visiting Ireland (ibid.: 5). Even with high costs, the TPRG concluded that there were also "high satisfaction levels and strong visitor appeal through [Ireland's] key brand attributes of 'people, pace and place'" (ibid.: 3). The "branding" of Ireland is utilized in any number of ways by government and private agencies specializing in Irish tourism. (This will be discussed further when addressing the marketing of Ireland as a destination.) The TPRG were explicit in the goals they set out; among the most important was increasing the visibility of heritage sites and adding sites and locations to the UNESCO World Heritage Site Designation list (both the Boyne Valley and Skellig Michael are currently listed). Such designation would, among other things, "add to the range of promotional products in Irish tourism for both domestic and overseas visitors in an area of strongly increasing interest to a more knowledgeable and discerning tourist base" (ibid.: 16).

There are so many symbols of national heritage on the Irish landscape that it would be nearly impossible to describe them all. Heritage Island, "the only marketing organization dedicated to the promotion of Ireland's major Visitor's Attractions and Heritage Towns" lists 84 attractions, theaters, and heritage towns in its directory, *The Group Organisers' and Tour Operators' Manual* (2004). "These attractions are as diverse as Ireland itself. They tell the story of kings and invaders, famine and emigration, priests and poets, encompassing the social and industrial heritage which has shaped not only the Ireland of today but also influenced Europe and the New World" (ibid.: 1). Twelve are considered "national monuments" by Heritage Island: the Adare Heritage

Centre, Blarney Castle, Bunratty Castle and Folk Park, Cruachan Aí Heritage Centre, Dublinia and the Viking World, Enniskillen Castle and Museum, Hook Lighthouse, King John's Castle, Kylemore Abbey and Garden, St. Patrick's Cathedral, St. Patrick's Trian, and the Waterford Museum of Treasures and Reginald's Tower. Peter Harbison lists nearly 900 sites throughout Northern Ireland and the Republic in the third edition of *Guide to National and Historic Monuments of Ireland* (1992), although there is no particular designation of "national" monuments.

IRISH IDENTITY AND IMAGE

As suggested above, Irish identity is tied to the landscape as well as the acknowledged personal and collective histories of the island. By acknowledged histories, I mean those notions of the Irish nation that are recognized as significant to the creation, maintenance, and continued development of Ireland and the Irish people. But questions arise regarding how the Irish understand themselves, their multiple histories, their landscape, and their position in the world, as well as how they are understood by others. Their status as part of the branding of Ireland ("people, place, pace") raises the expectations of those who visit the island; the wonderful *craic*, the gregarious atmosphere, the non-hesitant assistance are taken for granted by tourist populations. The unexpected snippy clerk, exhausted bartender, or irritated tour escort will be remembered, complained about, and reacted to in myriad negative ways. The Irish are often squeezed into a single theatrical caricature of themselves with little latitude for alternative common human qualities. Coach drivers refer to this as "putting on the Irish," whereby the performance of a certain cultural and ethnic identity becomes part of the job of simply being Irish in Ireland. Mike Robinson has referred to this as a "staged authenticity" (1999: 22), and others (for example, Bruner 1994; Lowenthal 1985, 1998; MacCannell 1976) have also questioned the role of the marketed expectations of tourists regarding "the other." Robinson goes on to suggest that the "packaging of cultures," such as that attempted with Irish culture, diminishes them to "a two-dimensional world carried by glossy brochures and generally reduce[es] distinctive cultures to superficial and readily substitutable narratives" (1999: 22).

Fintan O'Toole has also questioned the motives of presenting Ireland and the Irish as a single monolithic, homogeneous culture. He recounts the *Book of Invasions*, Ireland's foundation myth, as clearly illustrating the multiple influences that have had some bearing on the long historical development of the Irish people. "What you find is fifty four people making the first voyage from Spain to Ireland: the goddess Cessair, her father Bith, her brother Ladra, the helmsman Fintan, and fifty maidens, one from every nation on earth" (1999: 11). Likewise, in the case of how the Irish (and Irish-Americans) are portrayed on American television, Diane Negra suggests these overtly heterosexual, male-focused programs serve to embed a "myth of ethnic enchantment" (2001a: 229) that may unduly influence the expectations of Ireland-bound American tourists (2001b). Films such as *The Quiet Man* have also been influential regarding American expectations of Ireland and the Irish as "cute, quaint, and rural" (Rains 2003).

Image-based identities are a constant obstacle to the lived-worlds of tourism destinations. In Ireland, the urban, modern realities of the 21st century are often unexpected by those who visit the island for the first time. I took part in a seven-day tour of Ireland with 25 American tourists in 2000 that went to "standard" routed places: Killarney, Galway, and Dublin. One participant on the tour who had been to Ireland once or twice in the past and considered himself an "old hand" in Ireland, commented that he dreaded going into Dublin because "the real Irish" were not to be found there and the city was "not really part of Ireland." Others on the tour (all of whom were mature adults and all of whom were reasonably educated) found Dublin to be hectic, overly urbanized, emotionally cold, and unexpectedly modern. Many found the abundance of expensive automobiles, million-dollar flats, 5-star restaurants, and exclusive shops "un-Irish." Most in this group of tourists from a middle-class urban area in northeastern America are typical of the plastic hat, green-shamrock-sweater-wearing American-Irish who crowd into local bars for corned beef and cabbage on St. Patrick's Day. (In 2006, an American woman and her husband informed me that in seven years of visiting Ireland for three weeks at a time, they had never been to Dublin, preferring to stay in the "real Ireland" of the west.) Proud of their Irish ancestry, they are vastly underinformed about the Ireland that no longer floats in the ether of their grandparents' memories. After returning to the group from the General Post Office on a sunny spring morning, I was surprised that no one on the tour had any idea of the symbolic importance of the GPO to modern Irish history; equally disturbing was a comment by a school teacher as we drove through Limerick City that Frank McCourt's *Angela's Ashes* was patently untrue. According to her, his memories of a depressed Ireland with people mired in poverty could not be real because "it had always been heaven on earth" there, a presumably unconscious quoting from *The Quiet Man*.

The landscape of the island reflects the changing human attributes of the globalized island. Expectations of rurality can be fulfilled, but the expanding urban and suburban landscapes, necessary to accommodate the increasing populations centered on Dublin, Cork, Limerick, and Galway, are often seen as a blight by visitors. Ireland's position as a rapidly modernizing country is an unanticipated truth among tourists who understand Ireland as a rural, pre-industrial landscape. In terms of the physical impact that Ireland's economic rise has had on the land, it had the highest per capita house building rate in Europe in 2006 (www.finfacts. com/biz10/irelandhouseprices.htm). According to the Economic and Social Research Institute, "in terms of GDP per capita, based on current Purchasing Power Parities, Ireland is ranked fourth in the world. Ireland's GDP per capita in 2003 [was] estimated at US $33,200, with only the United States, Norway, and Luxembourg ranking higher" (www.esri.ie 2005). To further illustrate the booming housing market, in April of 2006 the RTÉ reported that out of 80,000 new homes constructed in 2005 only 3,000 were considered "affordable" housing (RTÉ 2 radio 19 April 2006).

The realities of the today's Ireland are often at odds with the expectations of its modern-day tourists.

THE CELTS OF OLD

The Celts of the Iron Age have been part of the symbolic creation and development of Irish identity since before the Celtic revivalism of the Victorian era. The heroic warrior Celt, linked with the Hill of Tara in the east, Emain Macha in Armagh, Cruachan in the west, and other "royal" sites, has been written into Irish history since the 8th and 9th centuries, when monks committed local oral lore to pen and vellum. Stories such as those of Finn MacCool, Cuchulainn, Queen Medb, and King Leary and the coming of Patrick to Ireland are felt to be stories of the Celtic peoples who migrated throughout Europe from the 5th century B.C.E. until the end of the Western Roman Empire in the 5th century C.E. Celtic tribes are believed to have arrived in Ireland around 400 B.C.E., replacing or absorbing the indigenous tribes of the island as they spread across the land. Their influence has been recognized in much of the material culture and archaeological remains that are found on the landscape. The Irish language is felt to be related to ancient Indo-European languages, of which the various "Celtic" languages are also related. This linguistic descent has been determined by many scholars to demonstrate the Celticization of Ireland by way of a substantial influx of Celtic-speaking peoples. The Celt has become synonymous with The Irish, so much so that even the Irish of the 19th, 20th, and 21st centuries have had their modern identities overshadowed by the mythic Iron Age warrior image.

The "Celts," called *Keltoi* by the Greeks and *Celtae* or *Galatae* by the Romans, never (apparently) proclaimed themselves by this label. They were a scattered grouping of tribal peoples related through artistic expression, language(s), weaponry, forms of architecture, and social structure based on a warrior aristocracy (much the way Native Americans throughout the Americas are "related"). They were first recognized as an archaeological culture in the latter half of the 19th century, with the excavation of Hallstatt in the Salzkammergut of Austria by Georg Ramsaur. A series of migrations beginning in the 5th century B.C.E. carried Celtic speaking tribes across much of Europe. On the shores of Lac Neuchatel in Switzerland, the La Tene culture—the brilliant florescence of Celtic creativity—developed. The distinctive stylistic emblems of the La Tene period (ca. 350 B.C.E. – Roman era) have been found throughout Europe, including Ireland. Leaf-shaped blades, vegetal-style plastic arts, fibulae, torcs, armbands, and other portable material culture; house styles, hill forts, burials, and earthworks—all suggest a highly influential cultural shift across the continent. Their legendary outspokenness, bravado, and aristocratic bearing seem to have also enveloped many of the existing cultures of Europe. The accepted cultural history of Ireland has been of a Celticization of the indigenous population(s) beginning around the mid-4th century B.C.E.; whether they were overwhelmed by an invading culture of marauding Celts from elsewhere in Europe, gradually absorbed into an occupying culture, or were only minimally influenced by Celtic trading partners or the presiding Celtic culture of the continent is a matter of much scholarly debate in recent academic discourse on the subject of ancient Irish history (for example, Chapman 1992; Collis 1997; Hill 1989; James 1999; Warner 1999 and others). These scholarly debates have begun to enter into the fringes of the tourist landscape, including the discourse of National Museum tours. Although the scholarly discussion may at times be heated and provocative, it has not found its way into the nonscholarly interpretations of ancient Ireland (such as those given by coach driver-guides on tours) that are generally available to the visiting public. The scholarly debates are also not widely known outside intellectual circles among the Irish themselves. This gap in knowledge dissemination creates a tension between those who advertise and market Ireland as destination, such as those who promote coach tours, and those who are rewriting Irish (pre)history and thus Irish identity in the New Ireland.

The following chapters focus on these areas: coach driver-guides and their positions within the tourism industry; the tourists (I focus on American tourists, although other nationalities are included for comparison) who engage with the heritage landscape; and the heritage of Ireland and the ways in which it is communicated and interpreted by and for visitors.

CHAPTER 3

Heritage and Archaeology in Ireland

HOW IRISH HERITAGE IS DEFINED

Thus far, heritage has been broadly referred to as the tangible and intangible aspects of cultural patrimony handed down through the generations—simply put, the inherited past. It is a far more complex issue than that, often engendering emotional responses to its very existence—or any real or perceived threats to its existence. Tourists to Ireland are often overwhelmed by the heritage landscapes that surround them; so, too, they can be oblivious to the symbolic importance of the heritage to the Irish themselves. Signs written only in Irish in the Gaeltacht region are many times seen as quaint, an anachronistic nod toward the "old ways" and not as a symbol of the multilingual Ireland of the new millennium or as a way for native speakers (or the government) to delineate a specific cultural area. Trim Castle and other such buildings are understood as "Irish" despite explanations by tour guides and written signposts pointing out their position in the past as strongholds of the invading forces of a foreign country only recently purged from Irish shores. Sites of the ancient past exist in many visitors' minds as somehow emerging organically from the earth—a past so far removed from their understanding as to have simply happened; the people who built and maintained the sites for generations are imagined as inherently different from people who live today. Cultures who built Newgrange or Carrowmore for the burial of their dead and to mark out territories are seldom compared to 21st-century cultures who build enormously costly buildings to house the living and to symbolize their own bounded territories.

This chapter examines on several levels the challenge of presenting and representing the heritage landscape of Ireland: through contested landscapes, archaeologically important sites, historic buildings and areas, and time periods; the constructed tourist landscape; the discourse of heritage presentation; and the labor, communities, boundaries, and frontiers of the heritage landscape itself. I begin with a discussion of the components of "the heritage" in Ireland and how those components are incorporated into the tourist landscape or tourist gaze (Urry 2002). As Ireland increases in popularity as a destination, there will be pressure exerted on driver-guides, tour guides, and tour operators to include more and more of the fragile heritage landscape into the tourist experience. Continued increases in tourist bodies in Ireland means that many popular sites and sights will be overcrowded, leaving the necessity of incorporating less familiar sites and sights into the tourist trail. For example, through the course of my directed observations at the Hill of Tara from 2000 through 2005, visitor numbers increased exponentially each summer season—parking is limited, resources are strained in the small village, and damage to the site is common. (For example, the Mound of Hostages is rarely open as it was only a few years ago; it has been fenced off from those wishing to view its interior in order to protect the mound from vandals and unintentional damage caused by visitors climbing on top of the mound.) However, plans are underway to expand the car park and extend the shop area to accommodate visitors who now commonly arrive by the busload from Dublin or while on organized long-haul tours. A highly controversial decision to extend the M3 national road in the area will enable more traffic to easily negotiate the general area of Tara as well, although its main intention is to relieve traffic congestion in and out of Dublin.

Until a few years ago, Tara would not have commonly been included in day trips or extended tours; instead, tours would have concentrated on the Brú na Bóinne, Trim Castle (only since its refurbishment in the mid-1990s), Avoca, Glendalough Abbey, and the Wicklow Mountains. (This may be due to a paucity of visitor facilities at Tara.) While many (including me) would argue that an extended stay at Tara and a detailed guided walk across the site are necessary in order to have even the most basic understanding of this complex and important area, few visitors on a bus tour are given the opportunity to view Tara at their leisure. The careful timing of the bus tours must be adhered to for them to run smoothly and within the bounds of Irish law. (Drivers are restricted to a certain number of hours they can drive and work per day to help insure the safety of their passengers.) The ability of the driver-guide to enhance the site visit through accurate and interesting previsit information is vital to establishing a baseline understanding of the depth of Tara's history and its significance to Irish identity and culture. Just as important is the driver-guide's capacity to answer questions in postvisit transit. Many of these questions emerge from the film that can be seen at the Tara visitor center and from the guided tours available on site, but many also can be posed by visitors who did not or could not avail themselves of these additional avenues of information. In many cases, the driver-guide is expected to correct or amend the assertions of the visitor in an effort to remedy misunderstandings.

One of the endemic problems that occur when visitors from North America visit Ireland is the idea that Ireland as a nation and the Irish as a people are not supposed to evolve. Again, premodern Ireland prevails in the minds of many of these visitors. A recent conversation with an American tourist in Donegal supports this notion. The tourist, a woman from Washington, D.C., asked me where I was living while in Ireland. I replied that I was living in County Roscommon in the village of Aghoo near Boyle in a small cottage I was renting from a musician who had relocated to Kildare. I went on to describe the rural setting near the Lough Key National Park. The woman shook her head in dismay and asked me how long I thought it would remain that way. She went on to explain in great detail how I was probably witnessing the last throes of bucolic Ireland, that soon modernity would rear its ugly head and vex cottages like mine with cable TV, electricity, and—horrors—running water. I replied that I already had those things and that everyone in the village also had those things, that in fact it was required by the state that people in Ireland have the basics such as electricity and running water and that nearly everyone had cable TV, educations, cars that passed inspection, and real jobs. She was truly saddened by this. "Ireland," she said, "is ruined. The modern world has completely destroyed it. Its culture is dead, its heritage is dead. I came here to see what was left of the old world, and all I've seen are expensive houses and developments." Her tour was a west-tour going from Shannon to Westport to Donegal back south to Ennis and then back to the United States. She was staying in hotels, eating in restaurants, and gazing at Ireland through the windows of a coach. She was with friends who all seemed to share her opinion that even the remote pockets of the country (such as my gaff in Aghoo) were slowly being absorbed by the modern world. It was implicit in their conversations that they felt the Irish were defenseless against this steady encroachment and that it was unwelcome by people who had suffered through generations of poverty.

As I drove back to Aghoo, these conversations kept playing over in my mind. Benedict Anderson would refer to this as an imagined community of old world Irish, but in this case the imagination is in the minds of the visitors and not those whom they visit (1983). To look out on the fields in front of my cottage or the view across the mountains to Lough Key or to walk through the Carrowmore Megalithic Cemetery outside of Sligo is to witness a heritage alive with the pulse of modern Ireland. Had modern sensibilities not been present as Ireland developed over the course of the last century or so, it is likely that few of the heritage landscapes we take for granted today would remain. It is equally likely, had tourism not become one of the leading industries in Ireland, that the sites would become unrecognizable with disuse or, more likely, misuse. Modern sensibilities, tourism, changes in economic fortunes, local concerns, and governmental decision making have all played a role in the preservation of the heritage of Ireland but have also played an integral part in exactly what is preserved, conserved, and marketed to the world.

Components of "the Heritage"

There are many components of the heritage in Ireland, most of which I will only lightly touch on in this book. The publication *The Heritage of Ireland: Natural, Man-Made and Cultural Heritage; Conservation and Interpretation; Business and Administration* (Buttimer, Rynne, and Guerin 2000) contains an extensive compilation of articles regarding the wide-ranging characteristics of the island's heritage. Briefly, here are the components included in this publication:

Natural and Man-Made Heritage

- Natural heritage
- Archaeological landscape
- Marine archaeology
- Urban archaeology
- Industrial archaeology
- Civil engineering heritage
- Architecture
- Vernacular architecture
- Urban heritage

Cultural Heritage

- Irish language
- English in Ireland (Irish-authored works in English language)
- Irish history
- Historical/cultural geography
- Place-names
- Genealogy
- Folklore and ethnology
- Irish storytelling

- Folklore and ethics
- Science
- Gaelic games
- Local studies

Heritage and the Arts

- Traditional music
- Irish dance
- Theater and performing arts
- Visual arts
- Irish film industry
- Film and Northern Ireland

As is clear thus far, I focus on the archaeological landscape(s), especially those that have been incorporated into the landscapes now commonly included in tourism experiences. The highly inclusive list compiled by the editors and authors of *The Heritage of Ireland* are those pieces of the heritage that are recognized as well by the Irish government (*Dáil Éireann*) and that are actively promoted, protected, and funded by it. They are understood as necessary components of a fully Irish identity and as having intrinsic value to the people and the State. They are also seen as potential attractions to visitors to the island and therefore have economic value as well.

ARCHAEOLOGICAL LANDSCAPES

The archaeological resources of Ireland are wide ranging. They include world-renowned sites, such as Newgrange, Skellig Michael, the Turoe Stone, the Rock of Cashel, and Trim Castle, less well-known sites, such as Loughcrew and the Legananny Dolmen, and relatively unknown sites, such as the hundreds of stone rings, ruined towers, and industrial sites scattered throughout the country. Irish archaeological treasures are kept by the State in hundreds of local, regional, and national museums, the most visited of which is the National Museum of Archaeology and History on Kildare Street in Dublin. Few of the sites and artifacts now visible in Ireland have survived into the 21st century without some degree of controversy. Although farming was once believed to be the biggest threat to the preservation and protection of the archaeological heritage, today infrastructural development and the expanding need for housing threaten the existence of thousands of sites throughout the island[1] (www. international.icomos.org/risk/irela_2000.htm; O'Sullivan et al. 2001). This threat is not new; for example, in the 1970s, Wood Quay in Dublin, the largest known Viking site in Ireland, had to be expediently excavated by Patrick Wallace to make room for Dublin Corporation construction. The same has happened in Cork, Galway, Limerick, and many other towns and cities. The contested nature of the Irish landscape has led to clashes between opposing groups, the most recent of which have been at Carrickmines Castle (M50 Roadway extension) and the Hill of Tara (M3 extension) (see Cooney 2004; Deevey 2005; Newman, Fenwick, and Bhreathnach 2004).

Archaeology

There are too many examples of contested archaeological sites in Ireland to name. In this section, I concentrate on a few of the more well-known sites that are considered highly contested or that have been contested sites in the past: the Brú na Bóinne located north of Dublin in County Meath; the Hill of Tara in Navan, also in County Meath; and Emain Macha (Navan Fort) in Armagh, Northern Ireland. These sites have common links: along with being sites of great archaeological and historical significance, they are also considered to be symbols of Ireland's rich heritage. Each has been incorporated into the tourism landscape to differing degrees, and each has been the subject of development controversies. As contested sites, they have been subject to many differing arguments regarding their "value," their importance to Irish history, and exactly what their use may have actually been in prehistory. Each site has regained a high degree of importance to local and national identities, if only as part of the viewed and commodified landscape of modern tourism. All have been investigated and excavated; each has been explored with a variety of remote-sensing techniques, which have helped to define their boundaries and hidden components.

Archaeologically, it is difficult to rank them in importance: all are outstanding and unique sites, and all have added immensely to our knowledge of both Irish and European prehistory and early Christianity. But they do not receive "equal billing" from the national tourism boards that represent them. Part of this discussion is the notion of memory making and memory keeping in terms of the tourist "orthodoxy of musts." These musts include the grander ideals of exotic locales and the freedom of foreign travel as well as the "keepsake"—that collection of transportable goods that verify the tourist's presence on that exotic foreign landscape. As these sites of archaeological and historical importance have entered the highly competitive and highly constructed world of tourism, they have been painted onto an intentionally recreated cultural canvas that represents them not only as hill forts, chambered tombs, or ritual areas but also as important stops on a visitor's holiday schedule.

Equally important to the discussion of memory are the notion of heritage and its increasing commodification on the world stage. Heritage is that which is inherited, and worldwide it has become a highly marketable commodity. The connections made among heritage, place, and time have been instrumental in the development of the tourism orthodoxy of musts. This is clearly visible in the explosion of interest in developing heritage sites such as the Brú na Bóinne and Tara and the European Union funding available to EU members willing to establish elaborate visitor's centers to accommodate high numbers of tourists and others. Heritage differs from history; much the way Eric Hobsbawm places tradition in the present (Hobsbawm 1983), heritage also exists in the present—it is processed and considered, chosen and produced. Unlike history that has already happened, heritage is current, tangible, audible, and precious. And, unlike history, you can visit it.

Brú na Bóinne. Five thousand years ago, at a bend of the Boyne River north of Dublin, the native people of Ireland built dozens of huge burial mounds and passage graves, erected standing stones and stone rings, and lived their lives among fields newly turned for an agricultural way of life. They carved magnificent artwork into many of the kerb stones and orthostats both inside and surrounding the tombs. They structured the passages to align with solstices or with other tombs of cultural importance. They utilized the passage graves for several generations, burying their cremated dead within chambers in and around huge stone bowls and slabs. Then they moved on, leaving the future to guess why they expended such enormous energy on their elite dead.

In the Boyne Valley, three of these passage tombs have risen to the status of World Heritage Site given by the International Council on Monuments and Sites (ICOMOS), a part of the United Nations. Dowth, Knowth, and Newgrange form a triumvirate of passage tomb sites that are the focus of the Brú na Bóinne Centre and the visitation goal of thousands of tourists and school groups each year. Dowth is the least visited, having not been reconstructed, while Knowth, only recently having its excavations completed, and Newgrange, excavated and reconstructed by Michael O'Kelly in the 1970s, are seen by hundreds of thousands of visitors each year. Carefully controlled access to the sites is monitored by the OPW and the site staff (the exception being Dowth, which can be entered from the road without supervision). Structured guidance and scripted information are given by specially trained personnel, some of whom are archaeology students and graduates from local universities. Each visit to Newgrange and Knowth is timed, and entrance to the sites is through the Centre and only by small transport buses driven by Centre employees. The Centre provides visitors with an exhibition area that explains the valley's sites, the culture that created them, and the methods used to excavate and reconstruct the tombs and associated sites. In addition, visitors can view a short film that focuses on the more mystical aspects of Newgrange, or visit the small shop, the café, and a re-creation of the inner passageway at Newgrange. From lookout points within the center,

Newgrange can be viewed through telescopes, helping to tantalize visitors prior to their actual site visit. (Knowth is barely visible, and Dowth cannot be viewed from the center.) The Visitor Centre is designed to mimic the tombs; it is round, built into the side of a hill (which may have been specially constructed to reflect the image of the tombs), and is decorated with the famous triskele design of the Newgrange passageway. It is a full-service heritage site.

Newgrange is the quintessential larger-than-life experience. Driving there and to the Brú na Bóinne Centre adds to the excitement. The tumulus is visible on the horizon, with its quartz façade gleaming even in the dimmest of sunshine (Figure 3.1). Entrance to the visitor's center is by way of a long passageway reminiscent of the entrance to the tomb. The visitor is supposed to feel as though he or she is beginning a journey.

The Brú na Bóinne Visitor's Centre is a huge multimillion Euro facility built especially for controlling access to the

Figure 3.1　The tumulus of Newgrange from the pathway leading to the site (© Kelli Ann Costa 2007).

necropolis at the Bend of the Boyne. Built shortly after the sites of Newgrange, Knowth and Dowth were added to the UN World Heritage List in 1993; the center, which opened in 1997, offers the only way into the sites (again, with the exception of Dowth) for the public. You can gain access to them only if you have a proper time-marked and colored sticker on your person. The center's exhibition area, mentioned above, is underutilized by visitors. As people enter the center, lines form immediately for the Newgrange and Knowth tours. Rarely is the center itself mentioned as an option for a visit. Should a tour be filled, it is suggested visitors "take a look" at the exhibition or to take some tea or go to the shop until their tour is ready. There is no real encouragement to take in the exhibits, and there is no intention by the management to make the center integral to the Brú na Bóinne experience. The center serves a different purpose—it is the staging area for the tours to the sites and a place of commerce where visitors can purchase a variety of goods and can have lunch or dinner in the café. Access to the Boyne Valley sites is highly controlled, timed, and restricted. Each group is clearly marked, hustled through the site by their guide, mesmerized by the recreated solstice show inside the tomb, and wedged into the central chamber for a few moments in order to experience Newgrange at its prehistoric best.

Newgrange is undoubtedly a tourist attraction. Visitors to the sight/site may have little knowledge of the Boyne Valley area, the archaeology of Neolithic Ireland, or of Newgrange, but they know they must visit it. It has not been without controversy over the course of its recent history. Maggie Ronayne (2001) found the area to have been overwhelmed with development as the visitor center was planned in the 1990s. Residents found their rather quiet hamlet of Donore overrun with traffic, signage was changed to focus on the site, and land was absorbed by the new center. The center was not developed expressly for the preservation of the necropolis; it was developed with the intention of increasing visitor (read tourist) traffic to the center and the sites of the Boyne. The excavations and recreation of the tombs at Newgrange and Knowth have also not been without a degree of controversy. Newgrange especially has drawn the ire of many critics (including me) who see O'Kelly's interpretation as questionable. The archaeology and preservation schemes are not explained to visitors with any degree of sophistication at Newgrange (this is currently not the case at Knowth, which, in 2007, has a rather thorough explanation of the site by trained guides). I visited Newgrange several times over the course of three years, and the concrete cap that protects the mound and gives it some structural integrity was never mentioned by guides, the fanciful quartz façade was presented as the only possible reconstruction (based on "science" and experimental archaeology), and the relationships between the mounds of the Boyne were not explained. Mention instead was made of the Pyramids and Stonehenge, further serving to exoticize Newgrange and lifting it to mystical iconic status among the better known ancient monuments of the Old World. However, if this propensity to exoticize is examined using the notion that the visitors overwhelmingly lack background, don't have similar points of reference, and also lack the sophistication once expected of visitors to sites of such significance, it becomes clear that an overly simplified presentation of the Boyne Valley sites must be given in order to have any success in passing on information (although an interesting contrast exists between Newgrange, where the presentation hinges on spectacle, and Knowth, which is presented as a living classroom).

The Hill of Tara. The Hill of Tara is located in the Midlands of County Meath and is the historic seat of the ancient kings of Ireland. It is also the place where St. Patrick is said to have had his first great triumph in converting the children of King Leary to Christianity. Central to Tara are the *Lia Fáil*, the crowning stone, and some of the most well-documented Neolithic, Bronze Age, and Iron Age sites of Ireland. The Mound of Hostages, the Rath of the Synods, Cormac's House, and the Banqueting Hall are found scattered across a wide expanse of fields open and inviting to the visiting public. Tara has been ingrained in the collective memories of the Irish and Eirophiles alike. It exists as a place of magic and power, a place memorialized in literature both ancient and modern, a place so invested with memory that it has been reused by successive generations eager to associate with its potency. Brian Boru and Daniel O'Connor arranged their forces there, and those ready for an independent Ireland gathered there in the early 20th century as a symbolic gesture to the English.

Today, the windswept and rain-soaked hills have been rediscovered by a new generation of the awe-struck. Visitors clad in an assortment of rain gear overrun the hill daily from early morning until late at night. The visitor's center in St. Patrick's Church is open from about 9:30 A.M. until 6 P.M., depending on the season. Visitors can access Tara even if the center is not open; gates are not locked, and little is done to prevent vandalism (although, according to both the OPW and locals, there is very little). There is not really much to the center. The entry is small, and visitors are funneled into the church to view the 25-minute film. Visitors who happen to get there when the film is already in progress can go back for it, skip it (and pay nothing), or buy some postcards or books available on the site. The staff is available to answer questions and organize tours. Despite its accessibility, few of the hundreds of visitors take advantage of the center or the staff who can arrange short tours of the main site areas. Many view the dramatic film but exit to the site immediately, barely acknowledging the staff as they leave.

After leaving the church, visitors can look at the two small standing stones in the churchyard as well as remnants of an early stone cross. One of the standing stones has a carving of a shee-la-na-gig near the bottom. Although not explicitly described in either the film or the literature, the standing stones are likely coeval with the Mound of Hostages. Most people take no notice of them. They bound through the gate toward the Mound of Hostages, which is visible to the right as visitors move through the entrance to the Hill. Just beyond to the south is the *Forradh* and *Teach Cormaic* with the *Lia Fáil* and the 1798 commemorative stone. At this point, visitors are within the *Ráth na Ríogh* (Fort of the Kings) but are likely unaware of it. The bank is very low and nearly invisible between the entryway and the Mound of Hostages.

The Lia Fáil is the premier picture-taking place at Tara (see Figure 3.2). Crowds of people gather around the standing stone and take picture after picture of one another standing next to it. Many of them also hug the stone to see if it will scream at them as in the tales. Then they laugh and take more pictures. Men tend to do this more than women do. Few visitors walk out to Leary's Fort and rarely out to the Sloping Trenches or *Ráth Grainne*. As most visitors cross the site toward the Banqueting Hall, they snap photographs of it from one end toward the other.

Even though there has been an increase in the amount of attention Tara has gotten from the State regarding funding and care taking, the site reflects few of the glamorous and energetic attributes of its neighbor Newgrange on the Boyne Valley Drive. There are very few onsite information areas, and the map of the site offered

Figure 3.2 The Lia Fáil, or Crowning Stone, at the Hill of Tara. On any given day, there can be crowds of visitors around the stone snapping photographs and hugging it. This photograph shows an "improvement" to the ground line where paving stones were installed by the OPW. Many locals believe that the new additions detract from the monument and are an eyesore (© Kelli Ann Costa 2005).

in the visitor's center is just that—a map. Visitors who may not have a familiarity with the site's history would know nothing more if left to wander the site on their own. Signage is minimal, and, with the exception of a new large view-board, there is scant reference to the archaeology conducted at the site and less still on the site's actual meaning and presence on the Irish landscape. Until very recently, the Hill of Tara received very little press from the government or Fáilte Ireland. The press recently has focused on the new motorway going through the area about a mile from the Hill between it and Skryne.

Parking at Tara has become a challenge as more and more people descend on the site as they drive through the valley or take bus tours from Dublin. Amenities are few as well; facilities are inadequate, and the small shop is not equipped for the crush of tourists who flock to the site on any given day. Even so, Tara remains virtually unchanged. There is an aimlessness to the site, a lack of excitement that may help preserve it. This is in stark contrast to its sister-site at the Bend in the Boyne.

Navan Fort (Emain Macha). The huge mound of Emain Macha is located in County Armagh in Northern Ireland. Although most of the sites referred to in this book are in the Republic (the "south" or "down below," as most people in Ireland call it), I reference Emain Macha here because of its importance archaeologically and historically to the entire island. The enormous ritual mound is also known as Navan Fort, a somewhat Anglicized translation of the Irish name (Flanagan 1997). The Armagh area has been important for several thousand years and has often acted as a focal point for a variety of cultural evolutions and revolutions, including serving as the seat of the Ulaid and the later Ui Néill, as the center of St. Patrick's Christian community, as the burial site of Brian Boru, and more recently, as a flashpoint in the Troubles. Even before, this the area was inhabited by Bronze Age and Neolithic peoples who built stone formations and hill forts and farmed the rich agricultural lands. The territory is dotted with archaeological sites, including Haughey's Fort (a large Bronze Age hill fort), Loughnashade, the King's Stables (a man-made lake), the Dane's Cast, innumerable standing stones, and

Figure 3.3 The Navan Complex showing the sites related both temporally and spatially to Navan Fort. Roughly 2,000 meters separate Loughnashade on the right and Haughey's Fort on the left (© Crown copyright, reproduced with the permission of the Controller of Her Majesty's Stationery Office).

burial mounds (see Figure 3.3). Emain Macha, a multicomponent hill site, has been the focus of cultural activity from the Neolithic through the early historic period.

Emain Macha is surrounded by a large ditch and bank formation that is roughly circular in pattern. Within the ditch and bank structure are a visible ring fort and a very large mound, which is also surrounded by a raised bank. Recent remote-sensing and excavation work at the site since the 1990s has also revealed an additional ring fort structure adjacent to and conjoined with the visible one, a processional way emanating from the southwest and climbing toward the interior mound, and a funnel-shaped and stone-lined entrance in the southwest highly reflective of Dún Ailinne (another of Ireland's "royal sites") near Dublin. Although an interesting and very unique site in itself, it is also the legendary home of the Red Branch Knights, Conchobar MacNessa, and the hero Cúchulainn, who fought against the armies of Queen Medb of Connaught in the *Táin bo Cúailnge*. Its legendary status as the home of these Iron Age heroes may have been a large part of its appeal to later inhabitants, such as the powerful Ui Néill and St. Patrick, and why Brian Boru may have camped his troops there in the 11th century during his battles with Viking invaders.

Archaeological work conducted by Dudley Waterman and Chris Lynn and others (1997) found that the site was extremely complex and that it had been used over a long period of time for a variety of purposes. Initially a settlement area for Neolithic farmers, the site became the center of ritual activity in the Bronze Age, possibly as a "sister site" with Haughey's Fort, which is visible from the hill at Emain Macha. The large mound located within the bank and ditch was found to be the remains of a 40-meter wooden structure that had been filled with limestone rocks and ritually burned and covered with turf sometime around the birth of Christ in the middle of the Irish Iron Age. During its period of ritual activity, the site, it is believed, was utilized as part of a complex of ritual sites along with Loughnashade and the King's Stables and other less important (or now less visible and less understood) sites in the area. It is an imposing site when first viewed from the road or the periodically out-of-use visitor's center across what is thought to be the "playing fields" of *Táin* fame.

Perhaps the most contested issue regarding Navan Fort is the visitor center, mentioned above. Opened to much fanfare in the early 1990s, the center was closed abruptly in 2001 owing to financial difficulties following a fire that damaged its audiovisual equipment and to its less-than-expected returns. It has only recently been re-opened with any regularity and is enjoying a resurgence of interest among school groups, incentive groups, and tours. Discussions surrounding the construction of a visitor center at the fort were often heated (personal communication, anon., 2003). Scholarly articles appearing in the journal *Emania* indicate that the proposed plans and subsequent construction continued to be a matter of contention on both sides of the argument. (On the one hand, a center would educate and attract a visiting public; on the other hand, it would affect the landscape and could destroy existing archaeological sites in the vicinity.) Until 1985, the site of Navan Fort was threatened by the expansion of the adjacent limestone quarry (Figure 3.3). The "Friends of Navan" group organized to hold a public enquiry, which halted the expansion of the quarry. The site was intentionally redeveloped for tourism, with the Navan Centre opening in 1993. Among those commenting in *Emania* on the center's development were J. P. Mallory (1987), Noreen Campbell (1987), Crawford Campbell (1987), Feargus McGarvey (1987), B. K. Lambkin (1989, 1993), and B. W. Musgrave and J. W. Crothers (1993).

Discussion

How is archaeology used and exploited by the site managers to attract visitors, and what messages do these sites and the presentations send to the visiting public? Archaeology is exploited in varying degrees by these sites. At Tara, there is some effort to include archaeology in the educational program, although there are few opportunities to educate a public that rarely questions the presentation. Employees at Tara wanted to educate but could not offer information to visitors who had little ability to articulate questions pertaining to archaeology. At Newgrange, the excavations done by Michael O'Kelly in the 1960s and 1970s are woven into the presentation, but misinformation is also given—the recreated environment is rarely explained as such, and questions regarding it are often brushed off by the guides with recommendations of "visiting the library" (the bookstore) before leaving. At Emain Macha, there is nothing to explain. The site, once the focal point of a people, is deserted and lingers without any recourse to its own history. The extraordinary discoveries at Emain Macha have been left to the experts, and visitors to the site are left to mull over its use and purpose on their own with no guidance or help in recognizing its importance—to many it is an enigmatic hill, nothing more. This symbolically important piece of Ireland's heritage has been ritually abandoned, much as it was by the people who burned the structure to the ground over 2,000 years ago.

What archaeological investigation and history have left us are memories for the making. The preservation of sites determined to have high heritage value has enabled the development of a booming market based on memory—the visit, no matter how cursory or uninformed, constructs the memory; the photograph, no matter how little is actually known of the place, preserves the memory and makes it transportable, an item of exchange, something to be envied.

As symbols of Ireland's past, Tara, Emain Macha, and Brú na Bóinne represent the complex life of the people of the Neolithic, Bronze Age, and Iron Age. As symbols of the present, they have become attractions and commodities—certainly not the intention of the builders of the necropolis of the Boyne, Emain Macha, or the royal site of Tara. Although "preserved," the sites may have been preserved to this extent only because of their marketability. Thousands of other sites, often those in out-of-the-way (nontourist) areas, have been destroyed, because their value to the tourist market was negligible. Questions of their possible value to understanding Ireland's prehistory (and history as well) have been outweighed by necessity: roads, municipal buildings, and housing.

Centralizing Sites

Claude Moulin and Patricia Boniface have written extensively on the "routing" of tourism flow and the importance of "honey pot," or anchor, sites to the development of tourism routes (2001). Several examples follow.

> The essence of a route is that it is a selected journey or progression among a series of elements. . . . Usually, the elements have an approximate equality. There is a type of route, however, in which the items at its beginning or end are centres and particular tourism goals. (ibid.: 238)

In terms of the sites mentioned above, Newgrange and the Brú na Bóinne serve as the center of the Boyne Valley experience, with satellite sites located along the designated trail or route through the valley. Newgrange is the "known" site, the site that visitors can most quickly recognize as a "must see," owing to its clever marketing and omnipresence in tourism literature. As stated previously, visitors may not know *what* they are seeing, but they know they must see it in order to record their visit through photographs, video, and souvenir collection. The Hill of Tara is also located on the Boyne Valley route, but, except for its name being recognized, few first-time visitors have a clear notion of what Tara is and what it represents; a friend from the United States who recently visited Tara remarked that he felt as though he were on a golf course. The creation of the Boyne Valley (Figure 3.4) route has served a number of associated purposes beyond attracting tourists to Newgrange. It has helped to fan visitors out across the valley's many attractions, several of which have benefited greatly from inclusion on the drive; it has somewhat eased visitation pressures on Newgrange by giving visitors alternate nearby choices; and it has helped in developing cooperative networks of marketing and management among sites. While this may demonstrate a form of horizontality as

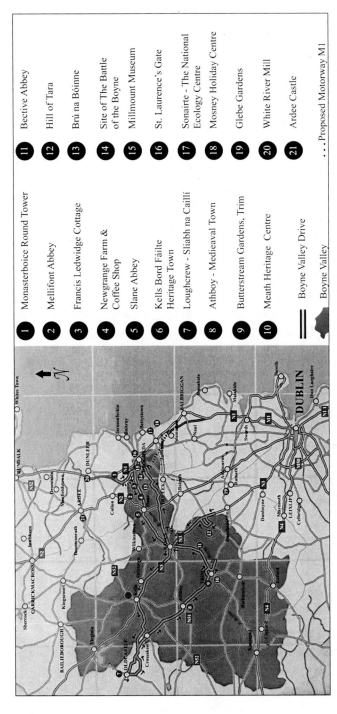

1	Monasterboice Round Tower	**11**	Bective Abbey
2	Mellifont Abbey	**12**	Hill of Tara
3	Francis Ledwidge Cottage	**13**	Brú na Bóinne
4	Newgrange Farm & Coffee Shop	**14**	Site of The Battle of the Boyne
5	Slane Abbey	**15**	Millmount Museum
6	Kells Bord Fáilte Heritage Town	**16**	St. Laurence's Gate
7	Loughcrew - Sliabh na Cailli	**17**	Sonairte - The National Ecology Centre
8	Athboy - Medieaval Town	**18**	Mosney Holiday Centre
9	Butterstream Gardens, Trim	**19**	Glebe Gardens
10	Meath Heritage Centre	**20**	White River Mill
═══	Boyne Valley Drive	**21**	Ardee Castle
	Boyne Valley	...	Proposed Motorway M1

Figure 3.4 Slí Na Bóinne: The Boyne Valley Drive. This route (maps such as this billboard are found throughout the region) has helped to make lesser known sites in the region more popular and accessible to tourists. The route also helps to compress the landscape and conflate the time periods that range from the Neolithic through the medieval and into the early modern eras (© Kelli Ann Costa 2007).

described by Moulin and Boniface (ibid.), in terms of access to sites beyond the Brú na Bóinne, the Brú na Bóinne is still the focal point of the region, commanding huge attendance numbers compared to its route neighbors (www.failteireland.com).

Dublin also acts as an anchor to areas beyond the city, but additionally the compact nature of the city lends itself to establishing much of the cityscape as a tourism route. With "hop-on, hop-off" bus tours, easy-to-negotiate pedestrian districts, and walking routes, Dublin has four of the top ten fee-charging venues in the country (Dublin Zoo, Guinness Storehouse, Book of Kells at Trinity College, and St. Patrick's Cathedral) and six of the top ten non-fee-charging venues in the country (National Gallery, Irish Museum of Modern Art, National Museum of Archaeology and History, National Museum of Decorative Arts and History, the Chester Beatty Library, and the Natural History Museum) (www.failteireland.com).

Elsewhere in the country, "Blarney Castle together with Killarney are probably the most visited areas of Ireland outside Dublin" (www.county-cork.com/Towns6.html). Killarney boasts Muckross House and Gardens, serves as the gateway to the Ring of Kerry (and, to a lesser extent the Dingle Peninsula), and is included in nearly every coach tour offered in Ireland. A short jaunt from Blarney Castle, located northwest of the city of Cork, Killarney has been established as the anchor site on the southwestern tourist route along with Blarney/Cork. Smaller and more easily negotiated than Cork City, Killarney bills itself as "Ireland's Premier Visitor Destination" (www.killarneytown. com).

Ireland West enters a competing claim that "Knock is Ireland's most visited town" (www.irelandwest.ie), with its Marion Shrine, airport, and proximity to Galway, Westport, Sligo, and Connemara. Understandably, the majority of Knock's visitors are "pilgrims," a category of tourist that has particular intent beyond sightseeing or visiting friends and relatives. The west of Ireland is often understood as the "real" Ireland, although it is much less developed for tourism than are the south and east of the country. Knock's location in an area of the country with relatively few "attractions" and its fame as a site of sacred apparitions, visits from Pope John Paul II, and a place where miraculous healing has occurred have aided in it becoming a magnet site on a west-ward swing through Ireland. The southeast has also fashioned a variety of routes that include Waterford Crystal (one of the top ten fee-charging sites), Kilkenny Castle, Glendalough and the Wicklow Mountains, and the Rock of Cashel (also one of the top ten fee-charging sites) among others. Although not all of the sites that are located along or anchor the various routes in Ireland are archaeological in nature, all are linked with Ireland's heritage and its past and are actively constructed to represent the Ireland of the here and now: vibrant and modern but equally traditional and rural, mystical and magical.

DEVELOPING AND PLANNING THE HERITAGE

It would be hard to argue with the statement that heritage sites are developed with tourism and revenue generation in mind. This is true of Ireland, as it is true for most areas of the world (McManus 1997). In a word of caution, Raoul Bianchi and Priscilla Boniface have written:

> A related concern . . . [is the] the centrality of tourism to the existence of many WHSs (World Heritage Sites), which raises questions about the appropriate balance to be maintained between consumption and conservation. While cultural/ heritage tourism provides one of the most effective means for bringing these places to the attention of a wider public, it may simultaneously expose them to the very dangers such designation is supposed to prevent (e.g., overcrowding, degradation, commercialisation). (2002: 80)

This is true not only of World Heritage Sites but of all sites open for public display that represent a culture's heritage. In Ireland, the impact of millions of tourist fingers rubbed across soft, carved sandstone and greywacke stones at Knowth, Newgrange, Loughcrew, and other places is evidenced in the rapid wearing away of the rock art so precious and unique to Irish passage tombs. The awareness of and attention to those places recognized as "heritage" have been a two-edged sword; these sites have been preserved, conserved, and rediscovered by locals and visitors alike, but their visibility has cost them in terms of the very things intended to be preserved for future generations, as visitor traffic far exceeds any site's intended use and carrying capacity. As MacManus has suggested for archaeological heritage sites in Ireland, there has been little effort to analyze the effect that high levels of visitor traffic has on the sites (1997). Instead, the effort has been on enhancing visitor facilities in order to attract more visitors to the sites (ibid.: 97). *The Stone Monuments Decay Study 2000* conducted by Sara Pavia and Jason Bolton for the Heritage Council describes the types and extent of damage occurring to stone structures throughout the country. Pavia and Bolton found "33.3% of 114 dressed stone monuments showed evidence of decay" (www.heritagecouncil.ie), not all of which was caused by direct contact with visitors; but 7% showed evidence of vandalism, and many showed indications of damage caused by increased fossil fuel pollutants and other detritus in the air. Very few of the monuments analyzed by Pavia and Bolton would be classed as prehistoric, and the authors suggest in their recommendations that prehistoric stone monuments be targeted in future surveys of stone decay. My own work at the Loughcrew Cairns near Oldcastle has supported their conclusions. Evidence of vandalism is obvious, and acid rain impact is indicated through higher than normal pH levels in the soils associated with the megalithic cemetery (Costa n.d., n.p.). Figure 3.5 illustrates graffiti on one of the inner chamber stones at Cairn U, as well as a lack of lichen. The lichen that is present is dry, scaly, and flakes easily off the stones. Although lichen may obscure the stone art, it also serves to preserve it. The increase in acid rain and other airborne pollutants has had a negative effect on the health of the lichen, has seeped into the soft stones, making the surfaces friable and extremely susceptible to flaking, and has also affected soil quality.

Figure 3.5   Evidence of vandalism at Cairn U, Loughcrew
Megalithic Cemetery. Lichen splashes along the bottom of the stone
also indicate that acid rain and other airborne pollutants have affected
the preservation of the stone art (© Kelli Ann Costa 2005).

In developing and planning the heritage sites of Ireland,
the Office of Public Works (OPW) and the Department of
Environment, Heritage and Local Government (DOEHLG)
have as their "primary concern" the protection and maintenance
of "Ireland's heritage for future generations" (OPW *Heritage
Sites of Ireland 2006/07*: 1). Of the 88 attractions listed in the
Heritage Sites visitor's guide, only ten would be classified as
prehistoric, the balance including gardens, castles, parks, abbeys
and churches, and nature preserves. Buttimer, Rynne, and Guerin
suggest two ways in which the heritage of Ireland can be best
served: through awareness of the country's heritage diversity and
complexity and "to entrust its advancement to people suitably
equipped to discharge this responsibility" (2000: vii). Training
programs, such as the Diploma in Irish Heritage Management
at University College Cork, were instituted in the 1980s to

provide a means to develop qualified personnel to manage and maintain the heritage of Ireland. As the European single market loomed in the early 1990s, the Irish government identified tourism as one of the key economic areas that could contribute to improving and sustaining "national regeneration" (Buttimer, Rynne, and Guerin 2000: vii). A series of development plans from the late 1980s through 1999 made the process of heritage development part of tourism development with associated funding and governmental support. However, Buttimer, Rynne, and Guerin point out that the National Development Plan of 2000–2006 had no such inclination, instead concentrating on infrastructural improvements and capital projects such as road construction (ibid.: xiii). The absence of heritage conservation and development programs is worrying, giving the impression that the earlier programs were simply a means to an end—that of economic growth and prosperity. As Ireland's economic position has improved exponentially since the 1989 version of the National Development Plan, the necessity of heritage improvements has been pushed aside for more basic needs such as roads, housing, gas pipelines, and retail development.

Gabriel Cooney, Tom Condit, and Emmet Byrnes suggest that Ireland see itself as a single, expansive "archaeological landscape" based on the number of associated sites and complexes located throughout the country (2000: 26–27). Recognizing the importance of the *National Monuments Act, The Heritage Act 1995,* and a series of other legislative decisions, Cooney, Condit, and Byrnes point out that sites and monuments on privately owned lands must also be incorporated into the planning process (ibid.: 27). They suggest that a multivocal approach of local communities, professionals, private landowners, and government, while being a major challenge, will "ensure the continuity of the past in the present, lived landscape of today and sustain it for future generations" (ibid.).

Although the concept of Ireland as a single, vast archaeological landscape is enticing, the country is made up of a series of both associated and discrete sites, many of which are jumbled into a confusing spatial and temporal mélange. The choice of which and what to conserve, maintain, preserve, and market is often at loggerheads with the reality of doing the work. An example of this is Ross Castle in Killarney, County Kerry, a 15th-century tower house with a surrounding bawn wall, circular towers, and later additions and reconstructions (Figure 3.6). Ross Castle was in desperate condition when work began in the 1970s, and the National Monuments Service saw it as one of their "most dangerous project[s] ever undertaken" (Rourke 2000: 353). However, the castle had a number of things going for it: it was located in a very popular and picturesque area of the country, it was historically significant, and it had great potential as a tourist attraction. Built around the same time as the neighboring Muckross Abbey, it was the home of the powerful O'Donoghue Mor for over 100 years. It was absorbed by the Anglo-Norman Earls of Desmond in the 16th century, whose relationship and loyalty to England was tenuous at best. The Earls

Figure 3.6   Ross Castle Killarney after reconstruction and preservation taken from the laneway leading to it
(© Kelli Ann Costa 2005).

and other Anglo-Norman families in Munster had adopted Gaelic customs and had intermarried with local families. In 1652, it was the last Kerry stronghold to fall to Cromwellian forces, eventually being converted to a barracks, then gradually falling into disrepair. Grellan Rourke describes the difficulty of dealing with the significant structural problems of the castle, as well as the funding issues that arose (2000). Work at the castle began in the late 1970s but was not completed until 1993, when the castle was opened to the public. Supported by European Structural Funds, private funding, and funds from the Irish government, the work progressed slowly and many times did not progress at all. Today Ross Castle is included in much of the Killarney and Kerry tourist literature with special boat tours of Lough Leane, including a castle visit, a visit to a 7th-century monastery (where King Brian Boru may have had his monks educated during his reign) and a 12th-century oratory on Inisfallen Island. It is questionable, with the economic climate in Ireland and the recent pressures to expand infrastructurally, whether such lengthy measures would be taken to preserve and reconstruct the castle had the work begun in more recent years.

Maggie Ronayne discussed the "valuing" of archaeological landscapes in the context of the construction of the Brú na Bóinne Centre in 1997 and the designation of the three monuments of the Bend of the Boyne (Newgrange, Knowth, and Dowth) as World Heritage Sites in 1993 (Ronayne 2001). A "contested landscape," or one that has myriad and often opposing understandings in the present (Bender 2001), the landscape of the Bend of the Boyne had already been a focus of visitor activity for several hundred years. Ronayne refers to a passage from Edward Lhuyd in 1700, who calls it a "remarkable occurrence," in order to contextualize its position as a magnet for the curious over time (ibid.: 149). More important here is Ronayne's discussion of the development of the Brú na Bóinne Centre, its location on the south side of the Boyne River (the monuments are on the north), and the relocation of signposts that directed visitors away from the historically traditional "launching" areas and local commercial interests that had sprouted up as the monuments gained popularity since the mid-1970s. Coinciding with Michael O'Kelly's completion of excavations and reconstruction of the mound at Newgrange, the local communities on the north side of the Boyne near the monuments had developed a number of cottage industries related to the monuments. The decision to construct the 7-million-pound visitor center (over $15 million) on the south side of the river took local control away from the people who had depended on the monuments' visitors for income. The changes in signposting steered visitors away from the monuments and toward the center, thereby clarifying access to the tombs as only through the center, as well as concentrating all Brú na Bóinne activity through the center. The rather clinical deposition of the center, the carefully controlled "tomb tours," the timed access, and the constricted flow of movement all contribute to a reduction in choice for the visitors who crowd into the center daily. The decision to exploit the monuments at the Bend of the Boyne as highlights in Irish heritage tourism correlates exactly with its designation as a World Heritage Site. It has since become the most visited of the ancient (prehistoric, pre-Christian) sites in Ireland that tally visitor numbers. (Note that not all sites in Ireland, even those considered as having great archaeological, historical, or heritage significance, have a process of enumerating visitor numbers. Many sites are simply present on the landscape and open to visitors free of charge and encumbrance.)

CHAPTER 4

Representing Ireland's Heritage

Thus far, we have seen that a number of factors have been used to establish and create a highly recognizable heritage landscape in Ireland. However, how has the heritage landscape of the country been exploited by the tourism industry? What aspects of it are considered marketable and presentable to a temporary, segmentary population? How are the heritage landscape and the components of the heritage landscape presented to an expanding multicultural audience? In what ways do the coach driver-guides act as intermediaries in the representation and presentation of the heritage?

In this section, a number of highly recognizable landscapes, sites, areas, and time periods are sampled within the context of tourism representation(s). In addition, I touch on the Irish as packaged heritage and the language of Ireland, including the slang, lilt, tone, and whimsy of spoken English, as well as the native Irish language. The important issues explored include the illustrations and language used in tourism marketing from both within and without Ireland and the actions and decision-making processes of the intermediaries who must validate, expand, titillate, and sometimes correct the impressions of Ireland brought to them by the tourist groups they escort.

LANDSCAPES

Although it has been suggested that Ireland could be seen as one vast archaeological landscape, in terms of the tourism land-scape it is segmented and bounded. It is common for coach driver-guides to announce to their groups that they are passing from one county into another or that they will soon be entering a new landscape. This is useful in preparing visitors for a new experience, as well as giving visitors a marker of identification when moving between landscapes and areas. The west, where this discussion will focus, is presented as authentic (Bruner 1994; MacCannell 1976), and the absence of urban landscapes in the advertising of the west appeals to those who may be searching for an Ireland of memory.

For example, Killarney, the popular and large town in County Kerry mentioned earlier, is a "focal point" for tourism, and many coach tours spend from a day to several days staying in the town and visiting the surrounding areas of the Ring of Kerry, the Blasket Islands, the Dingle Peninsula, and west Cork. Like the Brú na Bóinne Centre, it is a staging area for further exploration. Despite it often being choked with traffic and visitors, Killarney is considered symbolic of western Ireland's old world charm. Likewise, Galway to the north is not presented as a city but as an oasis of art and music; it is intellectual and stimulating, with the best of what a city can offer but without the urban masses, pollution, and stress. In reality, Galway is overcrowded and difficult to negotiate on foot, by coach, or by car on most days in spring, summer, and autumn. Its presentation is of something other than what actually exists.

Two of the landscapes commonly presented and visited are the Cliffs of Moher and the Burren. Typically included in even short coach tours of Ireland, they evoke notions of the "real Ireland"—the heartland spoken of by de Valera, celebrated by Yeats, and reluctantly abandoned by thousands of famine victims in the 19th century.

Cliffs of Moher

The Cliffs of Moher are located in western Ireland near the town of Doolin in County Clare on the coast. Soaring 700 feet above the ocean, the cliffs are visited by hundreds of thousands of people each year. Coach tours that get their start at Shannon Airport often move from there directly to the Cliffs; they are an invigorating and stunning way to begin a trip to Ireland. The journey takes about 90 minutes and gives jet-lagged visitors time to get their wits about them, have a quick nap, and ease into their role as tourists. If they have done any preparation, they know they are about to see a wonder of nature. Their driver-guide will begin his or her "Cliffs talk" about 30 minutes from the destination, complete with well-placed warnings not to get close to the edges and stories of people who have been blown off the cliffs by the relatively constant high winds that buffet the area throughout the year.

The cliffs are majestic and unique. They are often touted as the "last glimpse of Ireland" that famine émigrés would have had on their journey away from home. To further enhance the Cliffs of Moher as an attraction, the government took measures to sanitize the area by restricting the access of buskers and other street entertainers, improving walkways and safety procedures, and constructing a multimillion Euro visitor center. The center hits all the right buttons. It is high-tech, slick, well-presented, acts as a planning and excursion point, and has meal and toilet facilities. It boasts highly innovative, state-of-the-art architecture and design. It is paid for by visitors whose parking fees at the Cliffs have risen exponentially (for example, coach parking was €5 in 2006; in 2007 it rose to €60). Many coach drivers are concerned that the incredible increase in fees will result in fewer coach tours stopping at the Cliffs. A few suggested that a similar experience could be had on a day's outing on Inishmor in the Aran Islands, where visitors could spend an entire day on a ferry crossing, seeing the small island, and experiencing Inishmor's high cliffs out at the Bronze Age fort of Dún Aeonghus. It remains to be seen whether the added attraction of the visitor center at the Cliffs of Moher, and the additional costs of seeing the Cliffs, will affect visitor numbers in the future.

The Burren

The Burren is located just to the north of the Cliffs of Moher, also in County Clare, and is typically a "drive through" on coach tours, although there are many opportunities for hiking, dining, stopping for photos, or some other activity if there is time or it has been planned into the day's outing. Although it is another stunning landscape, the Burren, unlike the Cliffs of Moher, which are breathtaking, is desolate, quiet, remote, eerily resembling a moonscape. The landscape has become a facilitator in filling time between hotel zones for tourists. It is about 90 minutes south of Galway and is easily reached from the main Limerick-Galway road. In many cases, the Burren is a diversion off the main road, allowing tours to and from Galway to hug the Clare coast along Black Head and through Ballyvaughan with a possible stop in Lisdoonvarna (the town made famous by its matchmaking festivals) and lunch in Lahinch. On days when time needs to be filled, this route (which can also include the Cliffs) allows drivers and tourists to have a rather easy day of short drives and leisurely stops. Many tour groups traveling between either Shannon or Limerick and Galway stop at the Cliffs and drive through the Burren as they make their way through the west.

Geology, Human Geography, and Development. The Burren has been occupied from about 3800 B.C.E. by a variety of human groups, many of whom have, and do, depend on low-intensity livestock farming. While rich in scenic value, the land itself is difficult and reluctant to cooperate with human attempts to control it. Soil is of poor quality and is thinly spread across the landscape, which is dominated by bare limestone ridges and escarpments interrupted with scrub and occasional grassland. Within the Burren are located a 1,673-ha national park around Mullaghmore and a small 145-ha nature preserve. The Burren Uplands have been designated a "Special Area of Conservation (SAC) in recognition of its internationally important status" despite being privately owned (Lysaght 2005: 8). It is considered to be a "visually vulnerable scenic landscape" (ibid.).

Changes in land use in recent years have had serious impact on the Burren's viability as livestock farming has measurably decreased. According to Liam Lysaght of the Heritage Council, the fall off in agricultural activities has disrupted the balance between livestock grazing and species richness, resulting in, amongst other things, encroachment of scrub on the ecologically valuable grasslands. Tourism and recreation have become much more dominant economic forces, and the trend towards people living in the Burren but commuting to employment outside the region has increased. This has generated a vibrant local community, but it has also led to pressure for development. (ibid.)

Lysaght and others, such as the Clare County Development planners, have called for a decisive management plan in the Burren to address the issues surrounding the changes in this heritage landscape, suggesting that it is a "cultural landscape of inordinate importance" that requires protection.

The Burren as Attraction. Since 1997, tourism has outpaced agriculture as a major economic activity in Ireland. The same is true in the Burren and in other fragile and unique areas of the country. Tourism is considered the "key economic activity" in the area, and efforts to both increase and control tourist activity are evident in the barrage of ecological impact statements, proposals to stall or halt developments, and recent suggestions to turn the entire North Clare region into a national park (ibid.). The area is generally acknowledged in tourism literature as "stark and barren" but nonetheless as a place that is fundamental to an Irish identity and an experience of Ireland.

SITES

I have concentrated my interests on prehistoric sites, but perhaps of more significance to many visitors are the numerous ecclesiastical and monastic sites that are located throughout the country. This section discusses the sites of Clonmacnoise and St. Patrick's Cathedral within the context of heritage representation. Ireland's relationship to Christianity dates back to the 5th century and predates the coming of St. Patrick. Roman Catholicism was not the norm until the medieval period, when Celtic Christianity was absorbed into the Catholic Church. Among the most important landmarks in Ireland that help to illustrate the longevity of faith are the sites of Clonmacnoise in Shannonbridge, County Offaly, and St. Patrick's Cathedral in Dublin.

Clonmacnoise

The multicomponent site located on the banks of the River Shannon was founded by Saint Ciarán in the 6th century. Covering a wide expanse of land, the site allowed the inhabitants to see all movement up and down the river and across the flood plains on either side. Today the site includes the ruins of a large cathedral, seven churches built from the 10th to the 13th centuries, two round towers (thought to have been used in defensive strategies against Viking and Irish raiders; see Figure 4.1), several carved Celtic

Figure 4.1   This view at Clonmacnoise shows one of the round towers, part of the cemetery, a ruined chapel, and the landscape across the River Shannon. The Shannon is the longest river in Ireland and has been an important source of mobility and commerce since the Stone Age. Three of the high crosses have been moved inside the visitor center, which also features a film and further information on the site (© Kelli Ann Costa 2005).

crosses, and a large number of Early Christian grave markers. During the summer months, it is one of the busiest sites in Ireland and can often have long delays in scheduling guided tours.

The long history of the location on the Shannon predates the establishment of Ciarán's monastery. The *Eiscir Riada* (esker), one of the long glacial ridges that bisect Ireland, was used as a prehistoric highway, enabling people to move across the bogs with relative ease. Eskers are numerous in Ireland, but the *Eiscir Riada* passes directly by the site of Clonmacnoise. Archaeology in the area has uncovered Neolithic, Bronze Age, and Iron Age activity, suggesting that the flood plain of the Shannon was an active area for thousands of years.

Ciarán, who was taught at Clonard by St. Finian, a tutor to the early saints of Ireland, is also associated with the monastery on Inishmore in the Aran Islands. At Clonard, Ciarán's dun cow was so abundant in milk that she was able to sustain the entire community. When she died, her hide was preserved as a sacred relic. Shortly after founding the monastery at Clonmacnoise, Ciarán died in 549, after which the *clon,* or community, became a center of learning. It is known that the monastery was used as a scriptorium from the 8th through 10th centuries, and the earliest known manuscript in Irish, *The Book of the Dun Cow*, was produced there. Some believe that the vellum pages of the book are made from Ciarán's cow's hide. Smithwork in gold and silver and other high-end crafts were also produced. An example is the crozier of Clonmacnoise, now at the National Museum in Dublin.

The monastery was also a target for attack and was plundered 8 times by Vikings between the 8th and 12th centuries, 27 times by Irish raiders, and 6 times by Anglo-Normans. Its influence began to wane in the 15th century, and in 1552 the English garrison at Athlone reduced it to a ruin. However, it has held continuous religious significance with the Irish. St. Ciarán's Feast Day takes place in September, Pope John Paul II worshiped there in 1979, and pilgrims still go to Clonmacnoise to pray. In 1955, the Office of Public Works established a conservation scheme, many of the buildings and ancient grave slabs were cleaned up and preserved, and a modern visitor center built in 1990s was constructed wherein three of the high crosses and many other fragile artifacts are now housed to protect them from the elements.

Clonmacnoise and a number of other monastic and ecclesiastical sites are included on the "Monastic Way," a route stretching from Dublin to Galway that roughly follows the *Eiscir Riada*. It begins at Christchurch Cathedral in Dublin and travels through Maynooth, Enfield, Clonard, Durrow, Rahan, Clonmacnoise, Clonfert, the site of the 1691 Battle of Augherim, and finally ends at the Galway Cathedral. The route was devised by the Offaly Historical and Archaeological Society (www.monasticway. com). I was unable to find information on who and how many have used the Monastic Way since its creation.

St. Patrick's Cathedral

Founded in 1191, the cathedral is located on St. Patrick's Close in Dublin 8, and it is designated as Ireland's National Cathedral. Jonathan Swift served as Dean from 1713–1745 and was present when *Händel's Messiah* was first performed there in 1742. Its long history and its relationship to Dublin are illustrated within the cathedral in a permanent exhibit called "The Living Stones." In 2006, Afghan refugees occupied the cathedral and went on a hunger strike to draw attention to their continuing hardships as refugees and to the war in their home country. Within the cathedral, visitors can view a variety of artifacts and plaques recounting the long history of the site.

It is thought that there may have been a wooden church built on the site to commemorate St. Patrick's use of a holy well for local baptisms. The well is believed to be located under the modern car park. John Comyn, the first Anglo-Norman archbishop of Dublin, is responsible for raising the status of the small church to that of a collegiate church in 1191. It likely attained its stature as cathedral at some point while Comyn was in leadership, but this is not fact. It became Ireland's National Cathedral after 1870 with the disestablishment of the Church of Ireland (www.stpatrickscathedral.ie).

The cathedral as we now know it is believed to have been started in the early 13th century by Archbishop Henry of London. Considered a "natural attraction," it admits visitors daily throughout the year but is closed to visitors on Christmas Eve, Christmas Day, and St. Stephen's Day. Upon entry, visitors are reminded that St. Patrick's is a "living building," not a museum, and that it holds church services daily. The reminder helps to keep the atmosphere reverential and quiet even when the till in the gift shop is ringing.

AREAS

To further illustrate the segmented and bounded tourism landscape, areas such as Cork/Kerry and Connemara are used as focal points to attract visitors. In many cases, the areas will then be whittled down in the marketing plans to focus on a few particular sites or landscapes within them. In the Cork/Kerry region, the Ring of Kerry, Killarney, Kinsale, Cobh, West Cork, and Blarney Castle are given special attention, helping to attract visitors to these areas within areas owing to their abilities to serve the visiting public. In other cases, a "way of life" is the attraction, such as the Gaeltacht- or Irish-speaking areas in Connemara. Connemara is also one of the areas traditionally felt to be the "real Ireland." This feeling perhaps relates to the persistence of native Irish speakers and traditional customs but may also pertain to the high number of émigrés from the region over the last few centuries and to its peaceful and rural character (people, place, and pace).

Fáilte Ireland and Tourism Ireland have enforced the areal focus through a variety of regional schemes, such as the Super Regions initiative described in Chapter 5. Economic and infrastructural development has also tended to focus on regions with concentrations usually on urban or highly populated and developed areas within the regions. These regions are particularly important not only in terms of Irish economic development but also in terms of tourism development; they can accommodate high tourist numbers, while at the same time they help to deflect heavy traffic away from more vulnerable places in the countryside. "Routing" is also important in terms of decision-making regarding funding for the regions. Highly traveled routes and roads that are capable of sustaining heavy use and that direct travel to and from locales that can handle an intense tourism trade are especially targeted for infrastructural improvement (see, for example, the National Development Plans of 1999 and 2007).

This section examines Cork/Kerry and Connemara examined as areas or regions of tourism development in terms of their heritage value. The regions, although both located in the west, are very different. Their marketing and presentation are also approached very differently, internally and externally. Although clearly defined as "heritage regions," they offer the visitor different experiences.

Killarney and the Southwest

The southwest is the most visited region of Ireland after Dublin (www.failteireland.ie). Popularity of the area is driven by its honey pots: The Ring of Kerry, west Cork, Blarney, and the long picturesque coastal zone. The region adequately caters to visitors with a wide array of accommodation, restaurants, and activities. Killarney, the gateway to the southwest and the Ring of Kerry, is one of the most popular and highly utilized destinations in coach touring. For example, in the 2007/2008 Brendan Tours brochure, nine of ten Ireland-only tours include Killarney, and four of five combination tours (with U.K.) include it. This is typical of coach tours such as those of Brian Moore International, CIE, and Isle Inn, all of whom use Killarney as a stopover in most of their tour offerings. On any given day, international coach tours from Europe and the U.K. can also be seen in Killarney. Coach drivers and driver-guides overall find time in and around Killarney to be a favorable experience but overwhelmingly suggest parking and traffic problems as negative issues (see Figure 4.2).

Blarney and Blarney Castle in Cork, although real places, can be understood as created tourism experiences based on heritage. The idea of "kissing the Blarney Stone" in order to suddenly be blessed with Irish eloquence and the very action of doing so are tied to

Figure 4.2 Bus-only parking in Killarney taken over by automobiles is typical of the challenges faced by coach drivers and driver-guides in one of the most popular tourist destinations in Ireland (© Kelli Ann Costa 2006).

local lore dating to the time of Queen Victoria and her pointed exchanges with an Irish lord. Historical fact does not mention kissing an actual stone (a feat that includes hanging upside down while someone holds onto you and sticking your head through a gap in the castle wall as you plant one on a rock millions of other people have also kissed!). Kissing the stone was an exploit brought to life through active creation. Intellectually, visitors know that their communication skills won't improve, but the action, the taking part, the climb to the top of the tower, the meeting of lips to stone, and the photographic evidence of it, are part of the experience of Ireland's heritage, created expressly for tourists.

Connemara

It is an area commemorated in poetry and prose. A wild, tangled, mass of land. A traditional area where the Irish language is more natural than learned. A land devastated by famine and diaspora. A place that evokes emotional responses to its very landscape. A primordial experience. Unlike the Killarney area described above, Connemara, on the midwest coast, does not have an abundance of hotels and "activity areas." Its appeal is in its absence of these. There is a silence in Connemara, a mustiness, perhaps an Irish damp that has been re-created as an attraction and a destination. It is a stunning but empty landscape, dominated by the peaks of the Twelve Bens or Pins (*Na Neanna Beola*). The occasional manor house stands alongside small thatched cottages, and sheep roam the countryside in little danger of predators or traffic. It does have two significant points of entry though: Galway City to its southeast and Westport, a perennial "Tidy Town" finalist, to its north.

The 2005/2006 tourism guidebook produced by Ireland West contains a map that directs tourists from Galway to Westport along the N59, the road highlighted by its dark blue color, contrasting with the pale yellow of the map and the muted tones of lesser roads (Ireland West 2005). In the guidebook, we are told to "imagine a place where you are welcomed by a warm and friendly people, who give you the attention you deserve and are interested in making your stay the most pleasant and memorable you've ever had" and that it is "a rugged and most beautiful place that touches [the] soul and breaks [the] heart to leave behind" (ibid.: 5). The evocative passages penetrate the potential visitor with visions of a magical place filled with the most agreeable of people. The rugged scenes in the photographs conjure tales of survival, community, devotion to land, family, and an ancient way of life. Away from the text and well-framed images are advertisements for hotels, tourist shops, play areas, and heritage venues. It may be desolate, but a visitor can still find plenty to do in terms of distraction and commerce.

Coach drivers tended to like the cruise through Connemara, time spent in Galway (although all mentioned the parking in Galway City as atrocious) and Westport, and along the way in Clifden on the western edge of Connemara. Generally they pointed out that visitors enjoyed the landscape and the feeling of closeness to the land and people the area seems to evoke. Many coach drivers and driver-guides have developed stops on the Connemara drive where they are tipped by merchants either through a form of "kick-back" by bringing people into the shop or with free lunches, dinners, or some other bonus.

PEOPLE

One of the three core value concepts in the branding of Ireland is people. The 2005 Visitor Attitudes Survey conducted by Millward Brown IMS for Fáilte Ireland found that 39% of all holidaymakers believed that the Irish people gave Ireland a "distinguishing advantage" over other holiday destinations (2005: viii). The survey also found that 84% of all holidaymakers said that friendly people were the top destination issue, and 89% ranked the Irish as earning a high satisfaction rating (ibid.: ix). Advertisements for holidays to Ireland inevitably include visual enticements of happy, celebratory Irish folk in pubs with musical instruments, ordering pints of Guinness. Rural folk are also prominent, usually associated with sheep and thatch and wearing an abundance of earth-toned tweed—rural folk are usually male, unless an appropriate colleen can be found to balance the presentation. "The Irish" are inseparable from the heritage of Ireland; they created themselves and the landscapes to which millions travel yearly. People can also be absent from advertising, reducing Ireland to a patchwork of landscapes and buildings.

Advertising promotes in potential customers a particular expectation of a product. When the product is Ireland, the expectation is reinforced by a variety of other images gleaned from film, literature, and memory. According to Declan Kiberd, the "stage" Irishman or Irishwoman—the charming, talkative, wild, erotic, stereotypical "Paddy"—has become an easy conformity into which Irish natives have historically been able to retreat (1995: 29). Although this image was initially one used to adjust to life in urban centers away from homes in Ireland (such as London or New York), the image has also become one into which today's native Irish can slip when confronted with visitors. The "b'gosh, begorragh" Irishman, although a fiction of literature and English oppression, lives in the expectations of many tourists and must be folded into the touristic experience. Coach driver-guides utilize this disarming ethnic stereotype to keep visitors off balance; a shuffling, awe-shucks, "grand day isn't it?" can often diffuse a difficult situation without the surface of the holiday being disturbed.

Brendan Worldwide Vacations, begun in the late 1960s by Irish-Americans, is careful to include the Irish personality in its advertising:

> Ireland's people, history, culture, folklore, scenery and eccentricities . . . undoubtedly appeal to the American traveler. Reliving the past in a stately castle, the smiles and laughter of a B & B owner, the rolling emerald hills, homemade breads and soups and a pint of Guinness in a local pub—these are the memories Americans regularly take home and are eager to share. *Ireland is one of the few countries where the locals want you to experience their lives.* (2007: 2, *italics added*)

The 2007/2008 *Ireland and Britain: Escorted, Independent, and Self-Drive Vacations* brochure not only includes itineraries and descriptions of the tours (coach tours are highlighted) but also uses the branding principles of people, pace, and place throughout its guide: "friendliness is second nature to our staff," "skilled storytellers," "must-see" attractions, "the remote wilderness of Connemara," "distinctive Irish warmth and hospitality," "breathtaking scenery," and "vibrant cities" titillate potential consumers on the glossy pages. Accompanying the sparse text (the bulk of the content simply runs through a variety of itineraries) are well-framed photographs of Blarney Castle, the Abbey Tavern, Glendalough, Trinity College, the Killarney lakes, Dromoland and Ashford castles, and other places. Very few people are to be found on this rich cultural landscape, the exception being photographs labeled "always a smiling face" and "Ireland—expect a warm welcome." It is easy to assume the Irish pictured are there to serve. Native Irish who occur on tour are allowed to live during the present century but must essentially exude the past. Opulence and affluence, although becoming more common in some areas of holiday advertising (for example, spa vacations, city breaks, special sporting events such as the 2006 Ryder Cup), are situated in the remote past in most tourism literature. Ancient castles are now hotels, once occupied or owned by someone until a time when they could be rescued and rehabilitated and put to good use in the modern day. Few visitors associate these elegant culture-scapes with the Irish people's colonization and poverty-ridden past.

LANGUAGE

Language, whether the sing-song slang of a Corkman or the complex native tongue of the Gaeltacht, has also become a distinct form of attraction for visitors to Ireland. Irish-Americans who frequent "authentic" Irish pubs in their hometowns may have read the familiar *Cead Mile Fáilte* (a thousand welcomes) that typically appears within the context of many hometown pubs. They may also have listened to traditional Irish-language music. At the very least, most visitors, especially those who are descendants of émigrés, can recognize an Irish accent or the most basic of Irish language terms (*slanté* being a common term used for toasting in many Irish-American pubs).

While observing an American tour in 2006, one participant pulled me aside and asked if I was from Ireland. I told her I wasn't, I was from the Boston area, but I had been in Ireland for some time.

"Don't you just *love* the accent?" she asked.

"Which one?"

"The Irish one, of course!"

"Some of them can be quite challenging."

"No, I'm talking about an *Irish* accent!" she was clearly getting frustrated with me.

"It depends on which part of the country the accent is from," I said, "I really like a Cork accent, because it reminds of home. But I have a hard time following a Donegal accent or a northern Irish accent. And a Tipp accent takes some getting used to."

"They have different accents? They all sound the same to me. Just listening to this guy [the driver-guide] has made this the best vacation ever. I think it's sexy. I could sit on the bus all day long and just listen to him—even if I don't understand half of what he's saying."

"Have you learned any Irish since you've been over here?" The tour had been on for eight days and had a few more days to go.

"Yeah: wanker and slanté."

"You do know that wanker is a derogatory term, sort of like moron or bastard, don't you? And it's not Irish."

"No. It means silly. When you're a wanker, you're being silly. It's Old Irish." She then went on to tell me that a bartender in Killarney had explained the term to her and since he was a *real* Irishman and fluent in "Old Irish" he must be right. At that point I decided it was best to change the subject.

Interactions such as the one that took place between this visitor and a local could be understood as a form of resistance on the part of the bartender to the endless questions from tourists he is expected to answer. Driver-guides have also been known to "misinform" their charges when it comes to slang or the Irish language—just for the craic. Another form of passive resistance is for locals to converse in Irish when outsiders are around. On this same tour, a local guide was employed to do a city tour of Derry, and she and the driver spoke to each other in Irish in an effort to have a "private" conversation while in a public forum. Passengers found it "charming" and "beautiful," even though the actual conversation revolved around the mundane: the weather, the traffic, children, and work. At the end of the ten-day tour, several passengers remarked that the conversation in Irish they had been able to eavesdrop on in the coach was a highlight of the tour; one man in particular said it had made the trip feel somehow more genuine and added an air of authenticity to his ten-day quest. This encounter with the language—somehow familiar, yet so clearly alien—is part of the sought-for tourist experience among American visitors to Ireland who participate in coach touring. Turner has discussed this as part of a three-stage ritual: stage one is separation from the familiar; stage two is liminality, a truly unfamiliar period of time and place (in this case the episodic use of the Irish language in Ireland) that serves to validate the experience of travel; and finally, stage three, reintegration into the familiar (1973). These tourists, and many others, will return home feeling as though they have had a genuinely transcendent moment based on the spoken word; their gaze will somehow be sharpened, the ritual of travel more satisfying because of it. They may feel as though they alone own the moment.

TIME PERIODS

This final section on representing Ireland's heritage discusses time periods in terms of their presentation on the tourism landscape. In particular, I focus on the Georgian period, although nearly any time period in Ireland's history could be chosen.

Tourists cannot visit a time period, but they can visit markers of heritage that represent a particular period in time. Carefully chosen landscapes, buildings, routes, artifacts and objects symbolize these watershed stages in Ireland's history. Plantation homes, Georgian neighborhoods, bullet holes, statues, or in the case of the Celtic Tiger, unprecedented growth, expensive shops, and exclusive restaurants, have found a way to exist in symbiosis as part of the Irish touristic experience. In many cases they have become sacralized. As suggested by MacCannell, the sacralization of sites for the tourist begins with a simple naming—this is Georgian Dublin. This is followed by a process of framing and elevation—this is the best extant example of Georgian Dublin. Then comes enshrinement—this building will represent the architectural legacy of the Georgian period and will be used exclusively as a display. Mechanical reproduction of the sacred object (in this case Georgian Dublin architecture in its most pristine form) may be witnessed in the "discovery" of new Georgian neighborhoods worthy of preservation and conservation owing to their remaining attributes. (In 2006, there was a "discovery" such as this on Henrietta Street in north Dublin, where the entire street, much of which had fallen into disrepair, was considered to be worthy of this sacralization.) The social reproduction of sites is found in the active copying of certain stylistic forms. In this case, newly built stately homes and housing estates alike reflect certain attributes of Georgian style; the style becomes "preferred" and sought after, the value increases. This forces attention onto the original, making it even more symbolic, further imbuing it with historic and heritage value, thus completing the process of sacralization (MacCannell 1976).

Georgian Dublin

The Georgian Period is a historical period dating from 1714, at the beginning of the reign of King George I in Great Britain, to the death of George IV in 1830. It also designates a building style deriving from Palladian architecture. In the 18th century, it was stylish to live on the north side of Dublin. The Earl of Kildare (later the Duke of Leinster) moved his residence to the south side of Dublin in the late 18th century. This began a flurry of activity with the development of residential squares such as Merrion Square, St. Stephen's Green, and Fitzwilliam Square. The period represents a very difficult time in modern Irish history, the Act of Union in 1801 being one such attempt by Britain to step up its oppression of the Irish people.

In the 1920s, after independence, Eamonn de Valera's government discussed demolishing all of Merrion Square as a symbol of this oppression. Mount Joy Square was redeveloped and many other Georgian areas were destroyed. It wasn't until the 1990s that planning guidelines were enacted to protect the remaining Georgian buildings and areas of Dublin. Leinster House (the renamed Georgian residence of the Earl of Kildare/ Duke of Leinster) is ironically now used as the parliament building of Ireland (www.enfo.ie).

Number 29 Lower Fitzwilliam Street in Dublin 2 is one such protected Georgian building that has been restored and opened for tourism. It was restored by the ESB (Electricity Supply Board) in 1988 in exchange for land for offices with Dublin Corporation (now Dublin City Council). It is presented as a reflection of the life of a typical middle-class Dublin family between 1790 and 1820. It is furnished with "original artifacts" and was first occupied in 1794 "during a time of great change and expansion in Dublin" (www.esb.ie). According the ESB website:

> Visiting the exhibition gives young and old alike a chance to experience what life was like for the fortunate who lived in such elegant townhouses, and for the less fortunate who worked in them. . . . A survey of the population in Dublin in 1798 . . . shows for every three members of the upper class living in the Merrion Square area, at least two servants were employed.

Over 400,000 visitors have been received there since its opening in 1991.

CONSTRUCTING THE TOURIST LANDSCAPE

Thus far, the challenges of defining Irish heritage and representing Ireland's heritage have been discussed within the contexts of history, re-imagination, and re-invention. Several factors underlie the desire to create and display heritage. Of central importance is cultural patrimony: those things or actions that are felt to best represent a culture, those that show ownership, longevity, unique qualities, enigmatic virtues, and core collective values. They must be made available to the people, where they are made symbolic of the people. These may be highly insular or particular to a given culture, nation, or ethnic group. For that heritage to be understood by the outside world, it must be put forward in such a way as to be translatable, even if the translation objectifies the heritage as a thing of wonder and fascination. It is within this context of translation and objectification that the tourism landscape is constructed on the back of heritage. Heritage existed long before tourism became the most powerful industry in the world. It could be argued that heritage has existed as long as humans have organized themselves into defined cultural groups. But today heritage is more than cultural patrimony; heritage is itself an industry with strong bonds to the industry of tourism.

Heritage is a purposeful creation that continues to be created and recreated, in many cases to keep pace with the evolving tastes of the visiting public.

In this section, the tourism landscape as a purposeful construction and creation is examined as an aspect of heritage in Ireland. Although the choice of sites and objects is important, how those sites and objects are understood by tourists and those who present the heritage is equally so. How are routes defined? In what ways do the routes and frontiers help to define the heritage? Given a free rein, how would a driver-guide go about presenting his or her heritage to a group on a coach tour? Where would he take them? What areas would he deem more-, less- or unimportant in the great scheme of Irish heritage? Where wouldn't he go?

I begin with a brief discussion of cultural tourism and the process by which many heritage landscapes are chosen. The notion of a "site" is defined after which I return to the problem of routes and frontiers. I include a short reference to "No Man's Land"; not unlike MacCannell's "back stages," No Man's Land is a place that is off the tourism map for reasons that may be ill-defined. Entwined in these discussions are the opinions and thoughts of some of the driver-guides, whose responsibility it is to incorporate the heritage into the touristic experience of their clients.

Cultural Tourism

Cultural tourism, heritage tourism and indigenous tourism are often used interchangeably in scholarly discourse. But the actual meaning of the term(s) depends on a number of factors, including who is doing the defining, their particular disciplinary expertise, and the context of their actual definition. For example, McKercher and du Cros set out four categories within which this type of tourism is defined: tourism-derived (special-interest tourism, attractions based on culture), motivational (study tours, festivals, pilgrimages, and such), experiential or aspirational (cultural immersion, extended social contact with others), and operational definitions, which they contend are the most common and are based on active participation with or among cultural assets, such as castles, archaeological sites, and purpose-built attractions such as heritage centers (2002: 4–5). Valene Smith uses the term *indigenous tourism* when examining a certain kind of tourism that includes habitat, heritage, history, and handicrafts—a useful method of separating the cultural tourist from other tourists (1996). Heritage tourism can be an "identity-conferring" experience (Rojek and Urry 1997: 13), it can be reduced to a "cult of nostalgia" (Rojek 1993), and it can be transformative (Franklin 2003). It includes both the tangible and the intangible. It is a specialized method of touristic commerce.

While it could be claimed that cultural, heritage, or indigenous tourism appeals to only a certain faction within the traveling public, heritage itself has become less and less a specialized experience reserved for the chosen few. Heritage is also less situated within the realm of the unusual or unique and more within the approachable and marketable. As David Brett explains, constructing the heritage is a way of structuring the present (1996); heritage not only must appeal to the home nation in that it is immediately recognizable but also must be alluring to the outside world. It must resonate in its symbolic importance to the nation, the culture, the people in a way that demonstrates its universal value. At the same time, it must retain its mystery, the mythos of the past, the secrets of the culture. This is its appeal: that it can never be fully comprehended when one is outside; the cultural tourist must enter the space and time of the heritage experience in order to know it. It is both emotional and intellectual. Heritage is not history but a partner in the staging of historic places and times (Lowenthal 1998). Heritage "presents" and interprets. In the case of heritage tourism, it effects different outcomes: it captures a moment in time and offers a snapshot of the past, given as a symbolic representation of an epoch, or it conflates the past and the present, finding common features and recognizable facets from each to make the past somehow more palatable or understandable (Cooney 1996; Costa 2004; Lowenthal 1998). In essence, heritage does not parallel experience, it is experience—the tactile realization of memory expressed through the touristic adventure.

Choosing Heritage Landscapes

The methods by which heritage landscapes are chosen are as problematic as the difficulty in defining heritage or cultural tourism. In recent years in Ireland, the task has been complicated by the need to improve the infrastructure of the country through road building and other works, the need to accommodate the expanding population through housing schemes, and the pressure on farmers to sell their lands to developers who may be reluctant to protect potential areas of heritage as they occur on the land. In many ways, the heritage landscape of Ireland is already in place, having been recognized prior to the current explosion in development on all levels. Questions arise as to what and how much can and should be "saved" when the pressure is on to develop. Arguments exist that contest any development at the expense of the heritage, while opponents suggest that development must forge ahead for the country to remain prosperous.

Just how much of the landscape can be called a heritage landscape? And if limits are to exist regarding preservation and conservation, what are the steps to take to determine what gets saved from the bulldozer? Conversely, if heritage can be used to place constraints on development, who will determine the extent of the constraints? As Tim Carey has pointed out, heritage can be used as a weapon by people who seek out heritage issues to "support their objection to a particular development to hide reasons that do not relate to that heritage—for example, it will block their view or increase traffic on their road" (Carey 2006: 21). On the flip side, developers and others who support development projects can promote heritage as a "crank subject" (ibid.). Both cases are true in Ireland.

Choosing Heritage Landscapes in Ireland. Although heritage is that which we inherit, not all heritage is valued equally, and some may not be valued at all. Heritage can be highly selective in terms of what is preserved, conserved, and displayed, and its links to commerce are undeniable. Tourism has played a significant role in the development of heritage sites throughout the world. In 1992, when Ireland prepared to enter the Single Market in Europe, the *National Development Plan 1989–1993* (NDP) had finally recognized tourism as a venue through which the economy could be regenerated. Buttimer, Rynne, and Guerin note that the government saw tourism development as a "key sector" of the economy:

> Ireland has considerable assets which can be effectively marketed to international tourists: a rich cultural heritage, a tradition for friendliness and hospitality, a relatively unspoilt environment, and a folk tradition which is still reflected in a vibrant performing arts sector. (*NDP* 1989: 18, as cited in Buttimer, Rynne, and Guerin 2000)

Prior to this suggestion of combining the heritage of Ireland with tourism, there had existed no explicit or official program for this line of development (Bernadette Quinn, personal communication 2007). It seemed an obvious enough task, especially with such an extensive portfolio of heritage attributes to make use of. The key was sorting out which of the "assets" to focus on. For Ireland, this was also a journey of "self-discovery," as the country reacquainted itself with traditions and customs that had been pushed to the back of the cultural closet as the country pressed forward with economic and infrastructural plans over the course of the 20th century (Buttimer, Rynne, and Guerin 2000: xiii).

Barbara Kirshenblatt-Gimblett, in addressing the connections between heritage and tourism, proposed that the two are "collaborative industries," culminating in a series of "conversions" that may not be immediately obvious (1998: 151). A location converts to a destination when heritage becomes part of its marketing equation; the destination becomes economically viable when tourism enters the scene; finally, ways of life, buildings, artifacts become attractions and part of the destination (ibid.). She calls this the "value of pastness" (ibid.: 150). The goal is to get tourists to as many destinations as possible in as short a time as possible—the process of dislocation, of moving people from one location to another, is what tourism is all about (1998). Heritage adds an anchor to the touristic experience, evoking memories and establishing connections between visitor and place. The better the memory and more secure the connection, the more successful the visit. She uses as an example the Bunratty Folk Park and Castle near Shannon airport in the west of Ireland. Beginning in the 1960s, the stop in Shannon was promoted as a quick one-day medieval-themed tour of the region, the highlight of which would be an evening banquet and entertainment at Bunratty Castle. This is a tour scheme that many guides started with; the tour guide interviewed in Chapter 6 began her career as a guide on these one-day tours, and she mentioned that many of the original Shannon guides are still associated with tourism in different areas of Ireland. The Medieval Banquet is included in many tours today, especially coach tours, often as the farewell celebration. Promoted as an ancient part of Ireland's heritage, the castle, the entertainment, the landscape become entwined in the positive memories of the visitor. They have been to a castle, listened to traditional music, watched traditional dancers, feasted family-style in the keep—it is something they will not soon forget. A farewell dinner in a hotel, notwithstanding the quality of the food, would not evoke the same feelings of involvement and inclusion, would not be as memorable.

In Ireland, as elsewhere, many landscapes are considered to have heritage value. The natural heritage includes wetlands, such as lakes, rivers, and bogs, terrestrial habitats including woodlands and grasslands, coastal and marine areas, and the species that inhabit them (O'Donovan 2000). The inseparability of the natural and the cultural landscape is demonstrated in the close ties between how human groups view themselves and their world. We are "from" somewhere, we identify closely with place, and we have the strange habit of leaving our fingerprints all over the landscape through buildings, burial areas, tree clearing, and other alterations. The cultural landscape—that on which we have affected change and that includes archaeological remains—is steeped in heritage value in Ireland. Much of it has been subject to improvements through preservation and conservation and has become part of the "collaborative industry" of heritage and tourism mentioned above by Kirshenblatt-Gimblett. For heritage to be considered significant (and keeping in mind that significance and value are something we give it, in the present), a site, artifact, object, landscape, language, and so on should meet at least three criteria: scale (meaning its scale of importance to a local community or a nation), importance (how important it is at the level of the scale), and uniqueness or representativeness (meaning it is either the only one of its type or that it is the best representative of a type) (Aplin 2002: 20).

The establishment of significance is part of the process of inclusion in the tourism experience. For example, there are 230 or so passage tombs in Ireland, many of which rival Newgrange in size, yet Newgrange and its companion tombs have been described as "the greatest architectural achievement of tomb builders in western Europe" (Waddell 2000: 57). This statement alone is an indication of Newgrange's perceived importance on an international scale, and its inclusion as a World Heritage Site also supports this. Historically, Newgrange (or, more inclusively, the Brú na Bóinne) has also been understood as highly significant to Ireland and the Irish people; it is almost synonymous with Ireland. The late Michael O'Kelly, who conducted the excavations and reconstruction of Newgrange in the 1960s and 1970s, chronicled its historic importance (1982). It is mentioned in a series of ancient texts and tales, including *Tochmarc Etaíne, The Book of Lecan, The Book of Leinster, The Pursuit of Diarmuid and Gráinne,* and *Bruidhean Chaorthainn.* The *Annals of Ulster*, written in C.E. 862 mentions "Brug mic an Óg" (House of the Youthful Hero). In 1699, the Welsh antiquarian Edward Lhwyd went to Newgrange and recorded it after the entrance was discovered by the landowner who was mining the stones for construction. Throughout the 18th and 19th centuries, antiquarians were frequent visitors to the tomb. In 1833, George Petrie attributed the construction of the site to the ancient Irish, something those before him (and some to follow) were reluctant to do. He also established the link between Newgrange and many of the sagas and myths (such as those mentioned above) from early Irish literature. The discovery of gold torcs and other ornaments in the mid-1800s piqued further interest in the site.

Newgrange, Knowth, and Dowth were taken under State care through the Ancient Monuments Protection Act 1882, after the government was notified of increasing vandalism at the sites. At this time, some repairs and conservation measures were taken, and an iron gate was installed at Newgrange. In the 1950s, electricity was installed in the tomb, after which Newgrange was "left alone" for nearly a decade until O'Kelly's work commenced in the mid-1960s. O'Kelly wrote that Newgrange "plays a significant role in the mythology and heroic life of early Ireland and the corpus [of written work] . . . in which it has been mentioned has been common currency among scholars ever since the revival in native learning began at the close of the 17th century" (1982: 43). These are clear and linear connections to the historic development of modern Irish culture. The Irish renaissance, bolstered by the field work of the antiquarians and later professional archaeologists, helped establish the site's importance to the country and made people (and government) aware of the need and the obligation to protect and preserve the landscapes of memory around them. In terms of its uniqueness and/or representativeness, Newgrange can claim both of these valuable attributes. It is unique in its construction, quality of preservation, and its artwork. And it is highly representative as one of the foremost examples of passage tombs in the world. It ticks all the boxes.

Newgrange as a symbol of Ireland is also a political statement. It is a populist development, an easy-to-conjure image, a place of awe. It represents not just a distant and mysterious past but a past that is demonstrably of Ireland. Its unique qualities are continuously pointed out and emphasized when the site is visited. What those unique qualities may mean is likely lost on the majority of visitors, but the fact that they are unique, for whatever reason is not. Even though the tomb may have lain in utter ruin for thousands of years, its mere survival into the 21st century is given as reason enough to believe that it has held perpetual importance to the culture of Ireland. "This is us," a culture so long here that it disappears into the mists of primordial time, a purity of lineage and pedigree. If the visitor is of Irish descent, this implication can have enormous significance. A lesson in prehistory becomes the experience of walking the same ground as one's ancient progenitors, a moving and sometimes disturbing encounter. As a political statement, Newgrange can be seen to represent the survivability of the Irish themselves; to paraphrase Lowenthal, Newgrange gives modern Ireland a form of "biological fixity," a genetic time map of continuity (1998). The site, and others presented in a similar manner, "draws attention to the achievements of past societies who are assumed to be national ancestors" (Cooney 1996: 148; Trigger 1984). This coalesces in a hoped-for feeling of shared values, of a shared past, a national identity "which gives a sense of internal collectivity and external differentiation from others" (Cooney 1996: 147). This differentiation also sets Ireland apart from Great Britain. Tour guides' temporal comparisons to Stonehenge serve two distinct functions: one, the obvious establishment of deep time; the other less obvious, that Ireland too has a tradition of myth and mystery and splendid creativity—and look how close you can get to ours!

Routes and Frontiers

Nowhere are routes and frontiers more obvious than in coach tourism. Routes follow roads that lead to visitation sites and overnight stops. Frontiers are expressed as a movement through time or across county, provincial, or national boundaries. Sites may be located on the Boyne Valley Drive, the Táin Trail, the Ring of Kerry, or any number of other named tourism routes in the country. Locals rarely refer to their homes being on the Táin Trail, but some routes, such as the Ring of Kerry, have become so engrained that they are no longer just scenic drives but geographic locales.

Tourism brochures typically include small maps of Ireland with the routes of individual tours carefully drawn on them. Usually stops or overnights are highlighted, but this is not the only reason the map and tour route are included. The map is tied to the text of the itinerary. The text is peppered with titillating descriptions of stops and visits, evocative photographs tantalize the reader with snapshots of what could be. Potential customers can follow the description on the map, can use the map and the route to reify the journey and to locate a site within the tour within Ireland within Europe within the world. "Where are we on the map?" is a question often posed to driver-guides as passengers get ready to embark on a day's journey. Their location gives them a frame of reference (often then marked on the map) and also contextualizes distance and time. Knowing where one is and where one is going to seem comforting as well as adventurous; the map collapses the journey from one of miles to inches. At the same time, if the place is somewhere never visited before, then the question of "knowing where one is" is only in relation to the map and not the actual geography.

The driver-guide must continually update his clients with location presentations by pointing out markers on the landscape that could be identified on maps. He also will justify distance through time announcements, telling passengers how long it will take to get to where they are going, how many more minutes they will be, how long a particular delay may cost them. Although on holiday, and in a liminal space, time-consciousness prevails on a coach tour. A poorly chosen route can ruin a day's travel in terms of scheduling and time-keeping. With this in mind, coach driver-guides are continually monitoring road conditions, either through official channels such as national radio or through their own networks of other coach drivers, who may be traveling to similar destinations. Again, in some cases, delays are unavoidable but can be tempered through creative means, such as "bonus" tours and "diversion" tours through unrouted territories. A driver-guide's ability to incorporate intrigue, curiosity, or excitement into a diversion often makes or breaks a coach tourist's journey. He will also relay heritage information pertinent to the traveled through landscape or to the traveled to site. Heritage success depends on the tale told, and the heritage tourist is a rough conduit of tales taken, remembered, and then given away.

No Man's Land

It is hard to believe, with a tourism industry as strong as Ireland's, that there are places few people go to while there on holiday. The mere pressure exerted on some places such as Dublin and the Cliffs of Moher should send visitors careening across the countryside to far-flung corners of the island. But this is not the case. The Midlands, where I currently live, is such a place. Having moved from Aghoo to the town of Mullingar in the fall of 2006, I was fully aware that I was going from one nontourist place to another. Mullingar is a Norman town dating from the 1200s, an old market town on the Royal Canal with a tough reputation. As Dublin's shadow creeps across the east, Mullingar is quickly being absorbed into its abundance of bedroom communities. Despite the fact that it is relatively close to Dublin (about an hour by car or train), that it has its own train station, is located on the N4/M4, and has every possible amenity including a shower of hotels, Mullingar lacks tourists. This is true of the Midlands in general (Westmeath, Cavan, and Longford, especially). "People don't go *to* the Midlands," one coach driver-guide said to me. "They go *through* the Midlands." The Midlands is Ireland's highway, a modern-day esker making transport from one side of the island to the other simple and straightforward.

Targeted as one of the areas of improvement by the Irish Tourism Industry Confederation (ITIC) and Fáilte Ireland, the Midlands (part of the B-M-W, Border-Midlands-West and the "super region" of Ireland East that includes Dublin, the east coast, and the Midlands) still languishes as other regions hold steady or increase their tourism draws. The June 2005 report of the ITIC suggests that regional development plans, such as those in the 2004 Tourism Policy Review Group (TPRG) paper, should forge ahead. One of the major goals of the TPRG was "a doubling of promotable visitors staying at least one night in the

Border Midlands and Western (BMW) region" (ITIC 2005: 28). An admirable goal, but it remains to be seen if TPRG's goals will have much regard for Mullingar despite the town's location and amenities.

CHAPTER 5

Participants in Irish Tourism

Ireland has been a destination for millennia. Since the Mesolithic over 9,000 years ago, people have come from beyond the island's shores to put down roots, pillage, trade, colonize, and admire. It is only relatively recently in Ireland's history that outsiders have been welcomed—especially those who will make their stays temporary, preferably for seven days with an optional extra one-night stay over in Dublin. The development of Ireland[1] as a destination for tourists has been a deliberate, although occasionally shaky, enterprise. Today Ireland seems poised to continue as one of the premier holiday destinations in the world.

The participants in Irish tourism far outnumber those who will be highlighted in this chapter; taxi drivers, car rental agencies, hotel management, staff and ownership, airlines, ferries, and other businesses whose clientele are often tourists are not discussed in any great detail here. Rather I concentrate on the participants I understand as having the greatest impact and most influence on the construction of Ireland-as-destination: the government, tour companies and tour operators, tourists, tour guides, and coach drivers.

Despite its long record of attraction for colonizers and holiday-makers (Cusack 2001; Davies 1993; Heuston 1993; Kincheloe 1999), Ireland became a self-declared destination only in the years following its independence from Britain. Before this, beginning in the 1700s, spas in Mallow and Lucan and other places on the island were the first recognized holiday resorts in Ireland (Davies 1993; Gorokhovsky 2003). The spas, frequented by the English and Anglo-Irish, were followed by the rise in scenic tourism, in particular in Kerry and other coastal regions. According to Spurgeon Thompson, during the early years of independence (1925–1930), tourism efforts were mainly targeted toward its former colonizers and at the Irish themselves with campaigns such as "See Ireland First" developed by the Irish Tourist Association (2003). Thompson also points out that "until 1997 tourism would not become a larger industry than agriculture in Ireland" (2003: 264), in spite of its looming presence in tourism literature and the efforts of a variety of institutions and organizations to promote Ireland as a destination. This is in direct relation to the strengthening of the Irish economy in the 1990s and the firm hold that the "Celtic Tiger" has maintained on the world stage of commerce. Once a primarily agricultural country that exported most of its agri-products, Ireland today is an economy with a strong technology component, multinational corporations of every ilk, a variety of retail outlets, a thriving shipping industry, and a tourism sector that accounts for roughly 9% of its GDP (WTTC 2004). How did a country, considered among the poorest and most peripheral in Europe until a few years ago, become one of the fastest-growing economies in the world (Burnham 2003; Kockel 1994; Mays 2005; Volkman and Guydosh 2001)? In large part, it is due to a combined and continuing massive effort by national and regional governments, the European Union, industries, independent entrepreneurs, and businesses throughout Ireland.

THE GOVERNMENT OF IRELAND AND TOURISM

Even before the Easter Uprising in 1916, the Irish civil war, and independence, Ireland was included as part of many Grand Tours. It was idealized in paintings and poetry and also in the travel literature of the late 19th century (Cusack 1998, 2001; Kincheloe 1999). Even though Americans were explicitly discriminating against the waves of Irish immigrants who were coming ashore in Boston, New York, and Philadelphia, they were also looking east toward a mythical Ireland.

The "Celtic Twilight," a nationalistic Gaelic movement spearheaded by literati such as W.B. Yeats, would later leave an impression of Ireland "that was of an idealized, misty fairyland" (Kincheloe 1999: 41; White 1999). In the immediate postcolonial years of the new Irish Free State, the vision of the country expressed in romantic representations was to be found, with the right colored glasses, across the existing landscape. The country was in ruin—financially, culturally, infrastructurally—but the ruin was the path to re-creation. Eamonn Slater explains that Ireland's perceived position as an escape from modern pressures didn't relate to the socio-economic conditions historically encountered there (2003). Instead these perceptions were (and are) grounded in "specific ideological productions," such as the promotion of tourism and the romantic perceptions of visitors; the poverty of Ireland's situation was ensconced with the peasants bruising the landscape (who could be overlooked) rather than in the landscape itself, which was understood as pristine and picturesque (ibid.: 23). Ireland the relic became and remains to a great extent the central attraction to tourists.

The History of Tourism Legislation in Ireland

In 1925, the Irish Tourism Association (ITA) was created under the de Valera administration. Eamon de Valera was a prime catalyst in the Gaelic movement in postcolonial Ireland, and he moved quickly to ignite interest in restoring Irish as the national language, as well as soliciting support for the Gaelic Athletic Association (founded in 1884) and "to glorify traditional Gaelic culture" (White 1999: 51). Tourism was one way of glorifying the Gael through advertisements designed to focus on homeland and the traditions of an ancient race. Though manned primarily by ex-IRA (Irish Republic Brotherhood/Army) men (Thompson 2003), the ITA developed the framework of Irish tourism that remains today. Slogans (including "See Ireland First," referred to above), poetic descriptions of the land first and people second, and attractive and quaint representations of place were created to attract visitors from Britain, Ireland, and increasingly from North

America. The potential to create a market from the descendants of émigrés would exceed all expectations in years to come through the use of clever marketing that evoked an imagined Ireland in the minds of second- and third-generation Americans and Canadians.

In Ireland, the ITA eventually evolved into Bord Fáilte, which historically had been involved in all areas of tourism development: research and development, marketing, planning, and regulation among them. Bord Fáilte functioned as a semi-autonomous wing of the government until the 1990s, when the Irish government reorganized and began to take more direct control of tourism planning. CERT (Centre for Education, Recruitment, and Training, a national organization that coordinated education, recruitment, and training in the tourism industry) was established in 1963 with the intention of making marketable skills available to those with leaving certificates and to adults who needed to develop new skills in order to reenter the changing job market. CERT and Bord Fáilte worked together to plan and implement programs specific to Ireland's growing tourism market until 2003, when they were combined to form Fáilte Ireland, the National Tourism Development Authority (National Tourism Development Authority Act 2003). Its mission is "to increase the contribution of tourism to the economy by facilitating the development of a competitive and profitable tourism industry" (www.failteireland. ie). The new organization came about following the Irish Tourism Industry Confederation's (ITIC) paper, *A Recovery Programme for Tourism*, written in response to a rather disastrous year in tourism worldwide brought about by an outbreak of foot and mouth disease in Europe, the 9/11 terrorist bombings, and the war in the Middle East (2002). The government mandated that Fáilte Ireland work in partnership with tourism stakeholders "in order to be more competitive and more profitable and to help individual enterprises to enhance their performance" (www. failteireland.ie).

After progressive gains in the tourist sector over several decades, the events of 2001 brought about significant losses. The surprising shortfall was the catalyst for a reevaluation of the entire tourism industry and the government's relationship to it. The Irish Tourism Industry Confederation or ITIC, a nongovernmental organization that serves as a lobbying watchdog for all stakeholders in the industry in Ireland, published a report in 2002 outlining many of the underlying problems in Irish tourism during the 1990s. The gains had been extraordinary, but the market was shifting and the world-changing events of 2001 brought many of the weaker issues into sharp focus. The recovery program outlined by the ITIC included many of the recommendations and schemes already being addressed in the National Spatial Strategy and the National Development Plan set out by the government in the late 1990s. These suggestions included a commitment to strategies for distributing tourism development to areas that had either experienced a decline in tourism or that had never been strongly represented. Areas of particular concern included Shannon, the northwest, and the "BMW" (Borderland-Midlands-West). The ITIC also pointed out the market changes that the industry was undergoing in Ireland—in particular, the increasing popularity of short city stays in Dublin. Dublin tourism had climbed steadily over the decade (over 40% of all overnight stays) while other areas of the country had declined or gone static. They called into question the current status of tourism development policy and made several recommendations including business relief measures directed toward the small and medium enterprises (SMEs) that make up the majority of tourism related businesses, improving competitive access through promotion of "own car" touring, ferry service, and the restoration of airline routes and capacity, and destination and product marketing aimed at Britain, North America, Europe, domestic travel, and the emerging conference sector (ITIC 2002; see also TPRG 2003).

Dublin's popularity had spiked sharply upward in the late 1990s. A report by Tansey, Webster, and Associates for the ITIC in May 1995 found Dublin had "underperformed" in comparison with other regions of the country based on population. In 1993, they found that Dublin accounted for only 24.1% of all tourism revenue. By 2001, Dublin's tourism revenue had increased to over 30% (ITIC 2002). The Tourism Policy Review Group

(TPRG) reported that Dublin city breaks accounted for the greatest amount of growth, increasing from 95,000 in 1996 to 372,000 by 2002 (2003). City breaks (short stays with few trips outside of the city) were found to be particularly popular with tourists from Britain who have historically made up the majority of tourists to Ireland. Overall, Ireland's performance as a destination was far ahead of the rest of Europe during the time period of 1990–2001 (+6.1% Ireland; +3.2% Europe) with, again, "one of the contributing factors being the significant increase in short breaks in Dublin" (ibid.: 29).

The 2003 publication of the TPRG, *New Horizons for Irish Tourism: An Agenda for Action,* combined analyses of Ireland's tourism industry from 1990 to 2002 with strategies for performance and implementation for 2003–2012. Among its many findings, the TPRG reported that in 2002, the benefits of Irish tourism included €4 billion in annual foreign earnings, €1 billion in annual domestic earnings, 140,000 jobs, up to €2.2 billion in tax receipts each year, 4.4% of GNP, and its standing as a major instrument of national and regional development and as a sector of major opportunity for Irish-owned enterprises (2003: viii–ix). The TPRG also suggested that employment in tourism had increased by more than 70% between 1990 and 2002, demonstrating the strength of the industry and its importance to the Irish economy on a number of levels. Historically, the government had concentrated its efforts on job creation in the tourism sector as it developed policies; the TPRG and ITIC reports helped shift the focus away from job creation (which, it is assumed, will continue apace with industry needs) and toward supporting sustainable growth. Despite the strong indications that overall customer satisfaction meets or exceeds expectations, surveys conducted by Fáilte Ireland found that many visitors believed Ireland's value for money to be low. The Action Plan concluded with nine objectives:

1. To facilitate the development of the tourism industry through a range of tourism-supportive Government macroeconomic and other policies that enhance the business environment and encourage investment;

2. To address the deterioration in the competitiveness of Irish tourism in recent years (value for money);

3. To ensure that the price, quality, frequency, and route access of air and sea transport to and from Ireland are at least as good as that available to potential visitors of alternative tourist locations;

4. To accelerate the exploitation of the potential of information and communication technologies and e-commerce for the tourism industry;

5. To ensure that the tourism product that Ireland offers to overseas and domestic customers provides, and continues to provide, a positive and memorable experience beyond their expectations;

6. To focus marketing and promotion activities in the market prospects and segments that hold the characteristics and potential to best meet the expenditure, visitor number, and regionality objectives of Irish tourism policy;

7. To ensure that the people working in tourism in Ireland operate to the highest international standards of professionalism and that the generally highly positive experience of tourists with the people they meet in Ireland, well documented in successive surveys over the years, is maintained and enhanced;

8. To improve and enhance the effectiveness of Government leadership and interventions in promoting tourism;

9. To provide the essential foundations of comparative data, knowledge, and intelligence in which to develop the policies and actions by both the public and private sectors that promote tourism across the full range of the nine strategic success drivers outlined in [the] Report (TPRG 2003: 85–109).

The TPRG recommended that their extensive report and its proposals be followed up with consistent monitoring and evaluation by a representative group from the tourism industry and public sector for a period of two years with reports to the Minister for Arts, Sport, and Tourism every six months (ibid.: 11).

Three follow-up reports have been submitted and reviewed. The initial report of the Tourism Action Plan Implementation Group (TAP), published in August 2004, suggested that many of the difficulties outlined in the TPRG paper, such as Ireland's escalating inflation rate, were "outside the direct control of the industry" (TAP 2004: ii). But TAP also admitted that there had been some "opportunistic pricing" schemes at visitor attractions, problems in service quality in the industry, and a lack of innovation in the product itself (ibid.). It did find the industry to be recovering in terms of British numbers and occupancy levels, but overall the report mandated that the industry take serious action "if the intrinsic potential and the ambitious targets set for Irish tourism" were to be achieved (ibid.). The group outlined areas where it saw good progress (government commitment, industry commitment, human resources, tourism research), areas requiring further development (enhancing marketing and promotion to outbound tourists from Britain and abroad, developing a national conference center, closing "gaps" in the tourism product, improving roads and signposting) and areas it felt were barriers to progress (value for money, the Ireland-U.S. bilateral air agreement, Dublin Airport, access to the countryside, further enhancement of the arts community, changing consumer trends).

The second report, published in April 2005, and the final report, found a number of changing trends in Irish tourism, many of which were discussed by the TPRG and ITIC. Among its suggestions for "short-run responses" to these changes was to concentrate marketing efforts on traditionally strong markets showing economic growth, in particular, Britain. Surveys of British tourists to Ireland in 2004 found a number of problematic issues including British visitors finding no compelling reasons to come back to Ireland; not feeling that going on holiday in Ireland was actually "going abroad"; and knowing little about Irish culture or historic treasures and landmarks or about opportunities for special interest or activity breaks (TAP 2005). In light of this follow-up report, the Government has allocated at least 38% of the Tourism Ireland, Ltd. budget to British promotions. (Tourism Ireland, Ltd., a division of Fáilte Ireland, is responsible for island-wide marketing—including Northern Ireland.) It did find many positive areas, including increased air access, new markets (China, India, South Korea), increases in governmental tourism development budgets, further cooperation and development planning among Tourism Ireland, Fáilte Ireland, and the industry, and a more "pro-active" role of the Department of Arts, Sport, and Tourism (ibid.: 5–7). Despite these positive areas, the report found that the major stumbling blocks to further tourism enhancement reported in 2004 were still lingering and suggested that "Ireland's international image may not be as attractive as the industry here tends to assume" (ibid.: 9).

In 2006, a massive advertising campaign to increase domestic tourism to the regions was launched by Fáilte Ireland. Christened "Ireland 2006: Let's Play," the campaign capitalized on the Ryder Cup and the natural and cultural resources of the island. Among the multimedia advertisement slogans were: "Wake up to the West: Mayo, Galway, Roscommon"; "Find Fermanagh: Tell your own story"; and "Dublin: Make the city yours." Concentrated on the "holiday regions of the country" (2006c: 1), the €4 million 40-week campaign directed Irish holiday consumers to those regions that have historically been "the locations of choice" (ibid.: 2) for domestic tourists. The campaign was devised following a CSO survey that found that domestic tourism had grown "by 6% in 2005 to 3.3 million trips, [while] domestic holiday spending increase[ed] by 11% to €694 million per annum" (ibid.: 1).

The Government, Tourism, and Heritage

As suggested in Chapter 2, heritage is that which is inherited, including the landscape, the built environment, the songs, stories, and the memories handed down from one generation to the next. In Ireland, the inheritance of previous generations includes both tangible and intangible features located on the varied landscape, in the language, music and literature of the Gael, the architecture of the colonial powers of the past, the place-names that remain unchanged through centuries of unrest and development. Much of the felt attraction to Ireland by tourists rests in the heritage, both perceived and real, of the island. In recognition of this, the government has developed numerous departments and councils to manage, preserve, and conserve objects of cultural patrimony felt to be representative of the country's heritage. The Office of Public Works (OPW) has historically been most closely involved in the investigation, presentation, and preservation and management of sites of significance in Ireland. Dúchas (now disbanded and absorbed into the Department of Environment, Heritage, and Local Government), was associated with archaeological remains, excavation, mapping, and education.

Currently, in Ireland, the following government departments monitor a variety of heritage-related sites and undertake a number of tasks under the broad heading of "the national heritage":

- Department of Community, Rural, and Gaeltacht Affairs (*An Roinn Gnóthaí Pobail, Tuaithe agaus Gaeltachta*) (previously the Department of Arts, Heritage, Gaeltacht, and the Islands) established in June 2002. Its mission statement: to promote and support the sustainable and inclusive development of communities, both urban and rural, including Gaeltacht and island communities, thereby fostering better regional balance and alleviating disadvantage, and to advance the use of the Irish language.

- Department of Environment, Heritage, and Local Government (*An Roinn Comhshaoil, Oidreachta, agus Rialtais Áitiúil*). Its mission statement: to promote sustainable development and improve the quality of life through the protection of the environment and heritage, infrastructure provision, balanced regional development, and good local government. The Heritage Service is tasked with management of the State's responsibility for nature conservation and the built heritage as directed by National, European, and International law. (Includes the Architectural Heritage Initiative, GIS data, State-managed visitor sites, National Inventory of Architectural Heritage, and the National Monument Service, as well as the Office of Public Works, which has over 700 monuments in its care.)

- Department of Art, Sport, and Tourism (*An Roinn Ealaíon, Spóirt agus Turasóireachta*), whose mission statement is to contribute to the economic, social, and cultural progress of Irish society and the enrichment of its quality of life through promoting sustainable tourism; encouraging excellence in sporting and artistic achievement; facilitating greater access to sport and the arts; and preservation of our cultural inheritance (includes Fáilte Ireland, National Museum of Ireland, Shannon Development, Tourism Ireland Ltd., Irish Manuscripts Commission, Marsh's Library, Beatty Library, National Gallery, National Archives, and National Library).

In 1988, the government of Taoiseach Charles Haughey established the National Heritage Council "to look after both the natural and built aspects of the national heritage" (www. heritageireland.ie). Among the council's charges were these:

- To formulate policies and priorities to identify, protect, preserve, enhance, and increase awareness of Ireland's heritage in the specific areas of archaeology, architecture, flora, fauna, landscape, heritage gardens, and inland waterways;
- To promote among the general public an interest and pride in the heritage and to facilitate the appreciation and enjoyment of it (www.heritageireland.ie).

Initially funded through the National Lottery system, it included funding for the Archaeological Discovery Programme established by Haughey. Six committees reported to the National Council: Archaeology, Architecture, Natural Environment, Museums, Education, and Promotion. An additional committee was established to oversee the finances of the council. The National

Heritage Council granted monies to a variety of projects early on for heritage buildings and vernacular buildings (including thatch cottages). Beyond these early projects were the Botanic Gardens coming under State care, the acquisition of Castletown House, the extension of the National Museum to the Collins Barracks, excavations in Waterford City, and a major survey of Clare Island (www.heritageireland.ie). Between 1992 and 1997, 171 projects were assisted with funding and support from the National Heritage Council.

In 1993, the Council was placed within the Department of Arts, Culture, and the Gaeltacht, and this move was followed with the 1995 Heritage Act. The new legislation and structure within the Department led to the Heritage Council producing its *Heritage Plan 1997–2000*. The plan recognized "the importance of developing partnerships, particularly with local authorities . . . and the Community Grants scheme, which still forms the cornerstone of the Council's grant schemes, was established in 1997" (www.heritageireland.ie).

The Council recognizes that the economic position of Ireland, which is greatly influenced by visitor numbers, is vital to the continued ability of the government and archaeologists to preserve and protect the archaeological heritage for the future. Despite these pronouncements and the "cooperation" that is professed to exist between stakeholders in the heritage, infrastructural demands have continued apace, resulting in the destruction of massive areas of archaeological and heritage importance, such as the M3 roadworks, which demolished the Lismullin National Monument and other sites in 2007. Charles Mount of the Heritage Council detailed the history of the Heritage Council and its influence on the preservation and presentation of the heritage in Ireland (2002: 485–492). In what is primarily a discussion of archaeological resources, Mount recognized the value of the landscape to Ireland and its visitors:

[The archaeological resource is] a primary cultural resource
which contributes to the distinctiveness and sense of place
enjoyed by everyone in Ireland and the millions of people who

visit Ireland each year. . . . The Heritage Council recognizes
the need to preserve both the material and intellectual archaeological resource. (ibid.: 489)

Among other strategic investigations, the Council has examined
the rate of site loss and erosion, and strategies for combating
site loss. In the venue of archeological practice, the Council, in
partnership with the Institute of Archaeologists of Ireland, has
developed programs for continuing professional development,
has made grey literature (unpublished site reports) available,
and has continued to fully fund the Discovery Programme
(ibid.: 491–492). "Infrastructural expansion," often expounded
as a direct threat to the archaeological heritage, is seen as an
opportunity to expand knowledge (ibid.: 492). Mount suggests
that the economic state of Ireland and the rate of development
have allowed archaeologists to wield considerable power
regarding the process of development within the country. He
ends with a cautionary statement:

> The focus on development-led archaeology has obscured the
> need to manage Ireland's sites and monuments in the face of
> large-scale landscape reorganization. If archaeology in Ireland
> is to maintain its privileged position into the future, then it must
> quickly rise to the challenge of structural reorganization and
> professional development so that the advances made under the
> Celtic Tiger economy are consolidated. (ibid.)

"Core Values": The Branding of Ireland

It is clear from this brief history of the Irish government's relationship with the tourism industry that tourism has long been
recognized as a vital part of the Irish economy. Many reports
pertaining to the state of tourism in Ireland likewise recognize
its role as "the most successful sector of Irish-owned enterprise
since the foundation of the State" (TPRG 2003). The Organisation for Economic Co-operation and Development (OECD)
reviewed Ireland's national tourism policy in June 2004 and
found that the newly streamlined state offices helped to build

a more coherent focus for the implementation of the TPRG *Action Plan* (2004). The OECD also believed that the creation of Fáilte Ireland and Tourism Ireland in light of the *Action Plan* would ultimately "strengthen the partnership between the tourism stakeholders engaged in the implementation of the action plan" (OECD 2004). In this case, the stakeholders include not only the government but also Regional Tourism Organizations (or Agencies) (RTO/As), tourism companies and tour operators, tourists themselves, and the folks who work in the industry in roles of primary contact, such as the coach driver-guides.

Wooing of tourists through the use of the "branding" of place is utilized throughout the world and has been since the emergence of tourism as a trade in the 19th century. In Ireland, the branding has centered on the core concepts of "people, place, and pace" relating to Irish culture, landscape, and society. Tourism Brand Ireland was initialized in 1996 as a concentrated way to brand the island as a holiday destination and "has evolved into a highly successful global branding strategy managed by Tourism Ireland" (Tourism Ireland n.d.: 3). The idea of people, place, and pace as symbolic of Ireland is nothing new; it links seamlessly with prior attempts by the State to incorporate an image of Ireland, already widely recognized throughout the world, with a concerted advertising campaign to increase tourism commerce to the island. According to Tourism Ireland, the brand represents "[Ireland's] reputation—an *idea that resides in the hearts and minds* of our various audiences" (Tourism Ireland n.d.: 3, *italics added*). The promotion of the romantic Ireland is easily done, because the romantic ideal (or rural idyll) exists in absentia.

The OECD report of 2004 broke down the elements of the Irish tourism experience using three key elements as central to the tourist: (1) people, place, and pace, (2) value for money, and (3) safety and security. The study's compilers included facilities and services (roads, signposting, internal transport, communications, accommodation, restaurants, pubs/bars, entertainment, activities, things to see and do, shops, other support services), intellectual value system (people/way of life, history and heritage, arts and culture, folklore and beliefs, towns and villages, land use), accessibility (airports and seaports, airlines, shipping companies), and natural attractors (scenery and landscape) as additional elements in the Irish tourism experience that are integral to the country retaining high satisfaction ratings among visitors (2004: 13–14). Reiterating much of what had been reported in Fáilte Ireland's Visitor Attitudes Surveys prior to 2004, the OECD found that value for money was the most vexing issue among visitors. According to the OECD, visitors were overwhelmingly satisfied with the "people, pace, and place" of Ireland (2002 overall satisfaction rating of 93%); value for money however, had dropped from 63% satisfaction in 2000 to 45% in 2002, with U.S. customers having the most significant drop in value for money satisfaction, from 73% in 2001 to 48% in 2002 (ibid.: 14–15).

The core image of Ireland marketed to the potential visitor has changed little over the years since independence: a rural, quiet, friendly, welcoming, clean country with beautiful scenery and a lively, vibrant culture. The thatched cottage, Giant's Causeway, ivory-skinned lasses, and peaked-capped men (inevitably with sheep) are, repeated images that have engrained in the created memories of "promotable segments"—the potential holiday makers and business visitors across the globe who gaze at Ireland in travel brochures and on websites. In recent years, beginning in the 1990s, the urban landscape of Ireland has also been incorporated into its modern image. In 2004, Dublin as a destination outpaced other regions in tourist spending by nearly 100% (over €1.3 billion to its next nearest region of €686 million in the West) (Fáilte Ireland 2005: 2). The ITIC reported in 2005 that Dublin was the highest growth market in Irish tourism bolstered "by increasing demand for short breaks to urban destinations" (ibid.: 23).

> 1.9 million overseas visitors stayed for at least one night in Dublin in 2003, generating 6.7 million bednights for the city. This represents 29% of all holiday nights in the country, up from a 20% share in 1999. However, the increase in absolute volume of bednights is more impressive having grown by 41% over the period, at a time when bednights in the rest of the country fell by 14%.

> Almost three out of every five overseas visitors spend at least
> one night of their stay in Dublin. . . . For just over 1 million
> overseas holidaymakers to Dublin in 2003 it was their sole des-
> tination in Ireland. . . . The profile of leisure visitors to Dublin
> tends to be a younger age profile than the overall market to
> Ireland, shorter stay, and particularly in the case of Britain more
> seasonally spread throughout the year. (ibid.)

Advertising, brochurization, advertorials, and other forms of commercial communications have also increasingly featured urban modern Ireland as an alternative destination choice for visitors. Tourismireland.com lists "City Breaks" at the top of its menu, with Dublin, Cork, The West (Galway), Limerick, and Belfast as featured destinations for short break holidays (www. tourismireland.com). There is also an effort to re-imagine Ireland as a destination for highly discriminating visitors. Undoubtedly linked with the new affluence of the country, the changing patterns in visitor demographics include those with the ability to spend more, to consume more upscale items and lodgings, and to enjoy more exclusive restaurants, spas, and private holidays. Again, the efforts to attract these visitors are directed toward city breaks, whether in Dublin, Cork, Belfast, or elsewhere.

Visitor Attitudes Surveys conducted by Fáilte Ireland found that the positive response to Ireland as a holiday destination is very high among overseas holidaymakers (Fáilte Ireland 2004). Visitors pointed out that Ireland's scenery, the friendliness and hospitality of the people, the opportunity to relax or visit family and friends were among the most important motivations for choosing to holiday in Ireland. Negatives, as discussed previously, were value for money (71% were dissatisfied) and cost of living (50% were surprised with the high cost of living especially related to food, drink, accommodation, and car hire). A few remarked that the quality of roads needed improvement, but compared to previous surveys, it was clear that this problem had lessened over the course of the last decade. Customer Service was also pointed out as somewhat negative by those who took the survey. Despite these negative responses, the 2004 survey also had many positive findings: over 30% felt their holiday experience surpassed expectations, more than 60% felt it matched their expectations, and 75% said they would recommend Ireland to friends and family. Fáilte Ireland found the survey to be an overall positive indication that tourism in Ireland was an overwhelmingly satisfactory experience for visitors, noting that the high percentage of those who would recommend Ireland to friends is the most telling of all the results. They suggest that the "potential for positive recommendation is vitally important, given that word of mouth recommendation of friends, relatives, and others is the main influence in their choice of destination for almost half of holiday visitors to Ireland" (ibid.).

TOUR COMPANIES, TOUR OPERATORS, COACH COMPANIES

Tour operators are companies that specialize in the planning and operations of preplanned and packaged holidays that are normally sold and marketed to the traveling public through travel agents. Many tour operators have also developed niche or specialty holidays in sports, adventure, cultural, historic, or spa vacations, among others. In Ireland, tour operators are represented through a number of organizations, principal among them the Irish Tour Operators Association (ITOA). The ITOA has become a powerful organization with representatives from all sectors of the tourism planning community, including those who operate the largest and most influential companies, such as state-sponsored CIÉ.

The ITOA consists of both Irish and overseas member companies and represents almost all incoming tour operators. These include Professional Conference Organisers (PCOs), Destination Management Companies (DMCs), and Ground Handler or Handling Agencies (such as coach tour companies). The ITOA serves two major roles: it promotes Ireland as a destination among its 4,000 overseas partners, including tour operators, retail travel groups, and operators in the conference, incentive, and events sectors; it promotes every aspect of the tourism product in Ireland (www.itoa-ireland.com).

CIÉ (*Córas Iompair Éireann*) is Ireland's state-owned national transport company. In 1987, the CIÉ Group established three operating companies to provide bus and rail services throughout the Republic of Ireland and to and from Northern Ireland. CIÉ also has a specialized tour company called CIÉ International (www. business2000.ie). As a state-owned company, CIÉ enjoys a monopoly of routes and opportunities that have historically been closed off to private coach operators (such as city transport routes and other scheduled services). Recent (2005–2006) political issues have arisen, spearheaded by the CTTC (Coach Travel and Tourism Council), regarding CIÉ's market share and hold on these routes. A January 2005 Goodbody Economic Consultants report commissioned by the CTTC described the monopoly and made suggestions based on European Union proposals to liberalize the market. At the end of 2006, monopolization seems to be easing. Its touring company is arguably the largest in Ireland, offering an extensive worldwide menu of travel options to both visitors to Ireland and travelers venturing beyond the country. Its contingent of drivers is highly trained and competent, and opportunities to sit on the drivers' panel are rare and highly competitive.

The Coach Travel and Tourism Council (CTTC) represents many of the private coach companies in Ireland, most of which are associated with the tourism industry (Table 5.1). In 2006, there were some 1,800 private coach operators in Ireland operating a total of nearly 5,000 coaches in the tourism, private hire, school transport, and in limited scheduled services markets. This is about twice the number of coaches run by CIÉ. The largest number of private operators in Ireland run between one and four vehicles in their fleets (about 1,500 operators), while the remaining run over four in their fleets. According to research conducted by Goodbody Economic Consultants in 2005 (The Goodbody Report) for CTTC, more than 350,000 tourists took part in day coach tours, while approximately 300,000 were part of overnight coach tour services in 2003 (Goodbody Report 2005: 8). Most private coach companies in Ireland provide multiple services, such as coach tourism as well as private hire (81.7%, ibid.: 9). As the representative body of independent coach operators, the

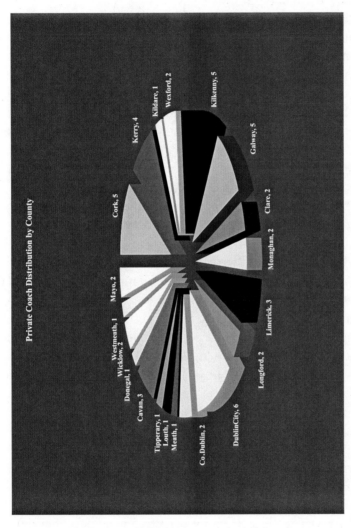

Private Coach Distribution by County

Kildare, 1
Wexford, 2
Kilkenny, 5
Kerry, 4
Galway, 5
Cork, 5
Clare, 2
Monaghan, 2
Mayo, 2
Limerick, 3
Westmeath, 1
Wicklow, 2
Longford, 2
Donegal, 1
Cavan, 3
Tipperary, 1
Louth, 1
Meath, 1
Co.Dublin, 2
DublinCity, 6

Table 5.1 Private coach company distribution chart showing the number of private companies per county. The companies shown are current members, as of April 2006, of the Coach Tourism and Transport Council of Ireland. It does not include coach companies in Northern Ireland (CTTC Membership list April 2006).

CTTC works in cooperation with Fáilte Ireland, the government, and other state agencies in setting strict standards of membership. Coaches are inspected annually and are rated according to age, onboard facilities, standard of comfort, and condition of vehicle (www.cttc.ie/about.php).

The CTTC serves to represent its members' interests "at all appropriate levels to all external bodies on coach tourism and transport matters" and to speak for "the industry as a single, fully representative and strong voice in all matters which effect the future of the industry" (www.cttc.ie/about.php). Membership in the CTTC is restricted to bona fide coach operators engaged in the business of coach tourism, private hire, and/or scheduled services who fully satisfy the Fáilte Ireland/CTTC standards (including licensing, compliance with EU regulations, insurance standards, and inspection compliance) (www.cttc.ie/cttcmembership.php).

New challenges for tour operators both within and outside Ireland are related to the most recent initiatives proposed by Fáilte Ireland and Tourism Ireland, among them the development of a €5 million plan "to drive new strategic marketing initiatives for regional tourism" (National Tourism Development Authority [NTDA] 2006). The funding will be concentrated in three areas: a €1 million local area marketing fund for the development of new attractive promotional packages; a €1 million "innovation fund" designed to "develop specific attractions that will attract and hold visitors in the rural areas" (Shaun Quinn, CEO Fáilte Ireland, quoted in NTDA 21 February 2006b); and a "Super Regions" fund to develop "strategic marketing alliances between adjoining tourism regions in Ireland for the purposes of overseas promotion" (NTDA 21 February 2006b). The targeted regions are Ireland South (South East, Cork/Kerry), Ireland East (Dublin, East Coast, and Midlands), and Ireland's Western Regions (Shannon, Ireland West, North West). These "programs of scale" are felt to be extremely effective schemes regarding overseas promotion. Paul O'Toole, CEO of Tourism Ireland, suggests that the Super Regions initiative will "[resonate] better with consumers in our key markets who are not as aware of regional boundaries" and that it will enhance access development, support for the car-touring sector, and themed cross-regional tourist routes (O'Toole quoted in NTDA 21 February 2006b).

The Super Regions initiative was announced following Fáilte Ireland's January 2006 report on the underperformance of rural regions within Ireland during 2005, which found that urban areas (Dublin, Limerick, Kilkenny, Waterford, Galway) continued to show impressive tourism growth, but the regions were suffering from trends in Irish tourism that include short breaks and shorter booking times. Gillian Bowler, chairman of Fáilte Ireland, suggested that the issue of regional spread had become a crucial one and that ideas regarding greater tourism spend equity may have been too simplistic, saying the idea of balanced tourism "may need to be reframed as thinking about rural *versus* urban tourism" rather than simply expanding marketing (Fáilte Ireland 4 January 2006a: 2, *emphasis mine*). Bowler also pointed out that changes in agricultural policies at the World Trade Organization and at the European Union level would have a great impact on the rural agricultural regions. She encouraged the communities to "consider tourism as a sustainable and attractive source of future income" (ibid.: 6). Her comment follows a similar one by Shaun Quinn, who suggested that "tourism is crucial to the maintenance and development of local areas and communities . . . [in order to sustain] livelihoods in areas which can have little in the way of alternative employment" (Fáilte Ireland 13 October 2005b). As agriculture continues to decline in economic importance in the country, alternative employment strategies in rural regions seem to be focused on tourism development in less-visited areas.

As new areas of tourism development are funded and focused on by the country's tourism organizations, tourism operators will be encouraged to incorporate the underutilized rural landscape into their tours. For example, farm holidays are becoming more popular, even for short half-day visits. Clever initiatives by local farmers include such activities as watching sheep dogs work, learning to play traditional Irish musical instruments, and having a traditional lunch with a farm family. These farmers, usually on farms not too far afield from tourism centers, or "honey pots," market their activities to tourism operators for inclusion in both day-trips and extended tours. Many of the activities are scheduled around the working hours of the actual farms, taking place from late morning through early afternoon. Coaches arrive; visitors tour the farm and engage in a variety of specifically planned activities and then depart within a few hours' time. Fees per person are in the €4–7 range and can amount to hundreds of Euro per day in additional income for farm families. Longer stays on farms are also gaining in popularity in a few regions, with some farms offering week-long or weekend stays for families who want to experience life on an authentic working farm.

The visitor farm industry in Ireland is concentrated on family-run farms throughout the island. The attraction to the visitor farms seems to be related to the theme of authenticity: these activities offer the visitor the opportunity to experience the "real" Ireland. A website dedicated to "Ireland's Top Visitor Farms" (www. esatclear.ie/~turoefarm/top/farms.html) suggests that the farms of the countryside express "a continuity of love for the land and its domestic animals. Farming is still a family affair, with a lifestyle which respects old courtesies: particularly the custom of being kind to strangers." Expressly aimed toward an urban audience, the farms offer guided tours of both cattle and sheep operations, and most will also give demonstrations of sheep shearing or shepherd dogs at work. Some of the farms among the top visitor list are highly specialized ones with rare breeds, organic crops and gardens, deer herds, or cheese-making. Most farms also have small restaurants or coffee shops, making the visit even more attractive to groups and individuals who may want to take part in the experience of a farm visit or holiday. Irish Farm Holidays, located in Limerick, offers extended-stay opportunities at working farms throughout Ireland (www.irishfarmholidays.com).

CHAPTER 6

Tourists in Ireland

TOURISTS

Tourists have been flowing into Ireland in ever-increasing numbers over the last 30 years. Beginning in the 1970s, Ireland's tourism economy began to evolve from a shop economy into a vital part of national development. As suggested, it was first noticed as a destination by the privileged and wealthy in the 1700s, when English and Anglo-Irish holiday-makers would flock to Mallow or Lucan (Davies 1993) to the spas, but the exclusivity of that tourism experience in essence no longer exists. As mass-travel has become cheaper, air-space agreements, such as the Open Skies Agreement, have been worked out between destination and point of departure, and the world has become smaller through mass media, Ireland should no longer linger in memory or myth. Potential tourists can "virtually" tour Ireland prior to arrival through innovations in internet presentation, eye-catching advertorials, and clever placement of banners, information links, and live webcams focused on holiday honey pots. The images related to these virtual communities are carefully chosen to represent an idealized Ireland. Very little is supposedly left to the imagination, and few visitors arrive in Ireland without having had the opportunity to surf through the country prior to landing. According to a seasoned tour guide from Cork, many of the American, French, and German tourists she worked with throughout the year had found Internet information and were "reasonably" prepared for their trip (though she admitted that many still expected a backward country filled with superstitious bumpkins and leprechauns). Not all tourists take advantage of the wide array of internet options available to them, but most at least have fantasized over the presentation of the Ireland that is packaged for the holiday visitor. Despite the availability of information, many (some would argue most) visitors to Ireland, especially those from the United States, Australia, and Canada, do little in the way of trip preparation and planning. Those linked with group tours tend to leave the decision making to others, are uninformed about the robust economic conditions of the country [*see the Epilogue for an update*], and have few insights regarding Ireland's deep history.

Trip Preparation

Ireland has responded to this particular aspect of visitor interest by increasing the number of information repositories and by making them highly accessible. Tourists can prepare for their island visit by accessing websites and other electronic media that assist in doing the groundwork on genealogical research. For example, the website *Irish Ancestors* not only has links that allow rudimentary surname research but also lists information on 8 family history societies, 35 local heritage centers, 14 "major repositories" of genealogical records (including the National Archives and National Library), 4 repositories considered to have limited relevance, and dozens of local libraries (scripts.ireland.com/ancestor/). Most of these are equipped with staff who will conduct the "nuts and bolts" of the research (usually for a fee), or they have detailed electronic databases with extensive information on family names. However, the difficulty of succeeding in finding one's family with limited information is considerable. I recently did a brief search on the surname Malone from County Clare (my own relatives) and found literally hundreds of Malones in the county, most of whom I doubt I'm related to, dating from the 1600s through the early 20th century. When I expanded the search to include all Malones without a county designation, it became clear that, without detailed information on exactly where my family was from, when they may have left Ireland, what their given names were, and where my relatives may be now, contacting my relatives would be close to impossible. A similar search using the name Daunt (descendants of French Huguenots who came to Ireland in the 1600s) revealed dozens of Daunts from the 17th and 18th centuries with the given name "Achilles," all from the general area of Cork. Visitors to Ireland intent on locating their relatives or information on ancestors would certainly need more information than I utilized in conducting my experimental search.

The Attraction to Ireland

It is difficult to determine exactly *what* attracts people to Ireland. But studies conducted by both governmental and private enterprises have found a number of distinct drawing points that appear to be common among many visitors to Ireland: roots, friends and family, culture, the environment, word of mouth (Fáilte Ireland 2005e).

Roots. For generations, Ireland has been an exporter of people. The vast numbers of émigrés from the island since the 19th and 20th centuries and their descendants eclipse the present-day population by several hundred million. Memory plays a significant role in attracting people to Ireland who are either recent émigrés intent on re-establishing contact with home soil or the children of famine survivors who crossed to other lands generations ago. As suggested, memory is often both highly mythologized and selective, and few challenge the traditional tales of homeland handed down through their families. Ireland's rains become a misty oasis of bucolic rural charm. The coal roads of Limerick and the quays of early 20th-century Dublin are remembered as urban wonderlands. Families, too, are transformed from the common-folk of Ballyfarnon to descendants of the last kings of Ireland. Seeking one's roots and finding evidence of family in Ireland is a considerable draw for many visitors to the island.

Expectations. As suggested, with the advent of the internet, many first-time visitors to Ireland can be reasonably well prepared for their holiday. Website brochures include a wide array of photographs of scenic Ireland and modern cityscapes. Stressing either relaxation and "getting away from it all" or the glitz and glam of urban life, the websites promise visitors that they will experience something unique and incomparable, something they will treasure and remember for a lifetime. The coach tourist will have the added benefit of sitting back and letting Ireland happen to them without having to go out of their way to find it. It is this passivity of coach tour participants that often lulls them into a state of unpreparedness when faced with an Ireland not of the brochure. Gangland slayings in Dublin, oil spills in Boyle, traffic jams in Corofin (caused by automobiles and not by sheep or cattle) are not expected by visitors and are certainly not mentioned in the brochures. Many times, the touristic idyll (Cusack 1998) can be disrupted by something as common as waiting in queue in the wind and the rain for a ferry to cross to the Aran Islands. Although visitors are told by tour guides and tour companies that rain is common, the fact that it does rain in Ireland while a holiday is in progress can be the deciding factor in whether or not they return to Ireland in the future.

An interview with a tour guide in Dublin in 2006 expanded on this. An experienced, professional, and qualified guide who has been in the business since the 1970s, she recognized most coach tourists as becoming less and less sophisticated over the 30 years she had been involved in the industry. This is in direct opposition to the TPRG (2003) report, which suggested that visitors to Ireland had grown more sophisticated; in general, sophistication may be understood differently by those who work on the ground floor of tourism and those who watch it from above. According to her, when modern Irish tourism was just gearing up in the 1970s, people who traveled had some degree of education and took their preparation for foreign travel with a high degree of seriousness. Travel was expensive, and few other than the elite or business travelers could afford to go abroad. When travel became more affordable (and people had access to credit cards), greater numbers of people began to travel on organized tours, which were relatively cheap. The expectations also changed. Thirty years ago, travelers would "stop over" in Ireland (usually Shannon) for a day or two before moving on to the continent, and 30 years ago in the west of Ireland, the rural "idyll" still existed without the façade of the premodern—it was premodern. In the new millennium, the rural idyll is hidden from view in areas of the island that rarely cater to visitors. Today's visitors, often expecting an Ireland of the past, are many times disappointed with what they get. At the same time, they demand modern facilities such as en suite rooms in out-of-the-way bed and breakfast accommodations and hotel-quality service from the families who run them. Complaints regarding the facilities are rarely directed toward the accommodators but toward the guides and drivers, who then must try to repair any damage while on the spin. Once the tour is over and tourists have returned home, letters and emails of complaint sent to the tour operator will then mention the success or failure of the guide or driver-guide to remedy situations that are often beyond their control. The tour operators may then decide to discontinue using a guide or driver based on letters of complaint by clients who have expectations that are at odds with reality.

It is this paradox of expectation of today's tourist—the rural idyll, the backward, suspicious country farmer, the countryside of thatched cottages, modern facilities, and being catered to by their guides, drivers, and hosts—that molds the end result of the coach tourism experience. Coach drivers, driver-guides, and tour guides associated with coach tours must bend over backward to provide their charges with a positive experience of Ireland even when things are beyond their control (such as rough seas on ferry rides). In the world of coach tourism, clients demand that their hosts take part in cheerful chatting, remember their names, have endless knowledge of local, regional, and national sites and sights, be approachable at all hours, and to enjoy what they do—even when they themselves may behave in ways that are anathema to a positive experience.

In return for this expected behavior, the tourists' guides and driver-guides are rewarded with tips. An industry standard in Ireland is €4–6 per day per person on the average tour (upscale tours may increase by €1–2 pp/pd), and this is explained by tour operators, included in tour brochures, and made clear in the personalized final itineraries each coach tourist receives. Unless the tip is included in the price of the tour (few tour operators and companies do this in Ireland, especially with American tours), it is left to individuals to put aside enough cash to cover the tip at the end of their tour. It is not unusual for tour guides and driver-guides to end a challenging tour only to be short-changed by the people they have catered to. One driver (who was not acting as a driver-guide in this particular instance) reported that he was once given a 70¢ tip by a French tourist he had driven for seven days. When I asked him if this happened often, he replied that there are sometimes class issues between tourists and drivers and suggested that tourists may feel that drivers should be grateful for receiving any tip for their work. Other drivers and driver-guides suggested that many times visitors simply run out of money at the end of their trip and that some tourists may not realize that drivers and driver-guides are not paid directly by the tour companies (many coach tourists I spoke to thought drivers and driver-guides received a "cut" from each seat sold) but by the coach owners, who generally pay the minimum required by Irish law (in 2007 this amounts to €8.30 per hour, averaging about €400 or so per week). At the same time, most drivers and driver-guides acknowledged the incredible generosity of coach tourists in general, who often tip in excess of the recommended amount; a few suggested that it would be rare not to receive substantial tips especially from American tourists, but only one driver-guide out of those surveyed regarding tips made the assertion that he was always tipped in excess of the recommended rate.

Pubs and Pints.

Dublin's pubs are slices of its living culture. They are the famous haunts of its literary set, politicians, rock stars and of course, Dubliners! Our capital city is home to some 1,000 pubs and no visit to Dublin would be complete without sampling a local brew in a real Dublin pub!
(Dubl!n: The Official Online Tourist Office for Dublin
[www.visitdublin.com])

Holiday-making in Ireland is synonymous with drinking. According to a recent survey (2005e) conducted by Fáilte Ireland, the Guinness Storehouse is the most visited place in Ireland. Electronic media have also promoted the availability and commonality of the "pub experience" in Ireland with significant presence on a variety of sites. In Dublin alone, a brief perusal of sites included *Dublin Pub Scene, Dublin Pub Guide, Dublin Pubs,* and *Dubl!n: The Official Online Tourist Office for Dublin.* Each site emphasizes Dublin's pub scene as central to Irish culture. The *Dublin Pub Guide* (www.dublinpubguide. com) suggests that Dublin is "the world's foremost drinking city" and that the site allows visitors to plan which pubs they will go to when they arrive in the city (although it lists only five of Dublin's 1,000 pubs on its site as of May 2006). *Dublin Pub Scene* goes so far as to include current Dublin drink prices and claims to list 900–1,000 of Dublin's drinking establishments on its site (www.dublinpubscene.com). Printed matter as well underscore the central theme of pubs as the center of the Irish social universe by emphasizing camaraderie, traditional music, the upscale market, "old" Irish pubs, or the legendary people who may once have held up the bars there (such as James Joyce at Davy Byrne's or Brendan Behan at McDaid's). Tourist brochures make repeated mention of "traditional" nights out, pub crawls, and experiencing Irish culture at the locals. An overwhelming percentage of tourists in Ireland (both foreign and domestic) visit at least one pub on their visit to the island.

Reality: A Day in the life of American Coach Tourists. Typical of most coach tours in Ireland is an included breakfast (a "Full Irish"), generally scheduled between 8 A.M. and 10 A.M., depending on touring schedule and hotel parameters. Most coach tours leave very shortly after breakfast is done, so most coach driver-guides emphasize the boarding time so that visitors will finish eating, put their bags out (if they are departing to another hotel), and ready themselves for what usually is a full day on tour. A Full Irish breakfast includes such things as rashers of bacon (most Americans remark that it's not at all like *their* bacon), Irish sausage, eggs, grilled tomato, beans (not at all like *their* beans, and why are they served at breakfast?), often grilled button mushrooms, toast, coffee, tea, and an array of yogurts (ditto—not like American yogurt), fresh fruit, croissants or some other pastry, and cereals. Once breakfast is over, tourists will be asked to quickly move along to the coach so their touring day can begin and their schedule can be adhered to. (What the tourists don't realize is that the coach driver has spent a good deal of his down time the night before confirming visits and the next hotel, deciding when to gas up or gassing up, cleaning the coach [including a full wash], taking care of grumpy passengers, swapping rooms with visitors dissatisfied with theirs [after all, he's just the driver, why shouldn't he give up his room?], talking to family and friends, checking in with the tour organizer and/or the coach owner, and trying to have a moment to himself when he is not bombarded with questions.) Generally, people are ready to go on time, but inevitably there is always at least one who can't seem to comply.

The coach departs as close to schedule as possible and the group settles down in the same exact seats they sat in the day before. (With Americans, there is always an attempt to have a row or a space in between each other). They will read the paper (I can't find a *Boston Globe*! I thought you said *The New York Times* would be in the hotel!), read a book, listen to music on their mp3 players, and eventually fall asleep at some point before arriving at their first destination. They rarely listen to the driver, who spends the time describing the landscape (What's that yellow stuff? Gorse. What's that yellow stuff? Gorse. What's that yellow stuff? Gorse.), previewing their destination, and giving them details on their next hotel, dinner times, what to expect in town, why there are these inconvenient bank holidays, and when the next bathroom break will be (every two hours). Driver-guides call this "talking to the wind-screen."

Tea and scones are usually scheduled with a bathroom break sometime just before or just after the first visit of the day. The group climbs off the coach, enters their destination (such as the Cliffs of Moher), takes a tour or is self-guided through the site, then immediately goes to the souvenir shop to fill up on trinkets. This scenario is repeated throughout the day—indeed for the duration of their stay. Trinkets and photos and postcards are indicators of a person's presence in a desired location—they are must-have parts of the tourist day and are emblematic of the tourist experience. The driver-guide escorts the group onto the site, exchanges vouchers with the personnel there, gets them started on their way, and then goes back to the coach to park it and have a few moments to himself. (As I mentioned earlier, I use himself, him, he, and so on throughout, because the vast majority of driver-guides in Ireland are men.) Within minutes of their return to the coach, the group is ready for lunch, normally scheduled between 12.30 P.M. and 2 P.M. along the way. In the course of a day, usually two stops at sites are planned unless sites are close together and a third can be squeezed in. In my experience, most coach tourists like one stop in the morning and one in the afternoon with ample breaks in between. While in the coach, the tourists will resume their seating pattern, go back to their reading or music, and generally ignore the driver until they are arriving at their next destination.

Dinner is included on most days on most tours (the common exceptions to this being Dublin, Cork, and Galway, where expenses are steep and many alternatives are available; this also encourages most visitors to get out of the hotel and experience the area). The menus vary from hotel to hotel, but most include beef or salmon—and so many do that a very famous race horse in Ireland is named Beef or Salmon, after this gastronomic habit. Ireland's hotels have learned to accommodate an array of tastes, including vegetarians. Dinner begins with a starter chosen from several options. Orders, depending on how busy the hotel is, are taken very quickly from a small menu designed for each tour group's budget. The main course comes with a variety of vegetables, and bread is always served throughout the meal. Drinks can be ordered; water jugs are on the table, and tea and coffee orders are taken with dessert. There are also a variety of desserts to choose from. Many visitors to Ireland are shocked at the quality and variety of the food, having been told of atrocities such as "boiled meats," warm beer, and menus consisting of nothing but potatoes and white fish. Drivers rarely accompany the group at meals, preferring to dine with other drivers or alone to avoid the constant questions, or because a particular tour company may request that they not fraternize with guests.

After dinner, guests have a number of options (some, for example, traditional nights at Johnny Fox's or Taylor's Three Rock in Dublin, are scheduled) including setting out on their own, spending time in the hotel pub, catching up on rest, or turning in early. Setting out on their own can be overwhelming to many American visitors, most of whom are convinced that crime will follow them from home and that their mere presence makes them a target for street criminals. American women will often be seen with their handbags slung across their bodies and clutched in a fist—a clear signal that they are carrying oodles of cash, credit cards, and traveler's checks. American men walk with their hands in their pockets—another signal to potential criminals that they have cash or valuables. They also tend to wear an abundance of green—no one in Ireland wears green except sports fans and tourists, especially American ones. A few will venture out; most retire to the hotel pub for a pint of the black stuff (Guinness— whether they like it or not); a few will take some rest. Those who go to pubs drink too much and talk incessantly about it the next day. Someone always badgers the driver to join them; most offers are turned down, but some will have a pint with a group and exit early, and a few will spend an evening with their group on occasion. The next day, it begins again, in much the same fashion. In an interview with a driver-guide in the spring of 2006, mention was made again of the total disinterest in Ireland despite his best efforts to make the visit of his charges interesting. He had even gone so far as to add stops and visits not outlined in their schedules to make them happy, with little result. His comment follows closely those of other driver-guides that many tourists are most interested in "going to" rather than "being in" Ireland and in their collection of trinkets and souvenirs and the number of places they had been for the photo album. Tourism as consumption.

By the end of the week, they are familiar and comfortable with the routine. In the event of changes to the schedule, they often have an inability to find things to do on their own and often lay-up in their hotels for the duration of the change. In recent observations of American tourists in Ireland, it was clear as well that it was an adjustment for many to accept the sometimes rough language of the Irish around them—many take exception to the colorful metaphors that pepper daily chat in Ireland, and mention is occasionally made in exit surveys of "harsh" or "dirty" language. Driver-guides and others associated with tourism have often been challenged with toning down their common talk to accommodate visitors. (There are a few exceptions to this, including a legendary driver whose colorful language is known throughout the industry and who continues to this day to be a favorite among Rugby teams touring the island.)

Discussion: Coach travel, Tourism, and the Pursuit of Heritage. Bob McKercher and Hilary du Cros have addressed the issue of passivity in cultural tourism at length in their book *Cultural Tourism: The Partnership between Tourism and Cultural Heritage Management* (2002). They suggest that tourism of any kind, including cultural tourism, must be understood as a form of entertainment, because "only a small number of tourists really seek a deep learning experience when they travel" (ibid.: 29). As suggested above in relation to coach tourism, McKercher and du Cros have found that tourists in general would rather receive a cultural experience (or "pseudo-event," specifically created for visitors) than go to the trouble of actively seeking one out or intentionally learning about a culture prior to arrival. They break cultural tourists into five categories:

1. *the purposeful cultural tourist*, . . . who travels for cultural tourism motives and seeks a deep cultural tourism experience;
2. *the sightseeing cultural tourist*, who travels for cultural tourism motives but who seeks a shallow experience;
3. *the serendipitous cultural tourist*, . . . who ends up getting a deep cultural experience [but does not necessarily seek it];

4. *the casual cultural tourist,* who identifies cultural tourism as a weak motive for visiting a destination and seeks a shallow experience; and

5. *the incidental cultural tourist,* for whom cultural tourism is not a stated motive . . . but who does visit cultural heritage attractions (ibid.: 39).

In Ireland, most tourists visit with some intention of experiencing the cultural heritage; this is borne out by the sheer numbers of tourists who visit heritage attractions on any given day (Fáilte Ireland 2005e) as well as by the way the tours are designed and marketed. Despite the numbers, I suggest that few coach tourists would match McKercher and du Cros' description of "purposeful" cultural tourists, nor would they be serendipitous, casual, or incidental (for the most part). Coach tourists are sightseers, intent on seeing the places and things listed and described in their brochure (which some participants may see as important cultural events)—essentially to say they had been there—but few return home with the "meaningful cultural experience" described by McKercher and du Cros. The majority of coach tours in Ireland are also made up of people who are in some way familiar with one another. (For example, university alumni, extended family groups, church groups, musicians, and so on are a few of the groups I had contact with during my research; the list is by no means exhaustive.) Although *individuals* on a given coach tour may be compelled to pursue more than a passing brush with Irish cultural heritage, as a *group* coach tourists are intent on soaking in the local color through osmosis rather than immersing themselves in it. The nature of coach tourism also prevents immersion, based on the often pressing schedules of the tours—it is not unusual for tours to arrive at their accommodation at 3 P.M., stay the night in a hotel, and be on the way to the next destination by 10 A.M. the next day. They also can afford to spend only a limited amount of time at a site/sight owing to the travel schedules, the scheduling of on-site tours, and the legal hourly limits placed on drivers. Coach drivers describe this as seeing Ireland through the coach windows. The object is to see as much Irish space as possible by covering as much ground as can be covered in a brief amount of time.

CHAPTER 7

The Coach Fellas

COACH DRIVERS AND DRIVER-GUIDES

My first experience with an extended bus tour in Ireland took place in 2000 when I observed a group of Americans (most of whom I knew) on a tour from Killarney to Galway to Dublin. To be honest, I didn't know what to expect regarding the tour itself except that we would be staying in the three cities in the brochure. I was especially unaware of the degree of responsibility that the driver (from Cavan) had for the group, the coach, and the entire organization of the tour. I was just a passenger on the trip—albeit someone who had spent a great deal of time in Europe and who had spent months on my own doing field research in Austria—and after two days, I was annoyed by the actions of many of the people on the tour. I could only imagine how the driver felt. Four days into the tour, I had the chance to talk with him about the trip, and I could sense his frustration with certain members of the group who were continually late for departures, complained about meals, were seemingly disinterested in the country and the people, and were there essentially to purchase souvenirs and have pictures taken of themselves in front of the symbols of Ireland. At one point, as we were arriving into Galway, a passenger began to badger him about the best place for fish and chips in the city. He carefully pointed out Quay and Shop Streets as we drove past the pedestrian district on our way to our hotel and told her that McDonagh's was without a doubt the best. She rolled her eyes and responded with "Why is that? Do they pay you to say that?" Needless to say, she didn't go to McDonagh's and never left the hotel once we arrived. At that point, after several similar interactions with her and other members of the group, he stopped giving any personal recommendations to his passengers. I would think this is not an unusual experience for coach drivers anywhere.

Coach driver-guides are the closest contacts to the visitor who also mediate the experiences "on the ground." They are responsible for the minutia of the daily tour; they organize breakfasts, times when coaches and other vehicles must be boarded, visits to sites, arrival times at hotels, dinners, they load and unload bags, and, most important for my research, they are the initial source of information for all things Ireland. Their rehearsed talks change little from tour to tour, although personal touches are encouraged by Fáilte Ireland. A recent trip to Dublin made this even more painfully obvious when, every ten minutes or so, a Dublin tour bus would drive past my Merrion Square hotel room with guides repeating the exact same script each time they approached Oscar Wilde's house on the opposite corner. What do visitors take away from these experiences? What do drivers and tour guides take away from them? Do they ever change the script? Is there room for flexibility? What are the expectations of both visitors and driver-guides before, during, and after tours?

Issues of class, status, tradition, consumption of the past, and communication are all integral to the study of tourism in Ireland. Drivers, more so than tour guides, are understood as working class and part of the service industry. Participants in the tours routinely ignore them, speak down to them, and tease them (this teasing usually centers on accents, drinking, sex, or being a "peasant"). Discussion with drivers over the past few years has brought to light their own feelings of inadequacy regarding their position in the tourism hierarchy, their mild to moderate disgust with some of their clients ("I just speak to the windscreen"), and an overall frustration that Ireland has become a massive theme park that no longer belongs to the Irish but to a world of visitors who come and go as they please.

The driver-guides, the "Coach Fellas" whom this ethnography focuses on, are the people responsible for "lead-in" and "lead-out" presentations of the Ireland scripted in the advertorials produced by the various tourism agencies in the country. As with most people in the tourism industry, their contact with their charges is fleeting and likely not to be repeated on an individual or group basis. The transient, ever-changing cycle of driving and touring enforces a distance of emotions that is at odds with their passengers' dependence on them and their knowledge. Truth and trust are assumed, implicit, and rarely questioned. The "coach fellas" are a fraternity of seasonal workers, most of whom are in continuous motion from March through October or November and who often get their assignments by text message on their ever-present mobile phones. How do they understand their positions on both the frontier and the backstage of a multibillion dollar industry? Given the opportunity, how would they present Ireland? What changes have they witnessed over the course of their careers? What is Irish cultural heritage? What are common expectations among different classes of patrons? What are common problems or dilemmas?

The discourse of the tour and the role played by driver-guides in providing information to their charges has been little studied. Often the coach driver is the first point of contact (or "primary interface," as the TPRG refers to them [2003]) that tourists have with the places they visit. In Ireland, where coach drivers also routinely act as tour guides, the blended responsibilities are extremely taxing. Coach drivers I have interviewed and observed over the course of this project often expressed the same frustrations as the driver mentioned a few pages ago had with many of their groups' lack of interest in Ireland and its culture. Many told stories of patrons "sleeping through Ireland" while on the bus, being afraid to leave their hotels, not paying any attention to their suggestions, and of others treating them like servants. Despite the demands and challenges of the job, most also told stories of passengers who became friends, who made them laugh for days on end, and of trips that still conjure fond memories of camaraderie, adventure, sexual escapades, and lawlessness.

The vast majority of coach drivers and driver-guides in Irish tourism are seasonal employees whose normal working schedule lasts from mid-March through the end of October (in some cases there are scattered tours through November, but these are sporadic and cannot be depended on). During their eight months on the road, they rarely have genuine days off; many work several weeks on end without a full day off, while technically staying within EU regulations regarding legal working hours. When the occasional day off occurs, it can be spent cleaning the coach, doing laundry, organizing the following days on tour, and catching up on sleep. After months on the road, sleep becomes a precious commodity. When the season ends (many drivers mention catching "October-itis" as the end of touring approaches), drivers begin to schedule holidays with their families or significant others or to look for off-season work. Many will go on the dole, at least for part of the off-season; others work under the table driving lorries, tending bar, or doing some other relatively "invisible" job. Drivers who stay employed by individual coach companies or who belong to a "panel" of permanent drivers for a given coach company may spend the off-season driving incentive groups on short-hauls, driving transfers from rail stations or airports, or working at the company's depot on the buses.

Training

Drivers and driver-guides must be licensed and trained to drive their vehicles. In Ireland, this can include hours of theory and road lessons with certified driving schools, or, in the case of EU-Nationals, a test that assures that the license in hand can be transferred to an Irish license. Any differences or lack of qualification in a certain area must be rectified before an applicant can be issued an Irish class D license. In addition to road training, drivers and driver-guides must also be familiar with current state and EU regulations, must have a working familiarity with the mechanical aspects of the coach, and be aware of all local road systems, including diversions. Since the 1990s, "Skillnets," an enterprise-led support body funded by the National Training Fund through the Department of Enterprise, Trade, and Employment, whose mission is to enhance the skills of people in Irish industry to support competitiveness and employability, has been available for those wishing to become tour coach drivers or those who want to sharpen their skills. The Coach Tourism Skillnet (promoted by the Coach Travel and Tourism Council of Ireland) notes:

> Coach drivers are . . . expected to interact with tourists intensively. To compete successfully, drivers must become qualified one-person driver-guides. . . . For most drivers, the [Skillnet] training provided the first validation of their knowledge by the award of a recognized qualification. This provided great motivation to those working in the industry. (The Training Networks Program 2005)

Not all coach drivers and driver-guides took part in this Skillnet, but Feargal Barton, of the CTTC, noted the necessity of coach driver-guide validation and training across the industry (personal communication 2007). Along with driving skills, they must also be able to diagnose technical and mechanical problems as they occur. According to Bus Éireann, "safety is primarily the responsibility of . . . drivers" (*Irish Times* online; www. business2000.ie). Once licensed, drivers and driver-guides must find employment with coach operator companies or become independent contractors.

Those working as guides may have gone through the system of training through CERT (prior to 2003), Bord Fáilte, or Fáilte Ireland. In many cases, driver-guides are not certified but are considered "experienced." A certified guide will have been badged or certified by the state on a local, regional, national, or city tour level. To receive certification, the guide must sit for exams on history, archaeology, current affairs, and other areas also offered as courses in preparation for the exams. They will also be observed and assessed by members of the examinations board during live tours, and they must have completed a number of city and national tours before receiving their certification. An experienced guide is often someone who has a long-term relationship with a certain area or who may simply have years of experience working in the industry. Guides' knowledge of Ireland is under constant scrutiny, whether they hold a badge or not. In some cases, tour operators may send someone along on the tour specifically to observe and assess the guide; in other cases, the tourists respond to the tour companies positively or negatively regarding the quality of the tour. Geva and Goldman (1991) found that the guide is often the most important factor in tourist satisfaction (as cited in Nash 1996). Likewise, the 2005 Fáilte Ireland Visitor Attitudes Survey found that "one in ten [holiday-makers] spontaneously mention their satisfaction with the quality of their coach tour in terms of organization, guiding, and comprehensiveness as a reason for their holiday expectations being exceeded" (2005e: 40). (See Table 7.1.) In a very unscientific perusal of client comments on a variety of tour organizer websites, I found few letters that did not mention the positive impression and professionalism of the driver or driver-guide.

Drivers and driver-guides in Irish tourism are overwhelmingly locals, although there had been an increase in foreign

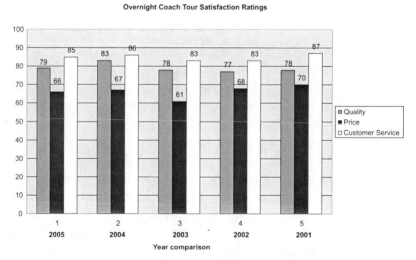

Overnight Coach Tour Satisfaction Ratings

Fáilte Ireland Visitor Attitudes Survey 2005 (Millward Brown IMS Limited) 39

Table 7.1 Visitor Attitudes Survey 2005 Fáilte Ireland. The figures indicate that ratings of customer service and quality, drivers, and driver-guides remained high from 2001 (*right*) through 2005.

national drivers, especially from Eastern Europe, as eco-nomic opportunities in Ireland attracted workers from Poland, Lithuania, the Czech Republic, and other emerging members of the EU. Irish-born drivers commented that, although they appreciated the expertise of many of the non-nationals, they worried that their willingness to work extra hours, to sleep on the coaches, and to endure adverse working conditions might make it increasingly difficult for Irish drivers to remain at the top of driving panels. They also have remarked that there is a lack of "young ones" coming up, meaning there are few Irish-born drivers coming into the business to take their places as many move toward retirement (Feargal Barton personal com-munication 2007). A high percentage of drivers who are Irish-born have between 15 and 20+ years of service in the tourism industry, and they worry that the environment of Irish tourism will become unrecognizable in the near future as drivers with no real history or interest in Ireland begin to be absorbed into the industry. This also raises questions regarding the quality as-sessments of the tours themselves—passengers on coach tours regularly converse with the drivers whether they are driver-guides or are only driving. The expectation is that the people associated with the tours will be Irish, at the very least they will be English speaking and have a strong relationship with the landscape and the culture of Ireland (14–16% of respondents to the Visitor Attitudes Survey conducted in 2005 for Fáilte Ireland mention "English speaking" as something that gives Ireland a competitive advantage over other destinations). With so much of the customer satisfaction ratings dependent on such factors, it remains to be seen whether the propensity to hire non-Irish nationals in these positions will affect the perceived quality of the coach tours in the future.

Participation

Driver-guides not only drive the coaches and give constant commentary to their clients while on the spin, they also rou-tinely participate in ground tours and other activities with their groups. Although it may not be required by the tour company that has organized the tour, many driver-guides believe that their participation and presence helps add to the sense of over-all well-being their customers ultimately feel. As the primary interface, principal point of contact, and leader of the group, the driver-guide provides continuous association with the group and personifies the interdependence extant between the tourist and the host. In my own experience observing and participat-ing in a number of tours in Ireland, driver-guides have will-ingly climbed mountains, crawled into caves, scrambled over fences, carried disabled tourists to places of interest, made ar-rangements for special visits to out-of-the-way sites that are not on the tour schedule, and gone to group gatherings (such as cabarets or banquets) that they may have gone to hundreds of times in the past simply to help maintain the cohesiveness of the group. With drivers being identified as "part of the group," tourists develop a common point of reference to the tour and may also attain the goal of the common experience. The com-mon experience, whether positive or negative, can also inten-sify the individual's perception of the tour, adding layers of information from various sources, enriching and expanding the felt memories of both the individual and the group.

Communication

After driving the coach, the principal duty and goal of the driver-guide is to communicate with his passengers. This seems an easy enough and obvious task. However, tourists begin their long-haul tours usually on the edge of exhaustion having flown from the far corners of the earth to their holiday destination. If they are coming from North or South America to Ireland, they have usually taken an overnight flight. (For example, from Boston's Logan International Airport, flights on Aer Lingus normally take off between 6:45 P.M. and 9 P.M., landing in Ireland between 6 A.M. and 8 A.M.—or 1 A.M. to 3 A.M. Boston time). They may have to spend an inordinate amount of time in the airport terminal gathering bags and going through customs, locating their travel companions, and finding their way through the airport. Most tour companies provide a "meet and greet" person who gathers the group together and introduces them to the driver-guide, who also meets them at the airport. In many cases, the greeter spends less than 20 minutes with the group, quickly passing them over to the driver-guide, who finishes organizing the mountains of suitcases, identifying people on his tour list, and then escorting them to the waiting coach. If group members are coming in at different times on different flights (not unusual), he may spend the entire day driving back and forth between hotel and airport until everyone has been accounted for. The driver-guide gathers room keys, hands them out, unloads suitcases from the lockers on the bus and labels them by room, organizes the room porters if the hotel provides them (often they aren't provided, and the driver carries and delivers all the bags himself), and makes any pressing group announcement as people are going to their rooms. He then helps them organize dinner if it is not included on the tour, takes them on a local or city tour, and makes any announcements necessary for the following day's excursions. If dinner is included, he shows them where the dining room is located and shows the group where they can find tour information on the announcements board in the hotel lobby.

While on tour, it is vital for the driver-guide to be both an effective and affective spokesman for Ireland. Annette Jorgensen has suggested that this necessity leads to a position of ultimate power:

> With regard to the touristic discourse, the most "local centres" of power might be the relations between the tourist and the tour guide. The guide possesses professional expertise, which gives him or her the power to construct what he or she is interpreting. The tourists are strangers to the place they visit, whereas the guide is a local, one who revisits it and re-interprets its meaning again and again. In addition, as the tourists are out of their culture (Crick 1989), they are dependent upon the explanations of the guide. So, if they are to "understand" the destination, they must accept the guide's expertise. Implicit in the touristic discourse lies the claim that the local culture,

history, or landscape can only be "understood" from the point of view of the guide. The locals are constructed as "other," to be gazed upon. Therefore, for a tourist, it is the guide, the person who "speaks one's own language"—culturally as well as linguistically—that one must turn to in order to comprehend them. Thus it appears to be the tour guide who has the power to speak, not the tourists and not the locals. (2003: 143)

This highly contradictory statement (for example, guides recognized as locals with power, but locals understood as objects without power) does not acknowledge the guide's explicit duty as teacher and interpreter. Visitors rarely possess the "power" to understand *a priori* the cultures and landscapes they are visiting, especially the nuances present in any culture and the often puzzling manifestations on the landscape and in the built environments of a given place. Even with the assistance of a guide, visitors are free to pick and choose the information given in terms of what they believe to be valid or invalid. I refer to my example of visiting Newgrange where, despite the guide's detailed lecture on the Neolithic peoples of Ireland, many visitors in my groups were still determined to believe that Egyptians, Romans, or space aliens built the passage tomb.

Driver-guides impart information along the way to a given destination; usually this involves describing the historical significance of a building, a specific place, or an area. There is rarely any perception of ranking or favoritism; for example, the smallest pub in Ireland will get the same delivery and billing as the Four Courts on a Dublin City tour. At the same time, driver-guides must take care not to slip into an overtly colloquial rendition of Ireland; the presentation must be phrased in such a way as to be easily digested by the group. Time lines must often be given in comparative terms, especially with American tourists who may have no real relationship with the deep history of Ireland; the Neolithic is beyond the scope of most American tourists' conceptions of the past, and the English occupation and the Norman invasions far predate most American perceptions of time, owing to their own country's and culture's relatively short history. The ability of the driver-guide to communicate in a nonthreatening, unobtrusive, polite way, while still maintaining an authoritative voice, is a learned skill.

Driver-guides not only must have an encyclopedic knowledge of general Irish history at hand but must also be able to discuss any particularities that occur along a given route. For example, during the summer of 2006, road works closed a large part of the main Dublin-Sligo road (the N4), and traffic was diverted through the back roads of northern County Roscommon and County Sligo. Despite the diversion not being included on the tour route, drivers I spoke to who were forced to take the back roads took advantage of the new route, pointing out unusual landscapes, famous buildings and cemeteries, and relating the views to their otherwise uneducated passengers. Many passengers on one of the rerouted tour buses delighted in the "adventure" and spoke highly of their driver-guide's knowledge and jovial attitude despite the slow-moving traffic and inconvenience of back-road bus travel.

Jorgensen (2003), McKercher and du Cros (2002), and others have examined tourism from above rather than from the point of view of the people who participate on the ground. The tendency in tourism literature is to understand the host community as overwhelmed by the visitors, as on inherently unequal footing, and as oppressed without recourse to the temporary colonization of their communities. In Ireland, this may have been the perception—in fact I might argue it was the case in the 18th, 19th, and part of the 20th centuries—but in 21st-century Ireland, control is firmly in the hands of the Irish, or at least those in the Irish tourism industry. Guides are in positions of power, as pointed out by Jorgensen, and driver-guides are trained first and foremost to drive buses, as discussed by McKercher and du Cros. However, I would argue that driver-guides are in the position of serving multiple roles: teacher, leader, organizer, driver, safety engineer, soothsayer, historian. Should the driver-guide fail as a leader—as the person with authority, knowledge, and power—the tour itself would ultimately fail.

DAY IN THE LIFE: EXPERIENCE
AND HUMILITY

Coach driver-guides, in their multiple guises of caretaker, lecturer, organizer, and taxi-service, are witness to myriad human stories on a continuous and daily basis. Over the course of this research, they have told me a variety of tales—too many to include in a short ethnography. Following are just a few of their stories, included here to contextualize the day-to-day relationships among driver-guides and between driver-guides and tourists and driver-guides and their employers.

Stories of the Road: A Series of "Real World" Narratives on Coach Driving and Tourism

Ashes. "I did a repeat job with clients I had had two years before, just a family group of a few people who were with [a well-known Irish musician]. The woman was after dying, and they were there to spread her ashes at places she was fond of. I guess because I had driven them before, they asked for me to drive them this time. There must have been about 25 family members who were along for this. At every place her niece would recite poetry the woman loved and then sing and play the tin whistle. It was all very sad and moving. She asked to have her ashes spread at the Ceide Fields in north Mayo, at Dún Aenghus Fort on Inismor and in the Doogh Valley leading to Louisburgh, the scene of a famine tragedy where hundreds of Irish people lost their lives walking to work houses." To me, this seemed like a very special situation to be involved in, and I asked him if they invited him along to the actual spreading of the ashes. He said the invitation wasn't explicit, but that he went along and helped in any way he could. "It was out of respect for the woman and the family," he suggested. I asked him if he had ever heard from the family again, and he replied that no, he personally hadn't heard back from them, and he didn't know if they had ever sent a letter of thanks or acknowledgment to the tour company either. "I was just there. I didn't expect anything in return."

Family Tragedy. "I had a group a few years back on a tour, and one of them was an older gent who brought his family with him. They'd been to Ireland before with me and were really happy to be back and about. We got to [a town], and I had taken the rest of the group to a pub for the night when I was informed that he was in the hotel unwell. The ambulance had been called but didn't arrive until 45 minutes later. The client had nitroglycerine tablets around his neck, because he had a dodgy heart, but it took another 40 minutes to get to [the] hospital. Sadly, he died at around 3 A.M. The family were put up at [the hotel] no charge, the undertaker was contacted and all. We had to carry on with the tour, which was difficult and sad for everybody. We met up with the family (his wife and two grown children were with him) at Shannon Airport four days later. He was all sealed up in a coffin and went home with the rest of the group." Driver-guides, drivers, and tour guides are not given specific training in any sort of first aid, yet they are expected to know how to handle difficult and dangerous situations seamlessly. This driver-guide had been with the rest of the group at a local pub and then spent the rest of the night at the hospital consoling the family. He also never heard back from this family.

Deported. "So I came off a tour and the boss calls me and says, 'Go on over to Belgium and pick up a double decker there.' I said 'I don't have my passport and I've never driven a double decker,' but he tells me it's no problem, all I need is my license and I'd be OK. So I get the boat at Rosslare and get over to England, then I have to get to London on a bus, then to Dover to get the boat across to Ostende. All is going well for about a minute when I realize I'm going to get stopped at the boat because everyone else has their passports out. I bullshit my way through ticketing [noticing my license is a year out of date], but then I get stopped by the security and they give me a hard time, but finally I somehow get on the boat. What I don't realize at the time is that there's some problem between Europe and England because of a beef import thing, so they've got loads of security out. I'm on the boat anyway and security reports me to Ostende and they hold me in Belgium for 10 hours because I'm of course there illegally. I asked if I could call to have my passport details faxed, and they agree to let me but send me out with a guard. So the boss faxes everything, and then they tell me that's fine, but I have to drive through France to Calais for the ferry, and the French won't let me drive through France because I don't have a legal license; remember it's a year out of date! So, I can't get the bus back to Ireland anyway. It ends up that they found a driver for it (it's also full of farmers from the Midlands), and it gets to the ferry. In the meantime, I'm getting deported back to the U.K. and getting marched around like a criminal. I get back on the boat with security all over the place and then realize I don't have any money with me, I haven't slept in two days, and I haven't had anything to eat. So they debate as to whether they'll even let me on the boat or keep me where I am. I throw what coins I have in my pocket on the desk and just walk on the boat after I tell them to charge the boss. So, I get back to Dover and I'm exhausted, but I know the ferry with the bus isn't in for a few hours, so I find a B & B, call the boss, and get that settled and go to sleep for a bit. I asked if I could sleep in, but the lady told me no, this is when we have breakfast and you need to be out (I tell her to get fucked, the cunt). . . . I get to Dover to pick up the bus and find out it's running 45 minutes late, so I decide to have my tea and freshen up (at least *they* haven't copped on that the license is out of date), and I'm just sitting down for my tea when I see the bus go by. So I drop my toast and tea and run after it. I have to drive six hours to Holyhead, then take the boat across to Ireland, and then drive all the way to Multyfarnham in the Midlands out near Mullingar with a load of farmers from an agricultural college. Mind you, I've had almost no sleep and I'm illegal. I get back to the yard with the fucker of a bus and the boss's biggest concern is the steep charge for my ticket back on the boat! I told him I didn't realize I was getting deported when I started the damn journey!

"A couple weeks later, I go back to the yard and I see the damn bus there with a trailer on the back. I said to someone, 'Jayzus, I pity the poor fuck who has to take that around!' And guess who gets it? Me. The fucking thing was impossible to drive; it was a country tour, so I was all over little boreens and kept getting the trailer stuck on little humpy bridges—disaster. Last time I ever drove a double decker and the last time I was ever caught without my passport!" This driver-guide, despite the hardship it caused at the time, said he spent more time laughing about the "Double Decker Deportation Debacle" than he did driving the thing. He also told me about another "royal cock-up" when he got sent to France with a group of Irish school kids and the teachers who came with them would go out and drink all day and night leaving him in charge. They were at a hotel in Paris, and the teachers came to him at one point and asked if there had been any problems, to which he replied, none he was aware of. Unknown to him, the students had been misbehaving for several nights, and when he went down to breakfast the next morning, the chef came after him with a cleaver and threw the whole lot of them out of the hotel. On another French excursion with Irish students, the three teachers crammed a keg of Guinness into a huge duffel bag and brought the taps and all with them to Paris. They unloaded the keg and filled a bathtub with ice and between the teachers and the driver finished it in three days.

The Crush. It would seem that "love on the road" happens with some regularity. This tale could have been told to me by any number of driver-guides, but the one who told me this story apparently has a habit of attracting admirers. "Just donkeys' years ago I was taking a group of Yanks around on a week's tour. They were all from New Jersey or New York. One of them was this fine lookin' woman who had her husband with her, and they were of Irish descent. Anyway, over the course of the week, we chatted more and more and eventually, well . . . we fell into the bed. It was just a flirt, but she took it really serious. The next year and the year after that she comes back, then she asks me to do a 'car job,' where I would be drivin' her and just herself like. So I think it would be good, because she tips well (always flashin' the cash like). Now, I'm married like and I have a girlfriend (which yer ones don't know about), so when this one shows up I'm in an uncomfortable position, because I want to be with my girlfriend, who is hiding in my hotel room, but this one is thinking I'll be diving in the scratcher with her. Anyway, after a week, my girlfriend has had enough, because she's copped on to what's going on , and I go to Miss New Jersey and tell her that I'm not going to sleep with her. So, she writes me this long letter saying she 'craves' me and would do anything and all kinds of shite. That was three years ago, and I don't go a week without hearing something from this woman. And just last week she rang me saying she was coming back and wanted me to drive her again. Ahh, yeah. Things like this happen all the time like."

MANAGING THE JOB

As is clear from the narratives above, managing the job of driver-guide is not a simple task. This section addresses health issues for the drivers and for others; emergencies and how they occur, are avoided, and taken care of; and social behaviors, communication, family and separation, temptations that happen during long separations, and interactions with management. Again, the multiple roles and complex tasks required of driver-guides are fundamental to understanding their interactions with clients; they are also central to maintaining the Ireland of the tourist imagination. The fine lines of the job are often difficult to negotiate and may not be readily visible to those unfamiliar with the world of the driver-guide.

Health, Safety, Emergencies

No matter how well-planned a tour is, problems related to health and safety can occur. In the past, driver-guides would have been willing to lend a hand in cases of injury or other health emergencies, but recent legislation has limited their role. Driver-guides can only notify gardai of emergencies and arrange for transport to medical facilities. Nonetheless, they must know the proper sequence of communications and have the ability to convey the procedures to their passengers.

Tour coach drivers have reported any number of medical emergencies, including heart attacks, deaths, broken bones, allergic reactions, flu, and other illnesses. To best serve their clients, drivers must know when and how to act and when to leave the decisions to the passengers. Tactful and proper action must be taken without passengers becoming implicated in causing or prolonging the emergency. One driver related the story of an elderly man who passed away while on the coach. He was seated by himself with a light blanket pulled up to his chin. Realizing something was not well, the driver tactfully let his other passengers off the coach at their hotel while telling "Joe" to remain where he was. He and "Joe" had made a habit of taking a pint together before dinner, so the other passengers were comfortably unaware of his condition. Once his passengers had disembarked, he took the man to a medical facility, where he was pronounced dead, and then returned to the group where he relayed the unfortunate news. Given the current requirements and the context of the tour, this was the only way forward despite the hardship it caused for this driver, who reportedly still worries when he sees passengers sleeping on his coach. Other drivers have informed me of people breaking arms because they missed a step climbing off the bus, stomach viruses that passed through the entire group (including the driver), vomiting on the coach, people being hit by cars while crossing streets, and one passenger who had his foot run over by a bus that was attempting to leave a car park. It would be hard to find another occupation that deals with episodes such as these as common occurrences and part of a day's work.

Behavior and Communication

Communication is central to a successful tourism experience for both the tourist and the driver-guide. Coach drivers are trained to communicate efficiently and effectively, but they can do so only within the bounds of their own language and accent, which, although expected by tourists, is often difficult for them to negotiate. Tourists have a cinematic expectation in that the Irish accents heard will be a "soft brogue," easily understandable, playful, yet lyrical. They are often not well prepared for the actuality of the lived variety of Irish accents, from the sing-song of Corkonian English to the inflections of the North. I saw many coach tourists who would not ask a driver-guide to repeat or explain something over again to avoid appearing confused or ignorant. Instead, they would ask one another what he had said, often relaying incorrect information to others. Given the number of hours that driver-guides spend on the microphone giving directions, pointing out places and landscapes, and explaining Irish culture and history, the opportunity for misunderstanding is constant. Alternatively, a few coach tourists may plant themselves in the seats directly in back of the driver and bombard him with endless questions. When this occurs, the driver then repeats the questions over the sound system so everyone will know what he is explaining. Inevitably on any given tour he answers the same questions posed by the same passengers several times.

Coach driver-guides are trained in culture, history, architecture, and heritage and spend a good deal of the day imparting their knowledge to the tour participants. Many driver-guides find it frustrating to look in the rear-view mirror and see half the coach asleep and the other half listening to portable music players; they often remark that they don't know why they bother talking at all or that they wonder why people come to Ireland to go "sight-seeing" when they spend most of their time with their eyes closed. Some drivers have tested their passengers' attention spans by telling wildly inaccurate and unbelievable tales as they drive along. Others simply stop talking altogether, passing along only necessary information, such as arrival and departure times, where and when they might be stopping for lunch, and when dinner time will be scheduled at the hotel. One driver (and I suspect others do this as well) would put his mobile phone headset on and tell his passengers he was waiting for a call from the tour company and then listen to his phone's built-in FM radio as the countryside rolled by.

Much the way there are expectations of Ireland and the Irish, there are certain expectations of the behavioral interactions between passengers and coach drivers. Although in positions of responsibility and authority, drivers are also in positions of deference, taking orders from all sides, including at times from the people on the coach. Their behavior at all times is expected to be professional, but this is complicated by the tourists' desire to be exposed to an imaginary Ireland complete with a slightly mischievous and somewhat naughty Irishman at the wheel of the coach. Driver-guides are in a constant state of behavioral role-switching, one moment in charge, the next negotiating with management personnel at hotels or in tour companies, and a moment later acting as entertainment for their clients (Figure 7.1). Unlike the driver-guides, passengers are given license to behave in amazingly unorthodox ways, often challenging the driver's patience and ability to maintain control over a tour. Drivers have reported women coming onto them in absurd situations, men

Figure 7.1 One of the many tasks a driver-guide must do is the loading and unloading of suitcases and bags. Although this appears at first glance to be a simple task, the bags must be routed to the right rooms, numbered and tagged for specific tours, and handled with care. Some passengers also overpack, and the weight can be a strain. Lost luggage is ultimately the responsibility of the guest, but it is the driver-guide who will spend hours (and sometimes days) tracking lost pieces while his guests enjoy the tour (© Kelli Ann Costa 2007).

falling down drunk on street corners trying to pick up prostitutes, and others behaving as though they were above the law by the simple virtue of their position as foreign tourist. As with health and safety issues outlined above, there are few occupations that would expect a single person to find ways to satisfactorily deal with such an array of situations while maintaining the integrity of an entire tour.

Family

On a personal level, family life can be anything but easy for coach driver-guides, many of whom spend eight to ten months a year away from home. For driver-guides living in popular tourist destinations such as Killarney, Dublin, or Galway, opportunities to steal away to spend time with family can occur on a somewhat regular basis. Other drivers, whose home base may be in less popular or rural areas, can literally go several months without seeing family, owing to the demands of their tour schedules. Many drivers have routinely missed birthdays, communions, marriages, births, and graduations among other occasions while driving tours. At first glance, this situation may appear to be grounds for leaving the touring life, but, in fact, many (if not most) drivers, once inducted into the profession, seem to have little problem being away from home. Spouses or significant others and children may feel abandoned, but the drivers themselves appear to adjust quickly to their independent nomadic lives. Constantly on the move, many have more difficulty in the readjustment to settled family life when the touring season is over than with returning to the road in the early spring.

The life of a driver-guide is primarily on the road, and they and their spouses or significant others and children must become adept at developing and maintaining long-distance relationships. Even though drivers have active social lives while on tour, they are not able to enjoy normal social or private relationships with those at home.

On average, the majority of Irish drivers currently employed in the tourism industry in Ireland are between 40 and 55 years of age and have been in coach tourism for between 15 and 25 years. Most were married before becoming drivers, and most either had children or became parents early in their careers. Drivers are unable to participate fully in the lives of their children and must leave domestic decisions and challenges to their spouses, including such things as dealing with childhood maladies, school issues, and adolescence. Separation and distance become the norm, leading to periods of discomfort upon their return in the late autumn. One driver, whose son was born a few months before his tour schedule started, remarked that when he returned home after ten months, his son no longer knew him and for several weeks wouldn't allow him to hold him or play with him. For several years, this happened each time his season ended, and he blames his job for the rather cool relationship he has with his son some 17 years on. It must be said that drivers have the choice to leave the profession, and many have and do. Those who remain in the job tend to have personalities appropriate for the demands of the profession, and many remarked that they would feel trapped in any other situation. One wonders if such a situation would include a "normal family life as well."

One driver remarked that drivers get "October-itis" as the season winds down and they begin to "switch off" and look forward to being home, but he added that the feeling is temporary and often followed by an oppressive need to be on the move within a few weeks. Many go on family holidays during the off-season, but there also are a number of drivers who vacation together, going on ski trips or other activity holidays. A number of drivers also forgo the family holiday and go off by themselves for weeks at a time, placing further strain on their relationships with those at home.

Since the legalization of divorce in Ireland in the 1990s, the divorce rate among drivers has risen exponentially. One driver suggested that as many as a third of his colleagues were either divorced or separated, and many more had taken up with other partners and were maintaining double lives with wives and kids at home and significant others or girlfriends they met on the road. (A driver used the term "my lady" when referring to his long-term girlfriend, who traveled the country with him while his wife was at home raising the kids.) Because drivers and their families are a relatively small community, rumors abound between and among them. Nearly every driver who participated in this study spoke of the rumor mill and how spouses, drivers, and friends would pass stories (real or imagined) back and forth along the grapevine. Because of the nature of the rumors (and the verified occurrences of affairs, out-of-wedlock children, and one-night stands), issues of trust are commonplace among drivers' families. The same driver mentioned above added that it was not without reason that marriages were strained to the breaking point, but he suggested that the nature of the job and the physical isolation of the men from their spouses were the catalyst for these indiscretions and peccadilloes.

Temptation(s) on the Road

So, it is the physical isolation of the job that may compel many drivers to affairs and other temptations while on the road. Then again, it may just be the opportunity to play away from home. Among the most common temptations are sex, gambling, and drink, all of which are readily available. Sexual partners can be members of the tour group, and there are certain advantages to this: sexual encounters will likely never happen again with any particular person, because she or he will leave the country; the affair will be brief, owing to the touring schedule; and there's little chance for the driver's spouse to identify the person. Although drivers acknowledge the ethical dilemmas of sleeping with tourists in their care, they likewise acknowledge the availability and ease with which these sexual liaisons often take place. "These [women] just want a ride with an Irish bloke," one driver said. "As you say in the States, it's like shooting fish in a barrel, they're just there waiting to get some in." On rare occasions, affairs with tourists on the road may blossom into longer-term relationships, but maintaining them is difficult and unlikely. Most longer-term romantic relationships are with people who already live in-country but who are far enough away from the driver's home life to maintain secrecy.

Drink, because of its widespread availability and cultural attachments, is the most common distraction and temptation for driver-guides. In many larger towns and cities in Ireland, certain pubs and hotel bars are known as driver hang-outs, and there are nightly gatherings at them during tour season. In Killarney, there is a "driver's den" attached to one hotel pub where they can get together as a group without having to mingle with tourists or others staying at the hotel. Many drivers maintain a certain level of alcohol consumption for much of the time they are on tour, only occasionally going over their personal limit in the after-hours, once they are done driving for the day. A few routinely go overboard, drinking to excess, and many of these men have reputations in the industry for "reeking of drink" on the coaches in the morning and being less than cordial to passengers until they have recovered from their hangovers later in the day. There is also an enormous amount of pressure exerted on drivers to drink with tour groups during the tour, and once in the bar with a group the pints keep coming. Most drivers learn to avoid these opportunities or have formulated excuses to leave the party without offending the group before drinking gets out of hand. On some occasions, drivers simply take advantage of the free drink and enjoy a night on someone else's bankroll.

A third example of temptation on the road is gambling. Betting offices are as common in Ireland as pubs, and the culture of gambling has been part of Irish society for hundreds, if not thousands, of years. Not all drivers gamble, but those who do spend much of their free time studying racing forms and going to betting offices or racetracks to chance a few Euro (or many Euro, as the case may be). In some cases, the excitement of winning develops into an addiction that results in a pendulum of substantial financial losses and gains, adding further stress to any relationships the driver may have. Addictive behaviors regarding sex, drink, and gambling, although not inherent in the occupation, are present and acknowledged by everyone associated with the coach industry in Ireland.

Dealing with Management

An important aspect of the driver-guide's job is his constant need to deal with management associated with the tourism industry, including that of coach operators, tour companies, hotels, and sites. Driver-guides spend a good deal of their day in contact with coach operators who own the coaches they drive in order to sort out mechanical problems, scheduling of particular coaches, upcoming tours, and other aspects of the job. The relationships between drivers and their immediate superiors vary greatly from a close and friendly partnership to one of subordination. Until recently, Irish coach drivers and driver-guides had some degree of control and power regarding their own destinies within the profession; with few young drivers coming on board, older, experienced drivers held sway over the better tour jobs and could negotiate freely with coach operators for jobs best suited to their tastes. In the last few years, with the expansion of the European Union and cheap labor from Eastern Europe streaming into Ireland, many old hands have witnessed their power ebb away as their colleagues are replaced by drivers from Poland, Latvia, and Lithuania among other places. One prominent coach operator has gone so far as to recruit drivers in Poland, taking a standard coach with him and testing their driving skills on the road as well as their spoken English. This has caused many Irish coach drivers to look at other options for employment and has been a subject of discussion throughout the tourism industry in Ireland.

Feargal Barton of the Coach Tourism and Travel Council has pointed out that, unlike many other tourism destinations in Europe, people who come to Ireland on a coach tour expect Irish staff on the tour (personal communication 2007). In Ireland, the coach tourist has certain expectations that are not common elsewhere: they expect a certain vision of Ireland and they expect everyone associated with the tour to be Irish. The bulk of the responsibility of delivering these expectations falls on the coach driver-guide, who not only must live up to these sometimes unreasonable and anarchic beliefs but must also guarantee a smooth and well-organized tour. The influx of foreign drivers may not only have a negative effect on the Irish driving force but may also have a backlash effect on tourism in general in Ireland. Already, hotel and bar staffs are becoming less Irish, and complaints about misunderstandings and break-downs in communication are commonplace among tourists visiting throughout Ireland. In late 2006, a coach operator, low on staff and needing to send a coach out on a Kerry run, sent a non-national driver out to do the job. He successfully drove out to the pick-up destination, but shortly after picking up his pas-sengers he got lost, ran the bus off the road, and then departed on foot, leaving the entire busload of passengers stranded for several hours. Despite this and other similar incidents, drivers fear that any rocking of the management boat will result in an accelerated turnover of drivers. Unable to come together effectively enough to form a labor union, drivers have found themselves relatively powerless in their ability to negotiate with coach operator management. Many believe that they will be placed in increasingly subordinate positions over time just to maintain what little influence they currently hold. With the 2009 downturn in the economy, many drivers are finding even fewer opportunities to earn a living as tourism projections for the year drop, reinforcing their feelings of powerlessness.

Management personnel at hotels and sites can also be challenging. Tour operators may schedule hotel nights for a specific number of people, but it is left to the coach driver-guide to work out when the group can arrive and when dinners and breakfasts can be scheduled, and to iron out any difficulties that may arise. Again, driver-guides spend a good deal of time phoning hotels in order to resolve any conflicts of schedule or trying to organize last-minute changes regarding room needs, dietary requests, and other such demands. Room assignments can be extremely delicate issues as groups become aware of others' room sizes or locations within the hotel. Drivers are often pressed into service to have people shifted around the hotel and are often assumed to be responsible for one person's room being somewhat nicer than another's. Drivers, however, are often put into converted broom closets with windows that don't open or that are located over the noisiest part of the hotel, while their passengers complain about the turn-down service.

Site managers are contacted throughout a tour as scheduling shifts and changes owing to unforeseen difficulties such as road works, weather, and traffic. Drivers believe that most site managers do their utmost to accommodate incoming tours, but they do also acknowledge that some site managers play favorites depending on the type of tour or number of guests. The greater the number of people and more exclusive the tour, the more cash flows into the site. Again, although tour operators may issue vouchers for site visits and work these costs into the tour, they do not normally schedule the actual visits. This responsibility is left to the driver-guide, who must call days (and sometimes weeks or months) in advance to make sure the passengers get what they pay for. I observed one driver on a large tour in 2007 who had to juggle several site visits and rearrange them because of weather constraints. Before the tour started, he had phoned the sites that were located throughout Northern Ireland and Donegal and set up a schedule that satisfied both him and the site managers. Unfortunately, the weather, which had been warm and sunny, turned gray, wet, and windy, making some of the scheduled visits hazardous. Two sites were unable to accommodate his requests for changes, so he deftly found alternative site visits, explained the situation to his passengers, and led them on a genuine adventure to two sites he had never been to. He eagerly joined in the visits, met the managers of the sites, and established new relationships with them. His passengers, although initially disappointed with the change, were delighted at the end of the day, and many mentioned in their post-tour surveys how enjoyable the day turned out.

The job of coach driver-guide is a much more complex one than that described by either Annette Jorgensen (2003) or Bob McKercher and Hilary du Cros (2002). Made to appear as a simple job done by equally simple men, it is a difficult task that is mostly invisible to the casual observer's eye. Driver-guides do indeed drive the bus and give their own synopsis of Ireland as they move along the countryside, but it is the unseen and undetected characteristics of their occupation that make the visible aspect of their jobs appear simple. Minus the drivers' adeptness at juggling multiple tasks, roles, and skills at a moment's notice, the coach tourism industry anywhere in the world would be anything but successful.

The following section discusses how coach driver-guides, in addition to the demands outlined above, communicate Irish heritage to the uninitiated.

COMMUNICATING THE HERITAGE LANDSCAPE

When planning a coach tour to Ireland, potential visitors are initiated through a series of images and narratives that describe a cultural heritage beginning deep in the mists of time. The temporal distance is so great that most visitors who partake in the tours have no real frame of common reference from which to draw analogous experience. As suggested, they are drawn to the landscape and the culture through these visual and written enticements, and they expect their tour to be supported through a set of verbal narratives that will be equally provocative. It is the driver-guide's task to satisfy their expectations.

In most cases, there is little choice in what heritage sites are chosen and visited on a given tour. Coach tours are preplanned and "packaged" with a prescribed series of sites scheduled that are representative of Irish culture and history. Although individual drivers may not share the tour operator's choice of representative sites, they will do their best to deliver the sites as symbols of not only a hoped-for Ireland but also an authentic Ireland. The better their delivery, the more genuine the experience is for their visitors. Driver-guides are not expected to join their groups on site visits, but many go along to see how site presentations have changed, if the tour narratives have been revised in any way, and to gather additional information on particular sites to strengthen their own pre- and post-arrival presentations. They often look for links between sites and refer back to them throughout tours, helping to contextualize Ireland temporally, spatially, and physically for their passengers. Most are also very successful in finding ways to incorporate the conjoining landscapes within their narrative, creating a regional, provincial, or national conflation of Ireland's histories. While this approach serves to collapse Ireland in a number of ways, these methods of heritage presentation annotate the more complete histories readily available to those who wish to pursue them once the tour is complete. It also helps create narrative flashpoints for visitors that can be repeated to those at home, adding authority and authenticity to the visitor's own post-tour presentations.

Misunderstanding Heritage

As with any discursive exchange, communicating heritage is not without misunderstanding and confusion. Again, owing to the often highly mythologized impression of Ireland that many tourists bring with them, the heritage presented is often not the heritage desired. There is a tendency among many visitors to hear only what they feel best represents their own imagined Ireland. This situation can often lead to heated discussion among coach tourists and between tourists and driver-guides. It is at this point when the local knowledge and training of the driver-guide are usurped by the imagination and memorialized cultural landscapes of the visitor. For example, while observing visitors at the Loughcrew Megalithic Cemetery in County Meath, I watched as several people gathered around a man from Australia who fancied himself a Druid. He explained at length that their driver-guide had misinformed them about the cairns, because in truth they had been built by his Druid ancestors as a center for ritual and sacrifice. He suggested that the driver's explanation (that Loughcrew was a passage tomb cemetery over 5,000 years old) was told in order to keep Druidic Orders away from the site. The people gathered around him asked for further magical explanations of Ireland, preferring a fictionalized tale over the factual one of the driver-guide. He neglected to say (and perhaps did not know) that druids were not in Ireland 5,000 years ago; that there is no indication of sacrifice at Loughcrew (human or animal); or that Celtic culture, to whom the druids belonged, may not have reached Ireland in any great numbers. By the time the Celts may have migrated to Ireland, Loughcrew and other passage tombs would have lain abandoned for nearly 3,000 years. But where's the romance in that? The driver-guide, upon the group's return to the coach, found it difficult to argue against the fanciful logic of his mystical guest and indeed found the balance of the tour a chore—because his "power" was taken by the modern-day magician from Oz.

Lethargy and Tourist Participation

An equally difficult challenge in the communication of the heritage is overcoming a group's boredom and lethargy. On a three-week tour of heritage sites in the early summer of 2007, I observed a group of about 20 university students with attitudes that ranged from mild distraction to complete tedium. Despite their professed interest in archaeology, heritage, and culture, few could muster the energy to even listen to what their driver-guide would say on the approach to sites. Their first and strongest inclination was to slump down in their seats and strap on their mp3 players, tuning out the countryside and the narrative. After a while, the driver-guide switched off the microphone and chatted with me. He suggested that he couldn't compete with technology and that any further guiding would be a waste of his time and energy. Instead, I received a lovely and insightful private tour of a part of Ireland I was relatively unfamiliar with from a man who was full of local knowledge and pride for the area. The students had no idea what they had missed, nor did they seem to care. Before our arrival at a major heritage site later that day, most students had drifted off to sleep and had to be awakened before disembarking. Needless to say, those who slept through the narrative were unprepared for the site visit and spent a good deal of time wondering exactly where they were and what they were doing there.

Driver-guides are also challenged with cross-cultural communication, especially when the language(s) of their passengers differ from their own. Though many driver-guides are proficient in more than one language (another fact of the job that goes unrecognized), it is often the case that last-minute scheduling of tours link together tourists who speak one language and a guide who speaks another. Not only does this situation complicate the interpretation of Ireland's culture to those on the coach, it makes simple day-to-day tasks equally difficult. For example, a driver-guide might be ending one tour and not have another scheduled for several days. The coach operator cannot allow the coach to remain idle and will put the coach and driver-guide on any of the tours the operator may have coming in. Driver-guides have been assigned Italian, Japanese, French, German, and other tours even though they may have no knowledge of the language of their guests, and their guests have little to no knowledge of English. One driver-guide related an incident (to be repeated throughout the tour) that occurred with a French group: the French tour guide (he had been assigned as driver) spoke no English and he spoke no French; even after giving very simple instructions regarding the time allotted for lunch and writing down the time they should return to the coach, the guide gave the wrong instructions, and the tour group returned to the coach after only 20 minutes instead of 60, as the driver had indicated. They milled around outside the coach in inclement weather while the driver relaxed in a cafe enjoying a leisurely lunch. Upon his return they were irate, not understanding that the guide had been the one mistaken, not he. He also noted that the tour guide had no previous experience in Ireland and read notes from a sheet of paper, barely acknowledging the actual sites and landscape as they passed by the window. Without a background in the language, he was unable to tell exactly what she was reporting, but his position as driver also prevented him from interfering in the communication or adding his own narrative to hers. He had no way of assessing the success of the tour and spent the entire week writing meal and departure times down for the guide so that the group had some degree of structure.

The challenges and tasks of the coach driver-guide far exceed what most of their passengers, employers, and contractors may recognize. As suggested throughout this chapter, the daily expectations of the job include such mundane things as helping people on and off the coach and the obvious task of driving. It is the less visible aspects of the job of coach touring that make the job of the driver-guide so complex. Along with the daily expected work of driver-guiding are the unrecognized and the unexpected chores, the hours spent on the telephone arranging the day, the time estranged from family, the temptations that occur on the road, and the challenge of living closely with large groups of strangers who cycle in and out on a weekly basis. As lynchpins in the huge tourism industry, coach driver-guides leave each morning shouldering enormous responsibility for their guests, their employers, and the business of coach touring in general.

CHAPTER 8

Components of Irish Coach Tourism

TOUR COMPANIES, THE TOURIST, AND BRAND IRELAND

Tour companies, and others involved in the business of tourism, understand the tourist quite differently than social scientists do. They also understand the nature of tourism differently. Ultimately, it is a form of commerce based on the movement of people from one area of the world to another (preferably one your company promotes) for a period of time and for a particular, or variety of, particular reasons. It is similar to a game of chess: the tourist is a pawn, moved by the chess master (the tour company or destination depending on circumstance); the place is the board. The tour itself is the game—the better the tour, the greater the chess master. The number of tourists per year and the amount that tourists spend are the measure of success.

This is, of course, an oversimplification. Tour companies seek out a particular tourist seeking particular experiences. For example, someone booking a week in a self-catering apartment on Gran Canaria would likely not be seeking the same type of holiday experience as someone who has booked a coach tour in Austria or a climbing holiday in Nepal. The sought-after experiences are different, and tour companies must know not only their clients (and potential clients) but exactly what they can offer them. Product must match client expectations as closely as possible. Tour companies, tourism organizations, government departments responsible for tourism—all have a hand in developing the destination through advertising, grooming, specialized accommodation, activities, and seasonal appeal.

The branding of Ireland through people, pace, and place seems an almost organic decision. The idea of Ireland already existed in the minds of those compelled to visit before the brand was developed. Bord Fáilte (later Fáilte Ireland) needed only to tease out the components of that idea and turn them into a highly recognizable presentation that not only would resonate with the visiting public but also was believable and doable. According to Anthony Foley and John Fahy, the relationship between brand promise and brand performance, once a fairly straightforward endeavor, has become increasingly more complex as consumers have grown more sophisticated and wary (2004: 210). In the case of tourism marketing, "destinations are not [necessarily] perceived as brands by the general public" (ibid.), but challenges remain. The images of place must be consistent with the impression of place. Ireland is envisioned as essentially rural and sparsely populated, although in recent years its cosmopolitan urban edge has also become part of the branding. Additionally, the images and presentations of Ireland are perceived and understood not only by those outside the country but also by the Irish themselves, adding to the self-consciousness of simply being Irish in Ireland (O'Toole 1999). Should the image not match and the expectation not be met, satisfaction levels decrease among visitors, as has been clear in visitor attitude surveys conducted over the last several years that have shown that "friendly people" quotients have declined (Fáilte Ireland 2005e). I would strongly suggest that the images of a "premodern" state filled with rural peasants have essentially been replaced in much advertising with images of landscapes with few or no people, with urban landscapes bustling with activity, and with photographs of Irish people in service positions such as those shown in the Brendan Tours brochure described earlier.

The Tourist: Self-Defined

Tourists hate being called "tourists." The vulgar and low-brow impression of tourists with their cameras, bad clothes, pack mentality, and lack of sophistication is not an identity that many people would voluntarily seek out. Theorists and the tourism industry understand tourists as very different beings altogether: on the one hand, they are socially inept, predatory, intrusive, and dissatisfied with their lives; on the other, they are consumers, target audiences, commodities, and clients. But how do tourists understand tourists? How do they understand themselves and their activities? Without the veil of industry or academy, can the tourist define him- or herself? Following is a suite of responses to these questions asked of tourists to Ireland over the course of 2006 and 2007. The ideas and thoughts expressed by the people visiting Ireland vary widely, at times coming close to academic notions, but in most cases tourists understand their roles and activities in much more complex ways than the scholars do. They also understand themselves as much more than mere consumers or target audiences.

1. Are you a tourist? "Am I a tourist? I suppose in some ways I am, but I really don't like to think of myself as one. I mean, I've been to Ireland many times so I know the country pretty well and I can get around. I don't go in for the kitschy stuff, no Ireland T-shirts, ya know? I guess when I'm on the bus a lot of people would see me as a tourist, but I think I prefer to call myself a cultural traveler or something. If I were here for my first trip I might describe myself differently, but after being here four times—and this being my fifth—I'd have to say I'm not your everyday tourist."—Connie, 49, USA

"No. Absolutely not. Tourists run in around in mobs. We're here finding our roots."—Jim, 31, and Marie, 31, USA

"I think the bus—or *coach*—gives other people the impression that I'm a tourist. I'm not though. I have a reason for being here. My family is Irish."—No name given (male), 26, USA

"God, am I a tourist? Let's see. I'm here with a bunch of people I've never met on a bus riding around a country I've never been to in weather only ducks would like—yeah, I'm a tourist."—Don, 34, Canada

"Just because I'm on a tour doesn't make me a tourist. I'll appreciate the trip when I get home. A tourist just wanders around taking pictures not mixing with the locals. I'll walk into a pub or a store and you can't tell I'm not from here—except when I start to talk. But this guy in Killarney who was waiting tables said I could do a really good fake accent, so even he was fooled. Tourist? No way."—"Trevor," 42, USA (Trevor also told me it wasn't his real name.)

2. Who is a tourist? What makes someone a tourist? "A tourist is someone who goes on an organized trip somewhere and doesn't actually have a real personal agenda except to see a place. They just want to see things and go to a lot of places. Like people who go to the beach for a break or a vacation, I wouldn't say they were really tourists. People who might go to Egypt to see pyramids would be."—Lynn, 39, USA

"I would be a tourist right now, because I'm letting someone else do the work for me. For instance, the driver is driving the bus and doing the guiding, someone else did all the hotel organizing, somebody else took care of the flights, all I had to do was show up at the airport on time and the rest is taken care of. I like it. No worries. I just sit back and let Ireland come to me—what could be better? I don't think everyone would feel that way—in fact, I know some people on this trip don't like all the organization, but I do. I want to relax and see the country, enjoy the scenery, the food, the company, have a beer in the evening, and have a good time. Other people might be coming to Ireland for other reasons, like finding family or something. I came to see some of it and relax. So far that's exactly what I've done."—Joe, 66, USA

"I think a tourist is someone who goes someplace they aren't really familiar with and stays for a vacation, then goes home. If they're just going somewhere close, like Disney® or something, they aren't really tourists; they have to be going somewhere a little farther afield like Canada or China or Ireland. They can't be going on business either; they have to be going on a vacation."—Jenna, 19, USA

"A tourist would be anybody who is traveling in a place they don't live in. They can't be traveling because of a job or something urgent like a family issue though. They'd have to be traveling to do sightseeing and things like that. And they have to be away for more than a few hours, more like a few days or a few weeks. It can't be a place that's around the corner either. Like I live in Toronto [Canada] and last year I went to Amish Country in Pennsylvania. I was a tourist then. But I also went to Montreal. I wouldn't say I was a tourist then, even though I rarely go to Montreal. So, yeah, it has to be somewhere exotic or different, and you have to be there longer than a day."—Kenneth, 29, Canada

3. What do tourists do? "They spend a lot of time looking at places and going to shops. They collect a lot of things along the way, too, souvenirs and the like. I think it's important for people to go to new places and learn about other cultures. I'm not sure all tourists would be doing that—at least not intentionally—but in the end, if they are in a new place and spending time there, that's what's happening. I think tourists learn about the places and people without really knowing it, too. I mean, they aren't in a place for the learning experience, but they end up learning anyway. But mostly they look around and buy things that will remind them of their trip and make other people aware that they've been somewhere interesting or different."—Lynn, 39, USA

"They jam up Grafton Street."—Enda, 17, Dublin

4. Are tourists a good thing? Who isn't a tourist? "I hate tourists, especially American ones. They have no clue how to behave when they're away from home. Just no class whatsoever. I'm an American, and I do my best to stay away from most of the other Americans on this tour. I guess tourists are a good thing, because they spend a lot of money in the places they go to see, and Ireland would go broke without them. I'm not a tourist though. I know how to behave in foreign places."—"Trevor," 42, USA (Trevor went on to snap his fingers at the waitress and yell for a pint while eating his chips with his fingers.)

"Tourists are a very good thing, aren't they? I guess I should say 'we.' We are a good thing. We bring a lot of money into the places we visit, and we keep economies going in some cases. We show foreign people our culture and we learn about theirs, what could be bad about that? I like touring and seeing new places, meeting new people and things like that. Some people aren't tourists, just travelers. Like I would say students who are away studying at school aren't tourists, like the ones from the States we met at Trinity [College] this morning. Business people, they aren't tourists. You have to be on a trip for enjoyment to be a tourist."—Claire, 44, USA

"Good for who? It depends. I'm not saying tourists go out of their way to cause damage or disruption, but just look at the traffic here [in Dublin]. Look at all the people; it's wall to wall everywhere. At the same time, they're spending money like it's going out of style. You can't tell me things would be this crazy and modern here if all these people weren't pouring in everyday. Tourists cause crowds, and they make my trip less enjoyable. I'm not a tourist. I'm not on one of those awful buses being driven around. I rented a car, and I go where I want. Tourists don't do that, they move around in big groups with guides. I do everything independently. It's tourists that have made Ireland such a crowded, crazy place."—Cassandra, 32, USA (When I mentioned Ireland's economic position in the world [in 2006], Cassandra corrected me, saying that I clearly was confused and that shops such as Brown Thomas wouldn't be for the Irish, because they couldn't afford it. I asked if she had shopped there, and she said it was far too expensive for her tastes. I reminded her that Dublin was home to over a fifth of Ireland's population, and Cassandra responded by saying: "Maybe, but that's like, what, 200,000 people out of a million?")

"Of course tourists are a good thing. Tourism is a good thing. Look at the trip we're on, for example. Ten days, we see an awful lot of Ireland, we have time to spend on our own getting to know the place and the people, we have a great driver in Lesley who takes care of us, we have no hassles. It's like a big cultural exchange—we learn about Ireland, the Irish learn about us. Not that there would be that much to learn, but you know what I mean. I think a lot of people who come to Ireland on these tours don't have an inkling about how mature a country Ireland is, how strong its economy is, how it is seen by the rest of the world. Some Americans still have a notion that Ireland is a rural backwater sometimes. But, with the internet, more people who visit Ireland are much more prepared for the sophistication of the country, the city life, the great food, nice hotels—all the things you would want on a vacation. And if you have a good guide like Lesley, you can ask questions and learn even more. I think we're all tourists at heart, don't you? We're just curious about things and other people."—Rob, 46, and Sarah, 41, USA

The Tourist and the Coach Driver

The relationship between tourists and the men who drive the coaches varies as widely as the responses to some of the questions above. In some cases, there is very little that could be called a relationship, such as when a coach driver is just the driver. Many tour operators and tour guides don't like anything more than necessary communication between clients and drivers, and I have both witnessed and heard of guides reprimanding drivers who do chat with clients while on tour. In many cases, the tour guide may feel as though the driver is invading his territory, but underlying some cases is the status hierarchy of the tour structure; the coach driver occupies the bottom of that hierarchy. Like a child in Victorian England, he is seen and not heard, speaks only when spoken to, and is present but invisible.

In other cases, such as when he acts as the driver-guide, the relationship is much stronger and emotional, although mostly one-sided. He is the tourists' conduit to the culture—he organizes everything, keeps them on time, gets them around safely, regales them with stories of Ireland, and digs them out of any variety of jams they get themselves into. In this case he "belongs" to his clients, and many of them quickly bond to him as their very own Irishman. This bonding—and the individual driver's ability to negotiate it—underlies the overwhelmingly positive responses to coach touring experiences in Ireland (Fáilte Ireland 2005d). It also conjures emotional attachments, enhancing the depth of the experience, positive or negative, of the coach tourists. They remark that they "love" their driver, that he "made the trip," or (rarely) that he "disappointed" them.

A rather low-budget tour in the spring of 2007 was surveyed for this project. Despite very poor ratings of accommodation, site visits, and meals, only one in 38 participants gave a less than excellent rating to their driver-guide. The one who did remarked that it was his doing that meals were bland and that more time was not allocated at certain site stops such as Newgrange. These problems were clearly not the driver-guide's fault, and he had no way of controlling food quality or site visit duration, both of which are dictated by outside forces. At the same time, the professionalism of the driver-guide, when mentioned in surveys or in interviews, is usually linked to expected Irish traits—wit, humor, storytelling and such—but rarely to his ability to organize, to drive, or to solve problems. It may be that these traits are taken for granted or equally that tourists assume that other people (such as the tour organizers) have taken care of everything ahead of time. Most tourists are unaware of the amount of "on the fly" organizing a driver-guide must do. The relationships between tourist and driver-guide will be further discussed below.

THE TOURIST EXPERIENCE IN IRELAND

As discussed, people visit Ireland for any number of reasons, but their reasons for visiting are not the sum total of their actual experience. The tourist experience includes far more than the reasons for traveling to a particular place. It includes things as mundane as the weather, the screaming child in the seat next to them on the plane, and the serendipitous chat with an old friend at Bewley's Cafe on Grafton Street in Dublin. It includes the unexpected, unprepared-for experiences, as well as the repetitive ones such as the climb onto the tour bus and the fry-up at breakfast. Some tourists seek out new experiences while on tour; others seek something that feels like a familiar living memory; and others may have no notion of what they seek, but when they find it, they'll know it.

This section examines the experiences of tourists in Ireland. A common thread here is the reason for choosing Ireland as a destination. Another is the sought-after memories created by the physical and emotional journey of traveling to Ireland—the unique and out-of-the-ordinary occasion of being in Ireland. The liminality of Ireland in relation to the coach tourist is central to understanding their presence there as a transcendent experience, one that does change a person's life. Tourists are physically removed from home, by their own choice, and placed into a culture that is at once familiar and foreign. Time is measured differently—they are on a wholly alien schedule, governed by someone else, and they must comply. They may be on a coach with people they don't know. They may be sleeping in a different part of the country every night. The place and the people are different, new, exotic, and temporary. In a literal sense, for the tourist, the destination exists only while they are physically present in it. Once they get back on the coach and are moving onto their next destination, they are suspended in a state of anticipation, the previous site now a memory and a topic of discussion. Their destination-world proceeds as a cinematic experience, unfolding in front of and around them. One tourist remarked that it was "like it was happening to someone else" and that he "was watching what was happening from a grandstand" (Personal communication 16 June 2006). Much like a traumatic experience, the tourism experience can feel somewhat unreal.

From an anthropological standpoint, the actual felt experience of the tourist has rarely been examined. Instead, tourism and tour-ists are objects that perform and occur. How tourists feel about their own touristic adventures and non-adventures has not been the subject of study *per se* but has been easily speculated on and viewed from above. The experience has been called "transformative," a "mediated activity," "harmful," and "inau-thentic." Rarely have the tourists themselves been asked about their experiences, or asked to consider what these experiences may mean. Anthropologists also rarely act as participants, de-pending more on observation from afar, post-tour discussion, document analyses, eavesdropping, or their own often jaded opinions of the tourist and the tourist industry. Exceptions are Edward Bruner and Barbara Kirshenblatt-Gimblett, both of whom have served as tour directors and guides on several occasions.

As mentioned earlier, the tourist experience in Ireland begins long before the actual arrival. In many cases, the tourist experience begins with family memories, exotic fabrications of place, movie trailers, or literary references. The power of suggestion in the realm of the touristic experience cannot be undervalued (Nash 2003; O'Connor 2003). Richard Prentice and Vivien Andersen have called this "evocation" and recognize it as a sensory process that begins through developing a familiarity with a destination through image, or, in some cases, imagination (2000). "For persons who have not visited a destination, image can be regarded as a pre-taste of a destination, leading to expectations about it" (ibid.: 492). They also suggest that potential visitors to destinations are attracted through marketing schemes that include "generic dimensions" that are easily recognizable across cultures, such as dance, art, music, and literature (ibid.: 494). They indicate that manipulation of the imagery in pretrip materials in these cases is utilized to evoke emotional responses to a destination brand. In Ireland, the imagery constantly evokes the brand triumvirate of people, pace, and place.

Tourists from America who visit Ireland overwhelmingly claim some familiarity with the country, whether it be due to family relationships or descent that may be several generations past. As David Lowenthal has written, many may also carry images of Ireland that are not their own (1985). Prentice and Andersen support Lowenthal:

> Non-visitors may hold complex images of destinations, gained from study or personal contacts with tourists or nationals. Family contacts in particular within a destination may lead not only to an increased propensity to visit but may also lead to complex images being held by family members who have never visited it. At its most extreme, the destination may be in essence "lived" in another place. . . . (2000: 495)

Michael Cronin uses the Irish Tourism Board publication *Ireland of the Welcomes* as an example of a preparatory device that many consumers of Ireland have utilized in establishing these destination images (2003). A magazine in circulation since the 1950s, *Ireland of the Welcomes* both represents Ireland to the nonvisitor as a glossy holiday, "a nomadic encounter with the culture, mediated through print and illustration" (Rojek and Urry 1997: 1–19, cited in Cronin 2003: 181) and serves a rhetorical function based on imagined ideas of who the visitor to Ireland is and what he or she expects. These images of expectation, as well as the actions of expectation or activities of expectation, are central to pre-forming the tourist experience.

Authenticity

Although an authentic experience may be important to the visitor, that authentic experience is preconceived and highly anticipated. It is waiting to happen. It is based to a high degree on imagery and expectation, rather than on something that may actually exist or have any possibility of happening. This feeling of intense expectation is particularly true of visitors to Ireland who anticipate their visit with powerful emotions and, again, that notion of connectedness or familiarity so common among them. An "authentic" experience must include Guinness Stout, hours spent in pubs, a visit to Newgrange or Cobh or Trinity College Book of Kells. And it must meet to some degree the romantic notion of the island of Ireland: the ethereal, stuck in the distant past, land of lads and lasses that is timeless, has forty shades of green, is slightly regressive, and is an altogether "airy-fairy realm" (Witoszek 2002: 347). But, this is the anticipated, the hoped-for Ireland. The real Ireland (not necessarily the same as the authentic Ireland in this sense) may never even be recognized or acknowledged by some visitors, who may float through their visit with their feet never actually touching the ground. The real Ireland may be a surprise; it may disappoint; it may be brushed off as "not Irish." For the tourist experience in Ireland to be positive, it must come very close to meeting the pre-experience expectations. How authentic that experience may be largely depends on how well the visit translates into an acceptable ideal for the individuals who participate in the touristic endeavor.

Attractions

Tourist destinations must also have attractions, or "demand generators" (McKercher and du Cros 2002). Attractions are assets and products; they are part of the process of commodity production and exchange in the world of tourism. Based on the work of Mill and Morrison (1985), McKercher and du Cros define a three-stage hierarchy of attractions: primary attractions are so important to most destinations that they play a critical role in shaping their image and influencing visitation; secondary attractions may be locally significant tourist attractions that complement the tourism experience; and tertiary attractions are largely convenience-based or occur by happenstance (2002: 109–110). They suggest that the greater the distance a consumer has to travel to a site, the more spectacular or unique it has to be (ibid.). They also indicate that "the more dominant the attraction is, the greater the sense of obligation to visit" (ibid.: 31). Attractions often attain this level of significance because of their symbolic importance to a nation or culture, such as the Arlington Cemetery or the General Post Office, through their natural beauty, such as Victoria Falls or the Giant's Causeway, or through their historic importance, such as Gettysburg or the Hill of Tara.

Whatever their status, tourists actively (sometimes inactively) engage with the attraction. According to Adrian Franklin, this engagement is because "tourists have an intimate and complex relationship *with* tourist sites, heritage buildings, museum artifacts, art gallery objects, souvenirs and postcards, cameras and videos, foods and drinks, tickets and passports, planes and trains" (and I would add coaches) (2003: 101). He goes on to suggest that in many cases this form of engagement involves a process of "interpellation," whereby an object (which could include sites, centers, works of art in museums, as well as kitsch) "speaks" to an individual in a deeply meaningful way, binding him or her not only to a moment in time but also to a place, an event, or a community that has also experienced a similar sense of connection (ibid.: 132). The collection of things, whether souvenirs, postcards, pebbles, dried flowers, or photographs, extends this interpellative experience into the post-event, back to the lived world and beyond the liminal space of the touristic experience.

Over and above the abundance of tangible attractions so well known in Ireland are the intangible attractions of memory, mythos, spirituality, and reputation. These can also be understood as primary attractions and may be equally appealing to the consumer of Ireland. Visitors may go to Newgrange, the Skelligs, the Burren, or the Ring of Kerry, because "they are there," but, according to many visitors, they are "drawn" or "compelled" to visit. In the course of planning a month-long study trip to Ireland with university students from Franklin Pierce College, I asked students to choose a variety of places they would like to go to and to write down the reasons why they wanted to go there. The majority of students chose places they described as having spiritual value, whether these values were Christian, Celtic, or prehistoric. When asked why they had decided to accompany me to Ireland when other field-school options were available at a much more affordable price, students overwhelmingly suggested that Ireland was a special place, full of meaning and history, a place they wanted to partake of. Many believed that it would be a life-changing and renewing experience. One student wrote:

> Just the thought of climbing up to the tombs at Loughcrew and
> running my fingers along the rock art makes me want to cry
> with joy. I can't wait to shed this old skin of mine and commune
> with my ancient self. For the first time in 15 years of school I'm
> excited about learning, about *being*.

Although clearly tinged with what Rojek would call "the cult of nostalgia" and a bit of bottled Celtic mysticism, the intangible qualities, the romance of Ireland, are as important to this student's decision making as are the tangible ones. There is a longing in the writing, a desire to feel the culture and the place, to affect change— not to Ireland but to or within oneself. It is, as Franklin would say, "the pleasure of possessing something in the imagination" (ibid.: 180). Nina Witoszek calls this the "prolonged agony of Romantic Ireland," the intangible and ethereal magnetism that attracts so many to its shores, a "fatal attraction of the Irish mystique" (2002: 345). Visitors want to experience the intangible, romantic Ireland; they want to feel touched somehow by a magic they are unable to articulate. Although the physical experience of Ireland may be fleeting, the psychic experience will linger, one hopes, long after they have returned to their mundane lived worlds.

Going and Being

In a coffee shop on Nassau Street in Dublin one sunny summer morning, a seasoned coach driver remarked that in his opinion ("and you can take it for what it's worth, so") most American coach tourists he hauled around Ireland were more interested in going there than actually being there. He went on to explain that too many people on his coaches were reluctant to "get on with it," meaning that they kept a careful distance from Ireland, they saw it but didn't really experience it. He told me that this was a relatively new occurrence and that it seemed Americans on the whole had become timid and cautious in some cases ("maybe it's that 9-11"). He had also seen many Americans who had a very hard time in Ireland: overdoing things, speaking too loudly, drinking too much. In their attempts to fit in, he had witnessed Americans "suiting up" by buying kitschy "Oirish" merchandise and trying to look the part or by "standing on a round" (continually buying drinks for everyone) in pubs.

Although these could be seen as more examples of finicky Americanisms, it may also be that the Ireland of recent years has become less recognizable in terms of the expectations of American tourists. The explosion of construction projects, housing estates, and office buildings, the increased traffic, the very clear displays of wealth and affluence, the increasingly consumer-driven culture that is the Ireland of the new millennium all shock rather than soothe. No matter how prepared or sophisticated the European Union or the Irish government believes its tourist population to be, the New Ireland's rapidly changing cultural landscape can be challenging for many visitors to contemplate. Despite these challenges, more than a few tourists find they are changed in significant and profound ways by the experience of Ireland. They move easily through the culture, explore it comfortably and with sincerity, observe with fresh rather than jaundiced and cynical eyes, and examine their own space and place in the world as they stand in a world removed from their own. They give Ireland and the Irish a fair shake and are touched by what they find.

Going to Ireland and *being* in Ireland can be two different things, and the coach driver above articulated this as a divergence in experiences. Going to Ireland is the passive participation often equated with mass tourism, especially that of coach tourism. Passive tourists observe the landscape and the people from a distance and interact in superficial ways with locals, often having little to no conversation beyond ordering food or asking directions. Instead, they interact with other tourists and quite often attach to their guide, driver-guide, and to a lesser degree, their driver. They are comfortable with this arrangement in most situations and make few explicit efforts to change their position as passive participants while on their tour. The notion of being "on tour" denotes a high degree of passivity; people on tour are literally sightseeing, they aren't actively learning, investing in the culture, or planning to move to the region.

Being, in contrast, involves active participation. I would suggest that few tourists have the luxury of actually being at their holiday destination or being deeply engaged with the people and place. There simply is not enough time. A week or two in a different place, especially when traveling through and across a destination as people do in Ireland, does not allow more than a tangential participation in the culture, no matter how determined the tourist may be. Despite the low opinion many scholars and others have of tourists, the fact remains that travelers, trippers, and all variety of visitor, even high-brow ones, are not fully and actively engaged with the cultures they visit—they are just passing through. *Being* also intimates a long-term association with a place and people, and in Ireland *being* often involves generations of living in a particular place. Descendants of French Huguenots who arrived in Munster 350 years ago are still considered "new" and outsiders by old Irish families in Cork. Families who may have only a generation or two in a town or village are called "blow-ins" by locals. In this context, tourists, no matter what their status, can never really "be" in the places they visit.

The Orthodoxy of Musts

Along with the difficulty of actually "being" in a destination during a coach holiday is the circumscribed route of visitation and limited selection of sites available to the coach tourist. The sites are repeated among tour operators. When viewing tour literature during pretrip planning, potential visitors to Ireland are confronted with itineraries and descriptions of places that have amazing redundancy. Even if potential visitors had no real agenda prior to studying tour literature, they can develop a desire to visit and to consume particular sites owing to the literature's repetitive emphasis on them. Much the way fast-food advertisements can make one hungry, these sites and places become part of an "orthodoxy of musts": sites that must be seen, visited, and recorded to demonstrate visitors' presence in a highly popular area that others may only dream of. As we have discussed, among the most popularized sites in the Irish orthodoxy of musts are ancient sites such as Newgrange, castles such as Trim and Ross Castle, and monastic sites such as Clonmacnoise, Glendalough, and Monasterboice. Regions such as the Ring of Kerry or Connemara are also highly touted. Tourists flock to these sites and areas that are typically included on coach tours and that construct a viewbook of Ireland that reflects the catalog of what is easily and commonly scheduled.

Coach driver-guides are challenged by this repetitive loop of sites. Although the familiarity is a positive notion in that it aids in scheduling, in finding parking, and in presenting the preparatory talk on the coach, it also can result in such numbing redundancy that driver-guides begin to script the presentation with little expression or genuine interest. Unless requested to do so by the tour operator, few driver-guides accompany their group on site visits. Instead, they spend inbound time to sites narrating, then sit idle in the coach while the visit is taken and gear up again to narrate while on the road to the next site visit. One driver-guide I interviewed in the course of this research drove the same tour every week for ten weeks, visiting the same sites, staying at the same hotels, and giving the same shop talk over and over again. "I could do it in me sleep now. Nothing about this interests me, and I'm thinking the people might have that notion too." He understood that he was taking visitors to places they might never see again, places they may have waited their entire lives to see, but he found the constricted and bounded nature of the orthodoxy of musts to be overly restrictive and stressful regarding his own part in the presentation of Ireland. He worried that his lack of interest in the tours might affect the impression of Ireland that visitors on his tours took home with them.

The Money Shot

The tourist experience anywhere would not be the same without the reproduction of memory through photography. The reproduced visual journey begins before embarkation; it begins in the preparatory phase with the review of the destination through advertising brochures, websites, a friend's or family's collected photographs. Typically, the preparatory phase is then reinforced by the in-flight "welcome film," which shows highlights of the destination, and by the airline magazine, which also splashes spectacular images of the tourist's ultimate desire (for example, Aer Lingus's film shown just before landing and its *Cara* in-flight magazine). Photographs are taken throughout all phases of the journey, including the trip to the airport, at the airport, on the plane, in the arrivals hall, on the coach or by the rental car. These are the same photographs taken by tourists everywhere. The photographs help to define and describe the liminal experience of the tourist. They will exist as substantive memory and validate or repudiate long-held assumptions of the destination. The collected photographs and those subsequently chosen by the tourist to exhibit and share with others become a distillation of the visual experience.

The "money shot" is a photograph that can be dreamed of before arrival at the destination, or it can be the photograph felt to best represent the adventure—a truly distilled memory. At heritage and archaeology sites visited by tourists in Ireland, money shots, such as the one at Malahide Castle (Figure 8.1), are used to demonstrate presence. In another example, at the Hill of Tara, the money shot inevitably is taken at the Lia Fáil, the Stone of Destiny, where tourists can be seen hugging, kissing, caressing, and gathering in large groups. "Look, we/I were/was here!" The proof is in the picture. Tourists jostle for position in front of or with the subject; they wait for the opportunity to take the "perfect shot"; they race to be the first to accomplish the task. Money shots are often copied—the Lia Fáil itself may *mean*

Figure 8.1   The "money shot" at Malahide Castle in County Dublin (© Kelli Ann Costa 2007).

nothing to some tourists, but the fact that others may be gathering for their photographs at the stone compel them to do likewise.

Understanding the Heritage Landscape

David Brett suggests that, for us to better understand the relationship between tourism and heritage, we reconcile "the heritage" as an engagement of "then" with "now" (1996). He also notes that the language of heritage tourism marketing "is being transferred from travel in space to travel in time" (ibid.: 14). Further, he proposes that the modern "preoccupation with the past is created out of the experience of continual change" (ibid.: 15), reflecting similar comments by MacCannell (1992, 1999 [1976]), Baudrillard (1988), and Eco (1986), among others.

Are coach tourists similarly preoccupied with time? With their constant inauthentic upheavals in the postmodern world? Or do they just want to see things, to walk around in new and unfamiliar spaces, and to interact with the landscape no matter what is presented? Are they more interested in collecting portable memories? Are possible preoccupations with the past linked more with consanguineal relations rather than with the inauthenticity of their lived worlds?

To contextualize the relationship between the coach tourist and the past and heritage in Ireland, the pace and continual sensory barrage of touring, stopping, moving, and experiencing must be taken account of. Tourists on tour are limited to what the tour offers: if you want to see Cork but the tour you are on doesn't go there, you won't be seeing Cork this time around. Likewise, when given leeway, tourists' choices can seem wasted. For example, on a day tour to Inishmore in the Aran Islands, a group of American tourists from the southern United States were taken out to the great stone fort of Dun Aenghus. The coach driver-guide had explained the island's most popular and famous site on the coach, and then on the shuttle to the site the shuttle driver reiterated his explanation. The explanations were well-presented, the tourists seemed interested, and many asked questions as they approached the site. However, once they were dropped on the road leading to the fort, many chose to remain in the shops near the visitor center buying trinkets, trying on "genuine Aran sweaters," and eating ice cream. They seemed satisfied to see the fort from afar (some clicked a few photographs and hurried into the shops, barely glancing at it again). The few who did walk out to the fort were pleased they had made the effort and felt that it was an exciting and interesting place, something they would remember and tell others about when they returned to the United States.

Afterward, at lunch, those who went to the fort busily showed their photos to those who chose to shop, while those who shopped busily showed their purchases to the fort visitors. Both seemed satisfied, yet both seemed to feel that they had missed out on something, vowing to either "hit the shops" at the next stop or to "see the next bit" at the following site. The time constraints of the coach tour, rather than a pre-occupation with time writ large, and what is on offer while on tour seem to be the pivotal factors in the decision making of the coach tourist.

COACH TOURISTS AND COACH DRIVER-GUIDES

Earlier in this chapter, I began a discussion of the relationships that can develop between coach tourists and their drivers or driver-guides. As suggested, these relationships can range from very superficial to extremely personal, depending on the groups and the individuals involved. In this section, I examine the varying connections that exist between tourists and drivers on the Irish heritage trail. Issues of power, status, class, and the interpretation of roles are central to understanding these relationships and setting a baseline for observing and decoding many of the verbal and nonverbal cues that pass between and among tourists, drivers, and driver-guides.

There are a number of things to keep in mind as the discussion progresses. First, even though drivers and driver-guides may at first glance appear to be a rather isolated group who spend their time being caretakers, drivers, and tour guides, in reality they are very well connected and socialize by mobile phone or in person with others in the industry and with friends and family on a regular basis. Second, although the coach tourists seem at first glance to be exposed and highly social, they are, in fact, inclined to limit their contact to others participating in the same tour. Third, very few tourists are privy to the backstages of the coach tourism industry and the amount of work and organization that is going on constantly behind the scenes. Finally, there is an assumption among most coach tourists that their driver or driver-guide is rather unmotivated, not terribly intelligent (though "well-versed"), and just getting by financially. But, he is the coach tourists' own genuine Irishman, and, usually with little encouragement, is included in group photographs or posed with wives, girlfriends, and kids as part of the coach tourists' memories of Ireland. As one coach driver said: "There's pictures of me all over the world with thousands of people."

The Interpretation of Roles, Class, and Status

When one thinks of high-status occupations in the West, "bus driver" is not one that ranks terribly high. In North America, service occupations such as driving a bus are not of particularly high status and therefore do not extend much prestige or power to the person performing the required tasks associated with them. Such impressions of prestige, power, and status are based on the social categories and roles constructed by and within individual societies and cultures. The role of bus driver implies a low form of service-related status, one based on manual labor, repetition, and, as stated above, an assumption that those performing this role also lack motivation or intelligence. Not so long ago, it was a social assumption that women were best suited to similar repetitive, "simple" tasks by virtue of their gender. Whereas today it would be considered highly discriminatory in the West to restrict women's participation in society to such roles, assumptions regarding the men who drive buses are equally limiting and made without hesitation.

Roles are the parts that individuals who are members of particular social categories or groups are expected to play in society. These established expectations make it easier to negotiate complex societies, because they lay the ground rules for what people can or should expect from one another in particular situations. Roles, and peoples' understandings of them, are linked to social status or the relative social position of individuals within society. We are not restricted to a single role or status but acquire and lose many over the course of a lifetime. "Bus driver" is generally a low-status social position, and it is assumed by many in society to be a one-dimensional role.

Coach tourists tend to understand their driver or driver-guide as equally one-dimensional: they are only bus drivers without social networks or interests outside the immediate tour, families, personal lives, or anything resembling a lived life beyond driving a bus. Allowing the bus driver to have human qualities would not only complicate the relationship between driver and tourist but in Ireland might also interfere with a tourist's impression and expectation of Ireland. An angry driver? A driver with a family emergency? A driver with plans other than escorting his group? These and other role interruptions have the potential of spoiling the nirvana of Ireland that many tourists hold in their imaginations. Ireland is idyllic (and possibly thought of as one-dimensional as well). The Irish are a class of people who are simple, happy, witty, and inviting. Irish bus drivers, as one of their main points of contact, are required to exhibit all the favorable traits of Ireland and the Irish. And they are expected to serve willingly and happily.

Drivers are equally guilty of compressing the roles of their clients. They are only "tourists"—somewhat harried, lazy, herdlike, and gullible. They require guidance, are easily confused, and like to see the places they visit from the windows of a bus. Drivers also generally possess a paradoxical understanding of status in regard to their clients. On the one hand, it is generally believed that coach tourists are of limited wealth, while, on the other hand, they are seen as having a high reserve of disposable income by virtue of their role as tourist. Drivers are also fully aware of the roles they are expected to play when engaged with their groups, and they overwhelmingly play them with little hesitation, putting off personal- and most work-related issues until they are in the privacy of their hotel rooms and away from clients. The stress of putting personal concerns off until there is private time to manage them has a multiplier effect in that those who may be involved are constantly in positions of coming second to groups of strangers on a bus. The fact that drivers and driver-guides may be miles or continents away from the genesis of a problem in their personal lives is an added dimension of difficulty. Unlike people in most other occupations, they cannot simply leave work and return home to remedy a situation. Arrangements for substitute drivers with similar qualifications and experience have to be made, and they will not be paid for days missed even in the case of an emergency.

Roles are also confusing in coach tourism. Coach driver-guides act as servant, go-between, and leader, resulting in a cycle of role-switching in which behavior moves from that of deference to command to negotiation and back again on a continual basis. To return to Bruner's idea of "borderzones," the coach driver-guide inhabits a liminal place when in contact with his groups (2004). His behavioral expectations, role(s), and status are likely entirely different from those in his "real" life. Equally true in the world of the driver-guide, tourists are both those whom they serve and those whom they teach.

Tourists can also find themselves in contradictory roles, often owing to the liminality of their position. They are served by those on the ground and are at their mercy as well. Understood as gullible or easily led, tourists, however, can be leaders in their "real" lives off the bus back home among their family or occupational peers. They may have others at their mercy on their own turf. They may be servants experiencing the role of the served and status of privilege only while on their tour. The learning curve is steep and quick and sometimes very difficult to negotiate in an abbreviated period of time. The perpetually changing landscape of the coach tourist with its constant movement and sensory exchanges may be partially responsible for the rather low opinion that many people hold of tourists in general and coach tourists in particular. Coach tourists' sensory bombardment, overload of information, jet lag, and lack of flexibility likely contribute to the sense that they lack certain qualities, such as independence, decision making ability, and self-reliance.

Scholarly assessments of coach driver-guides with regard to roles and status are nearly absent from the literature; in fact, there are few references to driver-guides in any capacity in the literature of tourism. The few that have been made treat the driver or driver-guide as part of the landscape, or as inherently unimportant to the success or failure of a tour. This dismissiveness directly conflicts with tourists' comments on their tours and with the consistently high ratings of coach tours in terms of guiding and organization (see, for example, *Fáilte Ireland* 2005e). McKercher and du Cros perhaps represent the overall view of drivers and driver-guides by scholars of tourism, suggesting that they are only and primarily qualified to drive a bus, not to instruct about their own culture (2002: 36). Although it may be true in *some* cases that the bus driver has no qualifications beyond a license to drive, in Ireland driver-guides are also natives and in a majority of cases also carry a guide badge, meaning that they have gone through state qualification and training in guiding tours at the local, regional, or national level. Opinions such as the one above are also at odds with the general opinion of much of the tourism literature, especially that of anthropologists and other social scientists. These scholars overwhelmingly suggest that local knowledge is good, positive, and authentic; that it adds a certain realism to the tourist-local encounter. They also suggest that tour guides (including driver-guides) are overly standardized, rehearsed, and inauthentic. There is no room in the discussion for those who may serve multiple roles, including that of a local, native tour guide who happens to drive a bus.

Power

Annette Jorgensen discussed issues of power during the tourism experience in her article "Power, Knowledge, and Tourguiding: The Construction of Irish Identity on County Wicklow Tour Buses" (2003). In the article (one of the few to consider power as a point of discussion regarding tour guiding), she suggests that the guide not only possesses expertise but is also a local with the flexibility of interpreting and re-interpreting sites repeatedly. For tourists to come to an understanding of a site, they must accept the guides' interpretation and point of view. Jorgensen considers this to be an incredibly compelling position for tour guides: they are looked to for their opinion, they are taken seriously, they command their audience. She firmly posits the tour guides whom she observed in Wicklow as "locals" while suggesting that their power comes from their authority as "tour guide" rather than from their local knowledge and ability to use experiential memory to interpret sites they are very familiar with.

In the case of driver-guides, power is continually negotiated between and among the stakeholders of the tour. At times, a driver-guide may be in a position of power through the use of his local knowledge, his suggestions, his experience and expertise. At other times, he is the clear subordinate, taking orders from tour operators, hotel management, coach operators, and often from his clients.

A driver discussed a particularly difficult tour he was on within the context of power and authority. A large group of Americans had come to Ireland on an *ad hoc* (self-designed) tour that included an odd combination of sites, stops, accommodations, and special tours. He admitted that it was a challenging tour from the point of view of hours on the road and far-flung destinations, but the most problematic part was the passengers, who were argumentative, clearly not getting on with one another, and overly demanding. At one point, after dropping his group at a site visit, he phoned the tour operator to explain how difficult the group was and used some colorful language in what he thought was a private discussion. Unknown to him, a passenger had chosen to remain on board the coach and was scrunched down in a seat and not visible. Having been overheard, the driver-guide, despite having done his best to accommodate his clients, was forced to make an apology to the entire group. Although the group leader later acknowledged the group's contrary disposition, he also did not hesitate in writing a letter of complaint to the tour operator, vilifying the driver-guide and suggesting he be fired immediately for insubordination and for clearly not "realizing his place" in society.

RETURNING HOME

At some point, the tourist will emerge from his or her liminal space and return home laden with goods and memories of the trip. Tourists may not be conscious of it, but they are changed by their experience. They have seen and done. They have slept in strange beds, eaten strange food, spent time in a strange place. They have come back and begun their lives again full of new thoughts and prepared to invite others to share in their memories. How good or bad those memories are depends in a large part on their driver-guide. Was he friendly? Did he represent the expected Irish personae? Did he appear to accommodate their needs? Did things go smoothly? Did his local knowledge support their assumptions? Was he handsome? Witty? Well turned-out? The positive memories of Ireland that return with the visitor are often linked to positive interactions with the driver-guide. Likewise, negative memories can be linked to negative interactions with the driver-guide. Occasionally, a bad trip (usually having to do with the weather or less-than-stellar accommodation) is offset by the positive relationship cultivated by the guide with his clients. What matters is that the positive experience be relayed by word of mouth to other potential visitors in an ever-expanding cycle of tourism development.

Discussions and Displays

All tourists share their experiences with others once they return home. Most also share their experiences with those who remain at home during the tour through calls home, postcards sent, and emails detailing each and every moment. There must be some "proof" of travel, some acknowledgment that the liminal space was inhabited, at least for a short while. Souvenirs, postcards, photographs, and other portable items are collected and passed between the traveler and the homebody, and stories related to each will be reported. The point is to garner admiration from the homebody (who could be anyone who was not along for the trip, including family, friends, and workmates). Stories about the trip will be repeated to everyone who will listen, even if the trip is mentioned only in passing to strangers and acquaintances. The banter may range from tones of excitement to bored-with-the-world renditions of the tour. People are glad to be home in their own beds and among familiar surroundings, but they "miss" the place they have been. Upon return, tourists also display their experience in myriad ways: photo montages on websites, blogs, articles of clothing that proclaim presence (Ireland or Guinness T-shirts, for example, or "Fisherman-knit" sweaters), framed photographs placed in prominent positions in "public" areas such as sitting rooms and offices. These displays serve not only as symbols of worldliness but also as reminders of a life-event for those who participated. The displays may encourage feelings of longing, annoyance, or jealousy among homebodies. They do not share the first-person memories and experiences; they can only live precariously through the traveler. It is at this moment that a potential customer is made and the seed of travel planning is planted. It is the moment that tourist bureaus, tour operators, and travel agents pray for.

The coach-driver guide who inhabited the liminal space takes up his place in the mythos of the returned-tourist imagination. The single pint he may have shared on an evening in a pub may transform into a wild night of drinking and storytelling. A quiet conversation with him may reiterate as a budding best friend or a come-on from a potential lover. An in-transit discussion becomes an argument whereby displays of "real Irish temper" flared. He may likewise disappear from memory or at least those memories shared with others, his clear significance during the tour and the tourists' dependence on him reduced and then washed away, returning control, power, and independence to the traveler, now safely returned to home soil.

The tourist at home is a changed person. His or her status will change in both his or her own mind and in the minds of others. The tourist now holds memories others do not and has experienced life in unique ways, ways that can be shared only through visual and oral means. Gift giving done upon return revolves around mementos. Tales are told of the places where they were purchased and the context of the gift-giver's presence in the place. Whether the gift is appreciated is not the primary consideration: that the giver can prove through this presentation that he or she has been somewhere and done something is. There is no reciprocation. At the moment that the exchange of information or presentation of the gift takes place, the giver's status elevates, even if just temporarily.

Conclusion

A COACH DRIVER-GUIDE PRESENTS THE HERITAGE OF IRELAND

To understand how a native Irish person might present Ireland's heritage to a visiting public, I asked a driver-guide to design a week-long heritage tour of Ireland. He has been active in the tourism industry for nearly three decades and is highly regarded by colleagues, tour operators, and visitors alike. He is a badged tour guide, having received his national certification in 1989.

Day 1: Dublin   National Museum
Dublinia
Kilmainham Gaol
Collins Barracks

"You have to go to these places; they're all so important to Irish culture and Irish history. People have to understand about our history. I think it's important that they learn about 1916 and that as well. Most people really don't have a clue so that's why I'd take them to Kilmainham and the Collins Barracks."

In my opinion, it goes without saying that the National Museum of Archaeology and History on Kildare Street should be visited by every incoming tourist to Ireland. A wonderland of archaeological and cultural treasures, the museum is a place that resonates with Ireland's unique personality.

Dublinia, located near St Patrick's Cathedral, contains a review of Ireland's Viking heritage. Although tuned to a younger audience, it provides visitors with an opportunity to glimpse the influence the Norse had on early Irish history. Responsible for the development of some of Ireland's great cities (Dublin, Waterford, Wexford, Cork, Limerick), it is not known by many visitors to Ireland.

Kilmainham Gaol is another place all visitors should see. A barren and frightening block of stone, the prison held thousands of the nameless and famous alike during England's colonization of the country. From the destitute and starving forced to steal in order to survive the famine to the heroes of the 1916 Easter Rising, visitors can experience the same cramped, cold, and dark environment that prisoners did. Kilmainham Gaol is also one of the first prisons to experiment with panopticon design, whereby prisoners could be watched and observed by guards and one another 24 hours a day. Graffiti etched into the walls express hopelessness, rebelliousness, and the joy of knowing that one's sentence is nearly up. In the yard, remnants of a gallows and the bullet holes of the firing squad that killed Patrick Pearse, John Connelly, and others after the Easter Rising are a somber reminder of those whose memories are forever linked to the prison.

The Collins Barracks located near Heuston Station and Guinness now houses the National Museum of Art and Design. An imposing structure, the museum stands as a mute reminder of the English troops that were housed there for hundreds of years. In the courtyard, paces are marked off on walls next to the area where soldiers marched and trained. Exhibits at the Collins Barracks range from small rooms recounting the evolution of society fashion to extensive permanent exhibits such as "Soldiers and Chiefs," which tells the story of Irish soldiers who have taken part in conflicts on foreign soil, including the American Civil War, World Wars I and II, and today's peacekeeping missions in many areas of the world. For several months in 2007 and 2008, the Sea Stallion, a replica of an almost 1,000-year-old Viking long boat that sailed from Scandinavia to Ireland, was kept in the courtyard before returning to Denmark.

Day 2: Dublin   Newgrange
              Knowth
              Hill of Tara

"This would give people a chance to learn about the prehistory and early Christian period in Ireland. People want to see Newgrange, but I think they get more out of Knowth—it's just more interesting and there's so much more to explore. Tara is a definite but for other reasons. Tara's been a center of Irish culture for about 5,000 years and not many visitors know really much about it. They know the name like, but not the actual place. They're all usually impressed with Tara after a visit, because the site (when it's presented well) shows them that it's been important from the Stone Age through the Bronze Age, with [St.] Patrick, through the rebellions [of 1798 and 1916], right up to today. There's also the M3 controversy that everyone's hearing about now." (Tara and the Brú na Bóinne have already been discussed extensively in this book.)

Day 3: Meath/Kilkenny/Waterford
              Glendalough (early Christianity)
              Jerpoint Abbey (Cistercians 1158)
              Kells Abbey (Augustinians 1193)
              Black Abbey (Dominicans 1225)

"This would be a really interesting day if I could do it all in one roll. This would cover the Christian period from the 6th century right through the medieval period. It would show the influence of the many orders, and it's also a great architectural tour. The abbeys themselves are really quite different even though some of the differences are subtle."

Glendalough is an early Christian monastic site founded by St. Kevin in the 6th century. About five hundred years later, in 1214, the Normans destroyed the settlement, and the monastery fell into disuse and ruin. It has been under restoration since the 19th century and represents one of the earliest monastic settlements in Europe. It is set in a Wicklow valley with two glacial lakes and has a round tower, stone churches, and several highly decorated crosses.

Jerpoint Abbey was founded in the second half of the 12th century by the Cistercians, or White Monks, near Thomastown in Kilkenny. It was commissioned by Domnall mac Gilla Patraic, King of Osraige in 1180, and was in active use through the 16th century. In 1541, it passed into the possession of James, Earl of Ormond. A Romanesque structure, the Abbey contains a variety of tomb sculptures, arcades, and transepts. The Cistercians practice the literal observance of the austerity of St. Benedict.

The Abbey of Kells is located in the town of Kells, County Meath, to the northwest of Dublin. This would be the first stop of the day for tourists leaving from the Dublin area. The original monastic settlement was founded in 554 by St. Columba, and many historians believe that the illuminated manuscript *The Book of Kells* may have been written there. It was certainly kept there for many centuries before being given to Trinity College in the 1660s, where it is now on display. In 1152, the Synod of Kells caused the Abbey's transition from a monastic to a diocesan church run by the Augustinians. On the Abbey grounds are a round tower, four Celtic high crosses (a fifth is located in the center of town), and an 11th-century stone oratory.

The Black Abbey, also in Kilkenny, was founded during the time of St. Thomas Aquinas by William Marshal the Younger in 1225 and is a Dominican Abbey. Suppressed in 1543 by Henry VIII, it was converted to a courthouse until 1603. It is the only original Dominican structure in Ireland still in use after 800 years. The Dominicans follow a life of community, prayer, study, and preaching.

Day 4: Cork   Cobh Heritage Centre

"I think everyone needs to spend a day at Cobh. There's such a connection between Ireland and the U.S., and Canada and Australia for that matter, and much of that starts at Cobh. This is where a good many of the Famine Ships left from. The Heritage Centre tells that entire story, and I think it's really well done. It also has exhibits on the Titanic and the Lusitania liners. The Titanic used Cobh as its final port of call. And the Lusitania was sunk by a German U-Boat right off the coast in 1915, and almost 2,000 people lost their lives."

Nearly three million people left Ireland from Cobh between 1848 and 1950. Located in a disused railway station, the Heritage Centre contains exhibits that recount the conditions of the famine ships and other passenger ships over that century. There are several statues in Cobh memorializing those who died on the Titanic and the Lusitania and one statue on the museum grounds of Annie Moore, who left Cobh for America and was the first person processed through Ellis Island when it opened on January 1, 1892.

Day 5: Cork/Kerry   Dunloe Ogham Stones
Stone Circles in Kenmare
Dingle bee hive huts; Staigue Fort

"This area is important, too, and I would bring every coachful of people here. It's not just the sites themselves, but the whole area around Dingle. The geology, the geography, the history—it's all ingrained in our brains here. I would take people to these specific sites, because they're not sites you'd see everyday—certainly not on a regular tour."

The Dunloe Ogham Stones are a group of eight stones carved with ancient Ogham writing. Ogham script is thought to have been in use in many areas of Ireland and Britain from about 2,000 years ago and is named for Ogmi, the script god. The Dunloe stones are not in their original site but are local to their present site near Dunloe Castle in Kerry. Ogham writing is usually commemorative in nature, and the Dunloe examples follow suit. They are believed to be from the time just prior to the Christian era in Ireland.

The Kenmare Stone Circle is the largest in southwestern Ireland and was built in the Bronze Age (2200–500 B.C.E.) for ritual and ceremonial use. It is believed that stone circles were linked to solar or lunar events. The Kenmare circle is unusual in that it has a large boulder dolmen at its center.

Staigue Fort is found near Sneem on the Ring of Kerry and is also known by its Irish name of *Cathair Na Stéige*. It is a large drystone ring fort, and its remaining walls are 5 meters high, 4 meters thick, and 27.4 meters in diameter. It is surrounded by a bank and ditch and was likely built in the 1st century B.C.E. during Ireland's Iron Age.

On the Dingle peninsula along Slea Head near the village of Fahan are a number of *Clocháns,* or stone beehive huts. They are difficult to date, because the stone corbelling used in their construction has been used in Ireland from the Neolithic through the 1950s. It is believed that the huts are habitation sites from around the time of the Norman Invasions in the 12th century, when native Irish were forced off good land and into marginal areas such as Fahan.

Day 6: Burren Poulnabrone Dolmen
       Ailwee Caves
       Limestone Plateau

"I'd end with them up The Burren. It's another area like Dingle that just needs to be seen. The area shows people how difficult it's been for the ones who live out there with all the exposed limestone and the barrenness of it all. The Poulnabrone Dolmen is the best in the world; you just can't find a better dolmen anywhere. And it's right there in the middle of a stone field. You have to ask yourself why they would have put it there and what for? But then I explain to them that the place wasn't always barren; at one time it had soil and trees and fields, and the dolmens were covered over with turf and people were buried in them. They have a hard time believing that the place was anything but what it is today. The Ailwee Caves are good craic—interesting to see and the tour is interesting. We have caves like that all over the place and people have been using them for thousands of years."

Poulnabrone is a portal dolmen or tomb and is thought to have been constructed around 2500 B.C.E. in the late Neolithic/Early Bronze Age. The remains of 16 adults and children and other artifacts were found when the site was excavated in 1986. The tomb faces north and is 2 meters high with a thin capstone measuring 2.5 meters wide by 3.5 meters long. It is situated in a karst limestone field east of the Ballyvaughan-Corrofin Road.

The Ailwee Caves, also near Ballyvaughan, opened to the public only in 1976. Originally formed when the glaciers retreated and water rushed through the cracks and crevices of the limestone plateau, the caves were once inhabited by large brown cave bears, the skeletons of which have been found throughout. They contain hundreds of stalagmites and stalactites and unique tunnels accessible by visitors.

"If I had ten more days I could think of fifty more places to take them to. It would take a lifetime to see it all, but I don't think people would come any closer to understanding most of it even if they had that kind of time. And some tourists just don't want any facts interfering with their versions of history, but I think that's the same everywhere. I could add castles and islands, Donegal, West Cork, Connemara, [the Book of] Kells and Trinity College, places in the North like the Derry Walls and Belfast. There just isn't enough time on a tour to do all the most important sites. I guess I would say they're all important, or important in different aspects."

When I asked him to elaborate on why he had chosen these particular sites and places, he took his time responding. He told me he had a difficult time designing the tour based on what he saw as important heritage symbols and sites and what he thought people wanted to see. He wasn't sure about the all-day abbey tour, nor was he positive about the effect he hoped sites like Tara or the Ogham Stones would have on people. There were too many variables to consider, and he felt the task was best left to the people who did the tour organizing. I reminded him that it was tour organizers, government agencies, and site managers who had determined what constituted Irish heritage. He responded by reminding me that so far they had done a pretty good job at it.

CONCLUSION

When I first began this project, I applied for several research grants from a variety of anthropological agencies in the United States. They are well-known groups, all professing to support research on the underrepresented and underresearched. Not a single anthropological agency saw value in this research. One of the largest in fact wrote back: "Bus drivers? What can you possibly learn from bus drivers?" I suggest that a lot can be learned from a bus driver: humility, compassion, pride, wit, patience, strength of character, a sense of fair play, and an astonishing ability to work under extremely difficult circumstances, among other things. The coach-driver guides who taught me about their lives, their jobs, and their heritage have opened up a previously unexplored aspect of tourism and the heritage business. They are not peripheral or epiphenomenal but key players whom the anthropological community should recognize. Unlike the bus drivers who inhabit the periphery of the tourist worlds of other researchers, I have met men who have written and produced documentary films, who have written volumes of poetry, who breed horses, who have survived IRA bombings, who work for the environment, who read the classics in Greek and Latin, who coach athletic teams, and who have raised families in spite of their lives on the road. Some paint and sculpt, some lie in the sun, some gamble their tips on Ruby Walsh. All of them, at the end of the day, are men of character and unrecognized ability.

Toward the end of this research, I rode along with two driver-guides who I believe represent the brotherhood at its best. They both expressed a transparent love for Ireland, its heritage, and its people. They both treated their groups with patience and respect. They both spoke eloquently and passionately on subjects ranging from the M3/Tara bypass to the GAA to the elections that were underway at the time of this writing. They both hoped that I would be fair in my analysis and presentation. In the end, it was fairness and honesty that most concerned them. When asked about the heritage and landscape, both expressed fears of encroachment, commercialization, damage, and development. In watching them examine the cultural and heritage landscapes of their home, I clearly saw that no matter how many times they might pass by a spot, it would resonate deeply with them. It was also clear that no matter how many times they showed sites to their vaguely disinterested or misinformed public, their feelings toward their heritage would never change.

The Coach Fellas helped me understand the difficulties, challenges, and triumphs of working with audiences who connect with Ireland mostly through hopes and dreams. I examined their personal lives and the ways in which they met the incoming hoards of visitors. Although admittedly exhausted at the end of a tour—and at the end of the season—nearly all welcomed the next group with anticipation and true warmth. A few over the course of the project hung up their keys and left the industry, tired of the grind and the strain it put on their personal lives. Some nursed outside interests in areas other than tourism, their real life-goals lying outside the coach business. Fewer Irishmen are coming into the business, and it is expected that there soon will be a dearth of young Irish drivers and driver-guides. What effect this will have on the Irish tourism industry remains to be seen, although most on the inside believe that this change will damage it beyond recovery.

Underscoring this examination of life on the road is the way in which the symbols and landmarks of Ireland's heritage are interpreted and presented to the visiting public, especially those on coach tours. The heritage of Ireland is vast both temporally and spatially encompassing—to paraphrase Gabriel Cooney, one huge cultural landscape. Archaeological landscapes are created and recreated perpetually; they are not just the remains of long-past societies and cultures but the materials of the present as well (and the impact that the present has on the remains of the past). It is the reuse of these landscapes within the context of heritage that gives them a commodified quality that extends far beyond their original intended use—Newgrange was never meant to be a spectacle for tourists; it was meant to be a place for the dead. Its value 5,000 years ago lay in its ingenious structure and the meaning kept private by the people who labored to construct it and those privileged enough to use it. We will never truly understand its original meaning, but we have found ways to make it meaningful to the modern world by reinventing it as heritage.

Coach driver-guides are expected to present the heritage of Ireland, in all its vastness, in small, easily repeatable sound bites. In my observations, attempts to go beyond these sound bites left driver-guides exhausted and tourists (for the most part) baffled. Learning when enough information is too much is a skill many of us could benefit from. The men charged with the responsibilities of presenting the heritage of Ireland as it passes by the bus have become adept at negotiating the frontier between the real Ireland and the imagined Ireland their guests expect. Using the mythologized Ireland to support their narratives of today's modern state, the driver-guides have passed along new interpretations of their heritage and culture, trusting their guests to distill their personal myths with the present-day realties presented through their discourse.

The heritage of Ireland is presented in tourism advertising as a nearly pristine vision: the countryside is exactly as imagined, the shorelines dramatic, the houses thatched, the people rosy, and the cities vibrant and pulsing with life. There is an open invitation to take part in the event that is Ireland. Once in Ireland, tourists (especially those from North America) are often overwhelmed by the contrasts in what they expect and what actually is. They can find it hard to reconcile the modernity of the lived Ireland with their memorialized one. But they nonetheless are generally enchanted, and few leave feeling dissatisfied (Fáilte Ireland 2005e). Tourists are happy to see the landscape and the heritage, even if they have no real time to seriously engage with it. A few good snaps of oneself in front of the statue of Molly Malone on Grafton Street (known locally as "The Tart with the Cart") will bring a flood of recollection upon returning home—the very action of taking a photograph with the marker anticipates the feeling of happy memories associated with a holiday to Ireland. The photograph, souvenir, or other memento can also become a status symbol used to express the experience of travel to those who remained behind and could not take part.

Archaeological and cultural heritage are also presented in dramatic fashion with guided tours, films, scripted presentations, heritage centers, and circumscribed pathways. But some bits of the culture escape this. Maeve's Fort, adjacent to Tara, lies quietly unmolested by tourism or heritage development. The vast landscape surrounding Rathcroghan in Roscommon remains in private hands, is difficult to negotiate without assistance from the Cruachan Ai Centre in Tulsk, and compared to sites of equal historical importance is rarely visited. Fore Abbey in Westmeath, despite its high degree of preservation, importance to early Christian Ireland, and interesting surroundings, is not part of the visitor's orthodoxy of musts, nor is it on the radar of heritage development. Countless other sites are either too far off the beaten path, too small, too ruined, or deemed too unimportant to be included on the tourism trail.

The Irish coach driver-guides who are charged with preparing their passengers to engage with the sites they visit are blessed with local knowledge and the willingness to learn. Their job is often difficult, and they find they spend an inordinate amount of time reconciling the "new Ireland" with the dreamed-of Ireland that their guests bring with them. On many tours, they spend more time shuttling passengers to gift shops than to sites, and many find the obsession with consuming Ireland mildly confusing. At the same time, they recognize the increasing consumerism of the Irish themselves as symbolic of the direction the country is now moving in. They have learned to walk the tightrope of political correctness, although many strain against the constraints of their expected behaviors. Members of a small brotherhood that shares many of the same experiences, they will also seek one another out at the end of the day to unwind from their hectic schedules. Many after-work conversations revert to their day jobs, but the downloading of the day between and among drivers seems to relieve much of the tension that can build during the touring schedule—and this tension is not allowed to surface until they are away from their guests. Part of the visitor's impression of Ireland lies with the coach driver-guide and his ability to overcome negative emotive reactions and to always remain cheerful and upbeat.

Ireland is changing rapidly. Bolstered by unprecedented economic success and more than a decade of Celtic Tiger affluence, the need to develop is overwhelming the landscape, especially the areas surrounding Dublin, Limerick, Galway, Cork, and Waterford. But other, less well-known landscapes are struggling under the weight of development. The Midlands, although not included in most tourist visits, are exploding with construction projects as the bedroom suburbs of Dublin reach across the area. Populations are increasing in towns once considered beyond the pale of Dublin, such as Navan, Mullingar, and Trim. Even towns further afield such as Longford, Tullamore, and Athlone, are experiencing growing pains. Leitrim and Roscommon, the least-visited counties in Ireland, suffer from holiday and second-home building clearly visible as one passes through small towns such as Carrick-on-Shannon on the border between the two counties. Roads projects, new schools, waste water plants, rubbish disposal, pollutants of all sorts also stress the landscape and the Irish people. Ways of life are no longer traditional even in the remotest areas. The country's economic success has had a multiplier effect in that the vision of Ireland is now different for those in the State and for those who visit it: the former appreciates and welcomes modernity and affluence, understanding it as symbolic of New Millennium Ireland; the latter is often dismayed by it, understanding it as symbolic of the demise of a culture.[1] Development is also seen as well deserved; after hundreds of years of poverty and underdevelopment, the explosion of houses, estates, and industry across the country reflects Ireland's potential and independence. It is also seen as dangerous and as a new form of oppression by many who observe from the outside in; the Irish, it is assumed, do not welcome it. Although many Irish people feel twinges of regret as the old makes way for the new, it is the visiting public who are the most indignant regarding development. As suggested, Ireland and the Irish are not supposed to evolve and are not supposed to welcome the 20th century (the 21st century is surely beyond their grasp!). They should be happily mired in history, innocent of the future that is now.

As this project came to an end, many drivers I spoke to believed that the industry was about to change in unprecedented ways. There seemed to be fewer tours, because so many of the big companies had consolidated or been bought out (among them Brendan Tours), and fewer drivers were happy with their schedules, because of the lack of "standard" tours. Very few new drivers who were Irish had come onto the scene, old venues were closing (The Burlington Hotel and the Jury's Ballsbridge in Dublin among others), and the structure of many of the tours was being revised. Tourism was also being affected by the dollar, which had been declining in value against the Euro steadily. There weren't many who looked forward to the coming years and most were concerned that they now lacked the skill or education to find other work that could be as financially rewarding or so suitable to their personalities.

Despite the dark clouds that appeared to hang over the industry, only a few had made plans to leave the profession. At one point, I showed a few drivers one of the new Fáilte Ireland campaign advertisements for 2007–2008, and a number of them pointed out that even though the ads suggest that tourism

Figure 9.1 But where are the coach fellas? (© Kelli Ann Costa 2007).

is for and about everyone, no photos of coach drivers were included (Figure 9.1.). One driver was about to comment on the photo when his mobile phone rang with a message concerning a passenger's bag that had been lost for a number of days through no fault of his. It had been located but was now 100 miles away at a hotel in Limerick. He glanced over the top of his reading glasses and said: "Yeah, and I'd bet none of them [in the advertisement] would leave an evening of pints and a fine dinner to go fetch a bag halfway across the fookin' country for someone either." And with that, he was out the door, started up his coach, and drove 200 miles to retrieve a piece of lost luggage.

Epilogue / Postscript

It is now February 2009, and Ireland, like most of the world, is in the grip of an extraordinary economic recession. The Celtic Tiger has died, and over 300,000 people are now unemployed and on the live register [the live register is Ireland's unemployment count]. As of today (4 February 2009), 327,861 people are on the dole (approximately 9% unemployment)—an unprecedented number of people are now dependent on the state (TV3 Midday News). This level of unemployment has not been witnessed since 1993, when 302,000 people were on the live register and does not compare to the 181,000 unemployed recorded in January of 2008 (ibid.). In response to these unemployment numbers, Fine Gael leader Enda Kenney stated there was "no prospect for the future" among many of those who had lost jobs, and Taoiseach Brian Cowen responded that the unemployment figures in the state could reach 400,000 by year's end (TV3 News at 5.30, 4 February 2009). It is estimated that every job lost in Ireland is costing the state €20,000 per year in social welfare benefits (ibid.). In the last month alone, IBM announced 120 redundancies, Waterford Crystal (a famous visitor attraction) announced 480 job losses and the closure of the Waterford Crystal Visitor Centre, Dell Limerick let 1,900 people go, and Celestica announced 380 job losses—and these are only the headline-worthy employers; hundreds of jobs are disappearing daily in every sector in the country. On average, Ireland is losing 1,500 jobs per week (ibid.).

The government has instituted new tax and pension levies on nearly everyone in Ireland because of a significant downturn in the exchequer revenues. Polish guest workers are leaving the country at a rate of 1,200–1,500 people per week as the Polish economy strengthens while the rest of Europe slips further into deep recession. Newspapers now carry advertisements for Irish workers to work in Poland on construction sites and in the Polish service industry rather than the other way around. And young Irish people are emigrating weekly by the hundreds to Australia, Canada, the United States, South Africa, and China, pursuing jobs that are no longer available in their own country. The Irish tourism industry cannot escape the recession. In March 2008, The Irish Tourist Industry Confederation (ITIC) Chairman, Dick Bourke, suggested that "tourism in Ireland is in good shape and is in a strong position to weather the economic downturn that will affect the industry in the year ahead" (13 March 2008 *ITIC Tourism News*). Two weeks after that, the *ITIC Tourism News* reported that Ken McGill, Executive Vice President and Managing Director, Travel and Tourism, at Global Insight, suggested that the recession in the United States was "mild" and that the negative growth it was then experiencing would last only two consecutive quarters, or the minimum time frame of a recession. McGill stated: "The global economy is a good-news story: slowing growth, then getting back on track" (4 April 2008 *ITIC Tourism News*). Fáilte Ireland's *Tourism Barometer 2008-Wave 4-December* stated that by September 2008 "it was evident that the deteriorating economic conditions in Ireland and in the primary source markets were having a major impact on the fortunes of the Irish tourism industry. . . . It is now clear that current economic circumstances have had a severe impact on the performance of each of the main tourism industry sectors" (2009: 4). In addition, the report suggested that 86% of coach operators reported a downturn in business in 2008 (ibid.: 22), and the same 86% predict a further downturn for 2009 (ibid.: 28). As of this writing, many of the coach drivers and driver-guides who assisted me in writing this ethnography have few or no scheduled tours in 2009. It would be unusual for them not to know their March and April schedules by the beginning of February. At the end of January 2009, "the European Tour Operators Association reported . . . that bookings for incoming tours to Europe are down by as much as 40% in some cases" (29 January 2009 *ITIC Tourism News*).

It remains to be seen what the future holds for the Coach Fellas. By mid-2008, the tone among them was sombre, and more than a few are now actively seeking work in other fields or considering retirement as the 2009 season beckons. Despite high satisfaction ratings in the latest Visitor Attitudes Survey conducted by Fáilte Ireland (2007), it seems unlikely that the industry will perform at anywhere near the level it has in the past during the coming months or years.

Notes

Preface

1. According to Fáilte Ireland 2005, the majority of those partaking in coach tours in Ireland are Americans (roughly 31%).
2. Recent reports in a variety of news media suggest that house prices are dropping as Ireland verges on recession in mid-2008. This economic position is directly related to the ever-weakening dollar and the rapidly rising oil prices. RTE reported that the tourism industry will be severely affected by the weak dollar and prices at the pump, and this situation has been personally witnessed in Dublin, Galway, and Cork in 2008, with a substantial reduction in tour bus and tourism traffic on the streets and at the sites normally swarming with people (RTÉ Nightly News 8 July 2008).

Chapter 3

1. Up to 34% of the State's identified archaeological monuments have now been leveled, and the rate of destruction has increased to an unprecedented 10% per decade. The National Monuments Acts, statutory Record of Monuments, and so on appear to be having no effect. This material is being destroyed at an alarming rate of about 1,500 sites per year, without any attempt to rescue the data being lost (H@R!: Heritage at Risk: Ireland *ICOMOS*).

Chapter 5

1. "Ireland" refers to the Republic here.

Chapter 6

1. One experience I had while observing a "day in the life" of a coach driver included racing off to Urlingford from Bunratty to pick up a coach on a Saturday, not getting the right sized coach because of over-booking, then going back to Bunratty with the wrong tour bus, having to pick up passengers at 6.30 A.M. at Shannon the following day, driving them all through the Burren, to the Cliffs of Moher, and onto Ennis, dropping the complaining lot of them at the hotel, driving the small bus down to Limerick, picking up a larger bus, cleaning the entire pig sty out, washing the windows and the outside, scrubbing the toilet (all in Bunratty), then driving back up to Ennis to escort them to dinner where they were still complaining about the temporary cramped quarters and badgering the driver about the quality of the travel conditions.

Chapter 8

1. John Urry (2004) and Dean MacCannell (1999 [1976]) have suggested that previsit imaging and the emotional anticipation and expectations that lead to these ideas of familiarity do not contribute to a high degree of cultural understanding; rather they expand and extend long-held imaginings of places and peoples.

Chapter 9

1. On 30 July 2007, it was reported by all the major news agencies in Ireland that they were the second wealthiest country in the world, ahead of France, the United Kingdom, Germany, Italy, and the United States.

References

American Heritage Dictionary. 2000. (4th ed.). Boston: Houghton Mifflin.

Anderson, B. 1983. *Imagined Communities.* London: Verso.

Aplin, G. 2002. *Heritage: Identification, Conservation and Management.* Oxford: Oxford University.

Baudrillard, J. 1988. *America* Chris Turner, (trans.). London: Verso.

Bender, B. 2001. Introduction, in B. Bender and M. Winer (eds.), *Contested Landscapes: Movement, Exile and Place*, pp. 1–18. Oxford: Berg.

Bender, B., and Winer, M. (eds.). 2001. *Contested Landscapes: Movement, Exile and Place.* Oxford: Berg.

Bianchi, R., and Boniface, P. 2002. Editorial: The Politics of World Heritage, *International Journal of Heritage Studies* 8(2): 79–80.

Boissevain, J. (ed.). 1996. *Coping with Tourists: European Reactions to Mass Tourism.* Providence: Berghahn.

Boissevain, J. 1996. Introduction, in J. Boissevain (ed.), *Coping with Tourists: European Reactions to Mass Tourism*, pp. 1–26. Providence, RI: Berghahn.

Bord, Fáilte. 1999. *Tourism Development Strategy 2000–2006.* Dublin: Irish Tourist Board.

Brendan Worldwide Vacations. 2007. *Ireland and Britain: Escorted, Independent and Self-Drive Vacations* (brochure).

Brett, D. 1996. *The Construction of Heritage.* Cork: Cork University.

Bruner, E. M. 1994. Abraham Lincoln as authentic reproduction: A critique of postmodernism, *American Anthropologist* 96(2):397–415.

Bruner, E. M. 2001. The Maasai and the Lion King: Authenticity, nationalism, and globalization in African tourism, *American Ethnologist* 28(4): 881–908.

Bruner, E. M. 2004. Tourism in the Balinese borderzone, in S. B. Gmelch (ed.), *Tourists and Tourism: A Reader*, pp. 219–238.

Burnham, J. B. 2003. Why Ireland boomed, *The Independent Review* vii(4): 537–556.

Butler, R., and Hinch, T. (eds.). 1996. *Tourism and Indigenous Peoples.* London: International Thompson Business Press.

Buttimer, N., Rynne, C., and Guerin, H. 2000. *The Heritage of Ireland: Natural, Man-made and Cultural Heritage; Conservation and Interpretation; Business and Administration* Cork: Wilton Press.

Campbell, C. W. 1987. A proposal for rehabilitation, *Emania* 3: 44–47.

Campbell, N. 1987. Comment on the draft proposal, *Emania* 2: 36.

Carey, T. 2006. Heritage and development, *Heritage Outlook: The Magazine of the Heritage Council*, Summer: 19–21.

Chambers, E. (ed.). 1997. *Tourism and Culture: An Applied Perspective.* Albany, NY: SUNY.

Chambers, E. 2000. *Native Tours: The Anthropology of Travel and Tourism.* Long Grove, IL: Waveland.

Chapman, M. 1992. *The Celts: The Construction of a Myth.* New York: Macmillan.

Collis, J. 1997. Celtic myths, *Antiquity* lxxi: 195–201.

Cooney, G. 1996. Building the future on the past: Archaeology and the construction of national identity in Ireland, in M. Díaz-Andreu and T. Champion (eds.), pp. 146–153. *Nationalism and Archaeology in Europe.* Boulder, CO: Westview.

———. 2004. Tara and the M3—putting the debate in context, *Archaeology Ireland* 18(2): 8–9.

Cooney, G., Condit, T., and Byrnes, E. 2000. The archaeological landscape, in N. Buttimer, C. Rynne, and H. Guerin (eds.), *The Heritage of Ireland.* Cork: Collins Press, 18–28.

Corkern, W. 2004. Heritage tourism, *American Studies International* Jun/Oct 42:2/3.

Corkman (newspaper). 2006. "Staggering" growth in Co. Cork house prices (www.unison.ie/irish_independent/Corkman, accessed 20 February 2006).

Costa, K. A. 2001. *The Brokered Image: Material Culture and Identity in the Stubaital.* Lanham, MD: University Press of America.

———. 2004. Conflating past and present: Marketing archaeological heritage in Ireland, in Y. Rowan and U. Baram (eds.), *Marketing Heritage:*

Archaeology and the Consumption of the Past, pp. 69–92.Walnut Creek, CA: AltaMira Press.

————. 2006. Loughcrew Cairns: Rock art at Cairn U, unpublished paper presented at the Franklin Pierce College Liberal Arts Faculty Seminar.

————. 2007. Globalizing heritage: Marketing the built environment in Ireland, in U. Kockel and M. Nic Craith (eds.), *Cultural Heritages as Reflexive Traditions.* Basingstoke, Hampshire: Palgrave Macmillan.

Crick, M. 1989. Representation of international tourism in the social sciences: Sun, sex, sight, savings, and servility, *Annual Review of Anthropology* 18: 307–344.

Cronin, M. 2003. Next to being there: Ireland of the welcomes and tourism of the word, in M. Cronin and B. O'Connor editors, *Irish Tourism: Image, Culture and Identity,* pp. 179–195. Clevedon: Channel View.

Cronin, M., and O'Connor, B. (eds.). 2003. *Irish Tourism: Image, Culture and Identity.* Clevedon: Channel View.

Central Statistics Office. 2005. *Tourism and Travel 2004.* Dublin: CSO (26 April 2005).

Cusack, T. 1998. Migrant travellers and touristic idylls: The paintings of Jack B. Yeats and post-colonial identities, *Art History* 21(2): 201–218.

————. 2001. A "countryside bright with cosy homesteads": Irish nationalism and the cottage landscape, *National Identities* 3(3): 221–238.

Davies, K. M. 1993. For health and pleasure in the British fashion: Bray, Co. Wicklow as a tourist resort, 1750–1914, in B. O'Connor and M. Cronin (eds.). *Tourism in Ireland: A Critical Analysis,* pp. 29–48. Cork: University of Cork.

Deevey, M. 2005. Archaeology, Tara and the M3 road scheme, *Archaeology Ireland* 19(2): 12–15.

De Kadt, E. (ed.). 1979. *Tourism: A Passport to Development.* Oxford: Oxford University.

Díaz-Andreu, M., and Champion, T. (eds.). 1996. *Nationalism and Archaeology in Europe.* Boulder, CO: Westview.

Díaz-Andreu, M., and Champion, T. 1996. Nationalism and archaeology in Europe: An introduction, in M. Díaz-Andreu and T. Champion (eds.), *Nationalism and Archaeology in Europe,* pp. 1–23. Boulder, CO: Westview.

Eco, U. 1986. *Travels in Hyperreality* (William Weaver, trans). New York: Harcourt Brace Jovanovich.

ESRI (Economic and Social Research Institute). 2005. *Quarterly Economic Commentary March 2005.* Dublin: ESRI.

Fáilte Ireland/ National Tourism Development Authority/NTDA. 2004. *Special Interest Tourism Plans.* Dublin: Fáilte Ireland.

———. 2005a. (March 15). 600 Irish festival and events to attract seven million people during 2006 (www.failteireland.ie, accessed 16 March 2006).

———. 2005b. (October 13). Local communities can play a larger role in tourism development—tourism chief tells Emo conference (www. failteireland.ie, accessed 16 March 2006).

———. 2005c. (November 17). Fáilte Ireland festival to recruit into 6,000 jobs a year in tourism—Ireland's largest recruitment drive: €16m to be invested in training at 70 centres nationally in 2006 (www.failteireland. ie, accessed 16 March 2006).

———. 2005d. (November 22). Fáilte Ireland urge move from accommodation to development of attractions and activities (www. failteireland.ie, accessed 16 March 2006).

———. 2005e. *Visitor Attitudes Survey.* Dublin: Fáilte Ireland.

———. 2005f. *Developing Regional Tourism 2006.* Dublin: Fáilte Ireland.

———. 2006a. (January 4). After record year in 2005, tourism businesses even more optimistic for 2006: Rural tourism under pressure while urban centres perform well (www.failteireland.ie, accessed 16 March 2006).

———. 2006b. (February 21). Additional €5 million to be invested in developing regional tourism (www.failteireland.ie, accessed 16 March 2006).

———. 2006c. (April 4). Fáilte Ireland launches €4 million marketing campaign to boost domestic tourism: Ireland 2006 Let's Play (www. failteireland.ie, accessed 15 April 2006).

ESRI (Economic and Social Research Institute). 2006d. (June). Preliminary tourism facts 2005 (www.failteireland.ie, accessed 17 July 2006).

———. 2007. *Visitor Attitudes Survey.* Dublin: Millward Brown.

———. 2009. *Tourism Barometer 2008 [Wave 4] December.* Dublin: Fáilte Ireland.

Finfacts: Ireland Business and Financial Portal. 2007. Irish house prices up 270% since 1996 rising at an average of 14.9% for each of the last 10 years; Construction sector may shed over 100,000 jobs by 2016 (www. finfacts.com/biz10/irelandhouseprices.htm, accessed 11 March 2007).

Flanagan, D. 1997. Introduction to the excavations at Navan Fort: Part 2—The identification of *Emain Macha* with Navan Fort, *Excavations at Navan Fort 1961–1671.* Belfast: The Stationery Office.

Foley, A., and Fahy, J. 2004. Incongruity between expression and experience: The role of imagery in supporting the positioning of a tourism destination brand, *Brand Management* 11(3): 209–217.

Foreign Policy. 2003. Measuring globalization: Who's up, who's down? AT Kearney (Carnegie Endowment): 60–72.

Franklin, A. 2003. *Tourism: An Introduction.* London: Sage.

Geva, A., and Goldman, A. 1991. Satisfaction measurement in guided tours, *Annals of Tourism Research* 18: 177–185.

Gmelch, S. B. (ed.). 2004. *Tourists and Tourism: A Reader.* Long Grove, IL: Waveland.

Gmelch, S. B. 2004. Why tourism matters, in S. B. Gmelch (ed.), *Tourists and Tourism: A Reader*, pp. 3–212. Long Grove, IL: Waveland.

Goodbody Report. 2005. *The Private Bus and Coach Industry in Ireland.* Dublin: Goodbody Economic Consultants.

Gorokhovsky, A. 2003. Tourism development in Ireland: An economic perspective, *Student Economic Review* 17: 97–105, Trinity College Dublin.

Graburn, N. H. H. 1989. Tourism: The sacred journey, in V. L. Smith (ed.), *Hosts and Guests: An Anthropology of Tourism* (2nd ed.), pp. 21–36. Philadelphia: University of Pennsylvania.

———. 2004. Secular ritual: A general theory of tourism, in S. B. Gmelch (ed.), *Tourists and Tourism: A Reader*, pp. 23–34. Long Grove, IL: Waveland.

Greenwood, D. J. 1977. Culture by the pound: An anthropological perspective on tourism as cultural commoditization, in V. L. Smith (ed.), *Hosts and Guests: The Anthropology of Tourism*, pp. 129–138. Philadelphia: University of Pennsylvania.

———.1989. Culture by the pound: An anthropological perspective on tourism as cultural commoditization, in V. L. Smith (ed.), *Hosts and Guests: The Anthropology of Tourism* (2nd ed.), pp. 171–185. Philadelphia: University of Pennsylvania.

———. 2004. Culture by the pound: An anthropological perspective on tourism as cultural commoditization, in S. B. Gmelch (ed.), *Tourists and Tourism: A Reader*, pp. 157–169. Long Grove, IL: Waveland.

Harbison, P. 1992. *Guide to National and Historic Monuments of Ireland.* Dublin: Gill and Macmillan.

Harrison, J. 2000. The process of interpretation, in N. Buttimer, C. Rynne, and H. Guerin (eds.), *The Heritage of Ireland.* Cork: Wilton Press.

Harvey, D. 2001. Heritage pasts and heritage presents: Temporality, meaning and the scope of heritage studies, *International Journal of Heritage Studies* 7(4): 319–338.

Heritage Council of Ireland. 2006. *An Chomhairle Oidhreachta* (www. heritageireland.ie, accessed 14 May 2006).

Heritage Island. 2004. *The Group Organisers' and Tour Operators' Manual of Ireland: Major Tourist Attractions and Heritage Towns.* Dublin: Heritage Island.

Heuston, J. 1993. Kilkee—The origins and development of a West Coast resort, in B. O'Connor and M. Cronin (eds.), *Tourism in Ireland: A Critical Analysis*, pp. 13–28. Cork: University of Cork.

Hickey, S. 2005. Tourism boasts 5pc hike as 7 million visit our island (www.unison.ie/irish_independent, accessed 28 December 2005).

Hill, J. D. 1989. Rethinking the Iron Age, *Scottish Archaeological Review* 6: 16–24.

Hobsbawm, E. 1983. Mass- producing traditions: Europe 1870–1914, in E. Hobsbawn and T. Ranger (eds.), *The Invention of Tradition*. Cambridge: Cambridge University Press.

ICOMOS. 1999. *International Cultural Tourism Charter: Managing Tourism Places of Heritage Significance* (www.icomos.org, accessed 20 July 2006).

Ireland's Top Visitor Farms. 2006. (www.esatclear.ie/~turoefarm/top/farms.htm, accessed 20 March 2006).

Ireland West. 2005. *Come and Discover Ireland's West: Galway, Mayo, Roscommon,* Guidebook 2005/2006. Ireland West Tourism.

Irish Times. 2000. *Business 2000* (5th ed.) online.

ITIC (Irish Tourism Industry Confederation). 1995. *Economic Effect of Tourism in Ireland 1990–1993.* Tansey, Webster, and Associates.

———. 2000. *The People and Place Programme Report.* Tansey, Webster, and Associates.

———.2002a. *The Impact of Tourism on the Irish Economy.* Tansey, Webster, Stewart, and Co.

———. 2002b. *A Recovery Programme for Tourism.* Tansey, Webster, and Associates.

———. 2005. *How Tourism to Ireland Is Changing: Regional Distribution.* Tourism and Transport Consult International.

ITIC (Irish Tourism Industry Confederation). 2006a. *Ireland's Competitive Position in Tourism*. CHL Consulting Co. Ltd.

———. 2006b. *National Development Plan 2007–2013*. Tansey, Webster, Stewart, and Co.

ITIC Tourism News [online] 13 March 2008, 4 April 2008, 29 January 2009, accessed 4 February 2009, www.itic.ie.

James, S. 1999. *The Atlantic Celts: Ancient People or Modern Invention?* Madison: University of Wisconsin.

Johnson, N. 1996. Where geography and history meet: Heritage tourism and the big house in Ireland, *Annals of the Association of American Geographers* 86(3): 551–566.

Jorgensen, A. 2003. Power, knowledge, and tourguiding: The construction of Irish identity on Board County Wicklow tour buses, in M. Cronin and B. O'Connor (eds.), *Irish Tourism: Image, Culture and Identity*, pp. 141–157. Clevedon: Channel View.

Kearney, A. T., Inc. 2003. Measuring globalization: Who's up, who's down? *Foreign Policy* January/February: 60–72.

Kiberd, D. 1995. *Inventing Ireland: The Literature of the Modern Nation*. London: Jonothan Cape.

Kincaid, J. 1988. *A Small Place*. New York: Farrar Strauss Giroux.

Kincheloe, P. J. 1999. Two visions of fairyland: Ireland and the monumental discourse of the nineteenth-century American tourist, *Irish Studies Review* 7(1): 41–51.

Kirshenblatt-Gimblett, B. 1998. *Destination Culture: Tourism, Museums, and Heritage*. Berkeley and Los Angeles: University of California Press.

Kockel, U. 1994. Culture, tourism and development: A view from the periphery, *Culture, Tourism and Development: The Case of Ireland*, pp. 1–14. Liverpool: Liverpool University.

Lambkin, B. K. 1989. Navan Fort and the coming of "cultural heritage," *Emania* 6: 48–49.

———. 1993. Navan Fort and the arrival of "cultural heritage," *Emania* 11: 61–64.

Lowenthal, D. 1985. *The Past Is a Foreign Country*. Cambridge: Cambridge University.

———. 1998. *The Heritage Crusade and the Spoils of History*. Cambridge: Cambridge University.

Lury, C. 1997. The objects of travel, in C. Rojek and J. Urry (eds.), *Touring Cultures: Transformations of Travel and Theory*, pp. 75–95. New York: Routledge.

Lysaght, L. 2005. The Burren: The case for a different kind of National Park, *Heritage Outlook: The Magazine of the Heritage Council* Summer/Autumn: 8–12.

MacCannell, D. 1999 [1976]. *The Tourist: A New Theory of the Leisure Class*. Berkeley and Los Angeles: University of California Press.

———. 1992. *Empty Meeting Grounds: The Tourist Papers*. London: Routledge.

———. 2004. Sightseeing and social structure: The moral integration of modernity, in S. B. Gmelch (ed.), *Tourists and Tourism: A Reader*, pp. 55–70. Long Grove, IL: Waveland.

Mallory, J. P. 1987. Draft proposals for a Navan heritage centre, *Emania* 2: 32–35.

Mays, M. 2005. Irish Identity in an Age of Globalisation, *Irish Studies Review* 13(1): 3–12.

McCarthy, M. 2005. Historico-geographical explorations of Ireland's heritages: Towards a critical understanding of the nature of memory and identity, in M. McCarthy (ed.), *Ireland's Heritages: Critical Perspectives of Memory and Identity*, pp. 3–51. Aldershot: Ashgate.

McGarvey, F. 1987. Rehabilitating Navan, *Emania* 3: 48.

McKercher, B., and du Cros, H. 2002. *Cultural Tourism: The Partnership between Tourism and Cultural Heritage Management*. New York: Haworth Hospitality Press.

McManus, R. 1997. Heritage and Tourism in Ireland—an unholy alliance? *Irish Geography* Vol. 30(2): 90–98.

Mill, R. C., and Morrison, A. M. 1985. *The Tourism System: An Introductory Text*. Upper Saddle River, NJ: Prentice Hall.

Moulin, C., and Boniface, P. 2001. Routeing heritage for tourism: Making heritage and cultural networks for socio-economic development, *International Journal of Heritage Studies* 7(3): 237–248.

Mount, C. 2002. The Irish Heritage Council, *Antiquity* 76: 485–492.

Musgrave, B.W., and Crothers, J. W. 1993. The Navan Centre Project, *Emania* 11: 55–59.

Nash, C. 1993. "Embodying the nation": The west of Ireland landscape and Irish identity, in B. O'Connor and M. Cronin (eds.), *Tourism in Ireland: A Critical Analysis*, pp. 86–112. Cork: Cork University.

Nash, D. 1989. Tourism as a form of imperialism, in V. L. Smith (ed.), *Hosts and Guests: The Anthropology of Tourism* (2nd ed.), pp. 37–52. Philadelphia: University of Pennsylvania.

————. 1996. *Anthropology of Tourism.* Oxford: Pergamon.

National Development Plan 1999–2006. Dublin: NDP/CSF Information Office.

National Development Plan 2007–2013. Dublin: NDP/CSF Information Office.

National Spatial Strategy for Ireland 2002–2020: People, Places and Potential. 2001. Dublin: The Stationery Office.

National Tourism Development Authority (NTDA) (see Fáilte Ireland).

National Tourism Development Authority Act 2003. Oireachtas May 2003.

Negra, D. 2001a. The new primitives: Irishness in recent U.S. television, *Irish Studies Review* 9(2): 229–239.

————. 2001b. Consuming Ireland: Lucky Charms cereal, Irish Spring soap, and 1-800-Shamrock, *Cultural Studies* 15(1): 76–97.

Newman, C., Fenwick, J., and Bhreathnach, E. 2004. Tara: A line in the sand, *Archaeology Ireland* 18(4).

O'Connor, B. 1993. Myths and mirrors: Tourist images and national identity, in B. O'Connor and M. Cronin (eds.), *Tourism in Ireland: A Critical Analysis*, pp. 68–85. Cork: Cork University.

O'Connor, B., and Cronin, M. 1993. *Tourism in Ireland: A Critical Analysis.* Cork: Cork University.

O'Connor, B., and Cronin, M. (eds.). 2003. *Irish Tourism: Image Cultrue and Identity.* Clevedon: Channel View.

O'Donovan, G. 2000. The natural heritage, in N. Buttimer, C. Rynne, and H. Guerin (eds.), *The Heritage of Ireland*, pp. 1–17. Cork: Wilton Press.

OECD. 2004. *Ireland National Tourism Policy Review.* Paris: Directorate for Science, Technology, and Industry.

Offaly Historical and Archaeological Society. 2007. www.monasticway.ie (accessed 12 February 2007).

O'Hagan, S. 2004. Bangers and machinations: From riverdance to the famine—The Disneyfication of Ireland's heritage continues apace, *The Observer Review*: 5.

O'Kelly, C. 2004. Being Irish, *Government and Opposition: Politics of Identity-V*: 504–520.

O'Kelly, M. J. 1982. *Newgrange: Archaeology, Art and Legend.* London: Thames and Hudson.

OPW (Office of Public Works). n.d. *Heritage Sites of Ireland 2006/07.* Dublin: Office Public Works.

O'Sullivan, Muiris, O'Connor, D. J., and Kennedy, L. 2001. *Archaeological Features at Risk Project: A Survey Measuring the Recent Destruction of Ireland's Archaeological Heritage.* Dublin: The Heritage Council Series.

O'Toole, F. 1999. *The Lie of the Land: Irish Identities.* London: Verso.

————. 2002. The clod and the continent: Irish identity in the European Union, *EurUnion* 1: 1–16. Irish Congress of Trade Unions.

Pavia, S., and Bolton, J. 2001. *The Stone Monuments Decay Study 2000.* Dublin: Heritage Council.

Pi-Sunyer, O. 1989. Changing perspectives of tourism and tourists in a Catalan resort town, in V. L. Smith (ed.), *Hosts and Guests: The Anthropology of Tourism* (2nd ed.), pp. 187–199. Philadelphia: University of Pennsylvania.

Prentice, R., and Andersen, V. 2000. Evoking Ireland: Modeling tourist propensity, *Annals of Tourism Research* 27(2): 490–516.

Rains, S. 2003. Home from home: Diasporic images of Ireland in film and tourism, in M. Cronin and B. O'Connor (eds.), *Irish Tourism: Image, Culture and Identity*, pp. 196–214. Clevedon: Channel View.

Ritzer, G., and Liska, A. 1997. "McDisneyization" and "post-tourism": Complementary perspectives of contemporary tourism, in C. Rojek and J. Urry (eds.), *Touring Cultures: Transformations of Travel and Theory*, pp. 96–109. London: Routledge.

Robinson, M. 1999. Is cultural tourism on the right track? *The UNESCO Courier*: 22–23.

Rojek, C. 1993. *Ways of Escape.* London: Routledge.

Rojek, C., and Urry, J. 1997. *Touring Cultures: Transformations of Travel and Theory.* London: Routledge.

————. 1997a. Transformations of travel and theory, in C. Rojek and J. Urry (eds.), *Touring Cultures: Transformations of Travel and Theory*, pp. 1–19. London: Routledge.

Ronayne, M. 2001. The political economy of landscape: Conflict and value in a prehistoric landscape in the Republic of Ireland—Ways of telling, in B. Bender and M. Winer (eds.), *Contested Landscapes: Movement, Exile and Place*, pp. 149–164. Oxford: Berg .

Rourke, G. 2000. Conservation and restoration: The built environment, in N. Buttimer, C. Rynne, and H. Gurein (eds.), *The Heritage of Ireland*, pp. 350–357. Cork: Collins Press.

Rowan, Y., and Baram, U. (eds.). 2004. *Marketing Heritage: Archaeology and the Consumption of the Past.* Walnut Creek, CA: AltaMira Press (Rowman and Littlefield).

Royle, S. A. 2003. Exploitation and celebration of heritage on the Irish Islands, *Irish Geography* 36(1): 23–31.

RTÉ. 2006. News report RTÉ 1, July 20, 2006.

St. Patrick's Cathedral. 2007. www.stpatrickscathedral.ie (accessed 13 February 2007).

Second Progress Report of the Tourism Action Plan Implementation Group. 2005 (April). Dublin: Department of Arts, Sport, and Tourism.

Slater, E. 2003. Constructing an exotic "stroll" through Irish heritage: The Aran Islands Heritage Centre, in B. O'Connor, and M. Cronin (eds.), *Irish Tourism: Image, Culture, and Identity.* Clevedon: Channel View.

Smith, V. L. (ed.). 1989. *Hosts and Guests: The Anthropology of Tourism* (2nd ed.). Philadelphia: University of Pennsylvania.

Smith, V. L. 1989. Introduction, in V. L. Smith (ed.), *Hosts and Guests: The Anthropology of Tourism* (2nd ed.), pp. 1–17. Philadelphia: University of Pennsylvania.

———. 1996. Indigenous tourism: The four Hs, in R. Butler and T. Hinch (eds.), *Tourism and Indigenous Peoples.* London: International Thompson Business Press.

TAP. 2004. *First Progress Report of the Tourism Action Plan Implementation Group.* Dublin: Department of Arts, Sport, and Tourism.

———. 2005. *Second Progress Report of the Tourism Action Plan Implementation Group.* Dublin: Department of Arts, Sport, and Tourism.

———. 2006. *Third and Final Report of the Tourism Action Plan Implementation Group.* Dublin: Department of Arts, Sport, and Tourism.

Thompson, S. 2003. "Not only beef, but beauty . . .": Tourism, dependency, and the post-colonial Irish State, 1925–30, in M. Cronin and B. O'Connor (eds.), *Irish Tourism: Image, Culture and Identity*, pp. 263–281. Clevedon: Channel View.

TPRG (Tourism Policy Review Group). 2003. *Irish Tourism: Responding to Change—Interim Report of the Tourism Policy Review Group.* Dublin: Department for Arts, Sport, and Tourism.

Trigger, B. 1984. Alternative archaeologies: Nationalist, colonialist, imperialist, *Man* 19: 355–370.

TV3 News at 5.30. "Dáil reacts to employment figures." 4 February 2009.

TV3 Midday News. "Country braces for more bad news." 4 February 2009.

Urry, J. 1990. *The Tourist Gaze: Leisure and Travel in Contemporary Societies.* London: Sage.

———. 2002. *The Tourist Gaze* (2nd ed.). London: Sage.

———. 2004. Tourism, Europe, and identity, in S. B. Gmelch (ed.), *Tourists and Tourism: A Reader*, pp. 433–441. Long Grove: Waveland.

Veblen, T. 2001 [1899]. *The Theory of the Leisure Class.* New York: Modern Library.

Volkman, K. E., and Guydosh, R. M. 2001. Tourism in Ireland: Observations on the impact of European Union funding and marketing strategies. Paper presented at the ASAC meetings 2001.

Waddell, J. 2000. *The Prehistoric Archaeology of Ireland.* Bray: Wordwell.

Warner, R. 1999. Celtic Ireland and other fables: Politics and prehistory. Paper presented at the Conference of the Irish Association, November 1999.

White, T. 1999. Where myth and reality meet: Irish nationalism in the first half of the twentieth century, *The European Legacy* 4(4): 49–57.

Witoszek, N. 2002. All that is airy solidifies: The prolonged agony of romantic Ireland, Textual Practice 16(2): 345–363.

World Travel and Tourism Council. 2005. *Ireland: Travel and Tourism: Sowing the Seeds of Growth: The 2005 Travel and Tourism Economic Research.* London: WTTC.

About the Author

Kelli Ann (Costa) níc Maoileoin spent many years in the horse business before turning her attention to anthropology in the 1980s. She received her Ph.D. in 1998 from the University of Massachusetts at Amherst, where she studied archaeology, heritage, and tourism under John W. Cole, Oriol Pi-Sunyer, H. Martin Wobst, Dena Dincauze, and Robert Paynter. Kelli was a professor at Franklin Pierce College in New Hampshire for ten years before taking a Fulbright Fellowship at the Dublin Institute of Technology in 2006. *The Coach Fellas* came about after her friend Lesley Daunt, an Irish coach driver-guide, suggested she study the industry in 2005. Now residing in Ireland, Kelli remains associated with the Dublin Institute of Technology and involved in the Irish tourism industry. She conducts accredited college tours of Ireland's archaeological heritage sites, is busy with research, and lives in the Midlands surrounded by the people and places she loves.

Index

B

H

Hallstatt 49

Handel's Messiah 88

Harbison, Peter 45

Harrison, John 37–38

Haughey, Charles (Cathal) 121

Haughey's Fort 65, 67

Henry of London, Archbishop 89

Heritage 9, 10, 30, 36–40, 42,
  51–52, 54, 58, 73–79, 81, 90,
  97, 99, 108, 120, 121, 164,
  174, 207–20

  Archaeological 57, 123

  Assets 36, 103

  Attractions 144

  Cultural 144, 149

  Industrial 44

  Interpretation 11, 37

  Irish 69, 73, 97, 99, 100,
    173–77

  Landscapes 37, 40, 50, 51,
    54, 81, 85, 102–07, 173–77,
    191–98

  Market 11

  National 44, 121

  Site management 11

  Sites 10, 36, 37–38, 44, 60, 73,
    175, 196

  Tourism 79, 100, 207

  Town 44

  Value 90, 98

Heritage Act 1995 122

Heritage Council 74, 84, 121,
  122

Heritage Island 44

Heritage Plan 1997–2000 122

The Heritage of Ireland 37–38,
  55–56

Heritage Sites of Ireland 2006/07
  75

History 33, 40, 42, 45, 49, 57, 58,
  69, 97, 101, 111, 134, 151,
  157, 164, 173, 191, 218

Hobsbawm, Eric 58

Holiday 19, 20, 32, 93, 95,
  109, 118, 126, 134, 136,
  167, 189

"Holy Grail" 22, 28

"Hollywood" 25

Hondarribia 21

"honey pot" 70, 131

Hook Lighthouse 45

Hosts and guests 21, 27, 29

Housing, estates 11, 98, 192

Hugenots 135, 194

I

ICOMOS 36, 59

Identification 20

Identity 45–48, 181

  Image-based 46

  Irish 45–48, 49, 56, 85

  National 57

Ideology

  National 24

Image 93, 180, 188, 189

Imagination 44, 188, 192, 200,
  205

Independence (Irish) 40

Institute of Archaeologists of
  Ireland 123

Internet 33, 133

Underclass 22
Unemployment 221
UNESCO 44
United States 33, 47, 54, 70, 134, 213
Urry, John 25–27, 32

V

Values 36, 56, 57, 93, 100, 104, 123–27, 191
  Cultural 23
Veblen, Thorstein 19, 31
Verisimilitude 23
Victorian Era 19, 31, 48, 185
Viking 57, 67, 86, 87, 207
Visitor Attitudes Survey 93, 125, 126–27, 152, 153, 223
Visitor 30, 38, 43, 60, 62, 68, 74, 90, 92, 95, 104, 124–25, 133, 135, 137, 148, 193
  Centre 39, 53, 58, 79, 83

W

Wallace, Patrick 57
Waterford 35, 45, 122, 131, 208, 218

Crystal 73
Waterman, Dudley 67
Wealth 192
West 22, 24
Westmeath 109, 217
Westport 54, 72, 92
Wexford 36, 208
Whiting Foundation 12
Wicklow 203, 209
  Mountains 53, 72
Wilde, Oscar 148
Witoszek, Nina 192
Wizard of Oz 23
Wood Quay 57
World
  First 24
  Third 24
World Heritage Site 44, 59, 73, 78–79, 105
World Trade Organisation 131
World Travel and Tourism Council (WTTC) 43
Working class 10

Y

Yeats, W. B. 82, 113